The Secret Club:
Why and How We Must Teach
Phonics and Essential Literacy Skills to Readers
of All Ages

Pat Doran, M.A.Ed.

Second printing, February 2005

Published in the United States by
Freedom Reading Foundation, Inc.
P.O. Box 794
Gilbert, Arizona 85234

Printed in the United States of America.

ISBN 0-9771101-0-9 (USA)

To my family:

my husband, Chris,
my children, Peter, Lisa, Jean-Marie, and Joy,
Lisa's husband, Jeff Cragg,
and my grandchildren, Yasmine and Jeffery.

About the Author

Pat Doran, M.Ed. has taught in the elementary classroom, has been an elementary school librarian for eight years, and has been an adjunct instructor, teaching remedial reading at the junior college level. She is the co-author, with her colleague, Theresa Manriquez, M.Ed., of a fast-paced, word-attack, decoding program, *Phonics Steps to Reading Success* that is the basis of a Rio Salado College online course. The course is designed to train educators regarding the teaching of secondary decoding and reading skills. She is the co-founder, president and CEO of Edu-Steps, Inc., a company providing strategies for teachers, educators, parents, and students and co-founder with Mrs. Manriquez of The Freedom Reading Foundation, Inc. to train tutors, instruct individuals, and develop instructional materials. Pat Doran is also the author of *The Secret Club: Why and How We Must Teach Phonics and Essential Literacy Skills to Readers of All Ages* and *My Steps Journal*, a character education journal. She is an effective teacher, trainer, author, dynamic conference speaker, and a champion for promoting literacy and eliminating illiteracy.

Pat Doran began her career in education in 1964, teaching elementary classes in grades 4-6. She took a hiatus to raise four children, re-entering education as a K-8 elementary school librarian where she remained for eight years. She has worked primarily with inner city minority students of low-socio economic backgrounds, many of whom were English learners.

A few years prior to her retirement, she returned to the classroom. Her students won all top Fresh Air Science Fair awards at Phoenix College, Phoenix, Arizona for three years in a row. When asked how she taught science so effectively, Mrs. Doran said, "I don't teach science. I teach reading. The students [then] are capable of great achievement on their own."

Her sixth-grade, inner-city class was skilled academically, averaging 51% SAT9 test scores improvement in one year. Moreover, these students were well-behaved, often quoting from the character education journal of motivational sayings that she had written or collected for them to adopt as aids in daily decision making. Student behavior problems were minimal-to-none, prompting a fellow teacher to ask, "How do you get all of the good kids?"

Pat is the former president of the Board of Directors of The John Corcoran Foundation, Inc. John Corcoran is the author of *The Teacher Who Couldn't Read*, a must-read autobiography of how he, an illiterate, was a high school teacher, never knowing how to read until age 48.

Pat is currently working with Jim Janssen who is writing his autobiography, *Honor Roll Illiterate*. He represents millions of individuals, 25 percent of the 2.5 million graduates each year, who are functional illiterates with high school diplomas.

Pat's successful work in the elementary and junior college classrooms as well as with adult illiterates fuels her passion. She adamantly believes that we must aggressively attack this problem for the safety and prosperity of our country's future. There are no excuses, no other options. With Theresa Manriquez and others, Pat is helping those stuck in the mire of illiteracy to get out, to change direction, and to find their way on a successful life's journey through reading. She encourages those who can read to help and to share this invaluable gift with others.

Informational and Strategies' Materials
by Pat Doran, M.Ed.
for Educators, Parents, and Students

The Secret Club: How and Why We Must Teach Phonics and Essential Literacy Skills to Readers of All Ages

Phonics Steps to Reading Success (PSRS) by Pat Doran, M.Ed. and Theresa Manriquez, M.Ed., a fast-paced, word-attack, decoding program for post-primary students and adults.

Multi-media format available:
- PowerPoint
- Full-color transparencies for overhead use for large groups
- Full-color paper format for tutoring—one-on-one or small group
- Black/white PSRS spiral bound copies for students
- Companion spelling journal/workbook for students
- Word-for-word audio

My Steps Journal: A Character Educational Journal

For information regarding Pat Doran's availability for speaking engagements, workshops, and seminars please contact:

The Freedom Reading Foundation, Inc.
P. O. Box 794
Gilbert, Arizona 85234
patdoran@edu-steps.com

Acknowledgements

I wish to thank the following important people:

- Chris Doran, my husband, for his generous and patient support and encouragement during the writing of this book and through all my endeavors for the past thirty years.

- Peter Doran, my son, and Lisa, Jean-Marie and Joy, my daughters, for their munificent willingness to help and provide wise suggestions and corrections.

- Theresa Manriquez, my colleague, for her friendship, honesty, integrity, insights and inspiration.

- Marianne Levin for her work in reorganizing and editing of the original manuscript.

- Joan Fay for rearranging her schedule to share her wisdom and editing skills.

- Sharon Hanlen, Norma Clark, Lorrie Hanlen, and Carolyn Nielsen for their attention to detail.

- Johanna Haver, author of *Structured English Immersion*, for her support, suggestions, observations, and friendship.

- John Paul Loucky and Wendy Arnold who so well articulated the importance of teaching phonics to *all* students. I am also grateful to Ms. Arnold for her words which inspired the title for this book.

- All who have been my teachers, within and outside of the classroom, who have modeled for me the excellence of the teaching profession.

- All who have been my students, for their love, learning, and all they taught me.

◆ ◆ ◆

- *Special thanks* to Janet Martin, without whose help, friendship, wisdom, and inspiration this book would not have been written. I also thank her for her gracious willingness to critique the ongoing process at my every request, correcting my grammar when it lapsed, and calling attention to material whether missing or superfluous.

Pat Doran
Chandler, Arizona
February 13, 2005

CONTENTS

"Hold on to the gift of hope."
Words of wisdom from my mother, Cecelia C. Reddy, 1986

INTRODUCTION

"Self esteem begins with the ability to read efficiently and fluently. Teach others how to read and their future will have no limits." Unknown

It is possible, necessary, and effective to teach the body of knowledge known as phonics to post-primary students and adults. This refers to those who are proficient speakers of the English language as well as for those who are English-language learners.

The purpose of this book is to help teachers, parents, friends, and mentors of older students to (a) understand the causes, complexities, and consequences of reading problems and (b) provide practical help to teach skills necessary for successful decoding and reading comprehension. Throughout this book, the term *phonics* means explicit, systematic, direct, and scientifically research-based instruction of sound-symbol relationships, unless otherwise indicated.

This book is for parents, educators, and other interested parties who ask these types of questions:

- Why do students arrive at the upper grades with poor reading skills?

- Why do post-primary students avoid reading big words, guess at words, or substitute incorrect words while reading?

- Why do students who struggle with reading and homework have negative attitudes about school?

- Why do students who struggle with schoolwork act as bullies, class clowns, disengaged students, truants, or dropouts?

- Why do some students without effective phonics/reading skills struggle with reading assignments and display *symptoms* resembling those of ADD/ADHD or dyslexia problems?

- What is the best way to teach basic decoding skills to post-primary students without damaging their self-esteem?

- What is the history of reading instruction and how did we get to where we are today?

- What is the best way to ascertain the general validity of research claims?

The following dialogue that took place on the Internet among reading instructors in the spring of 2004 helps to summarize the reason for writing this book. Dr. John Paul Loucky (2004), English instruction specialist and researcher at Seinan Women's University in Japan, wrote:

> Without help in reaching a 'minimal phonemic awareness,'
> learners will be at a frustration level virtually all of the time, just
> as they will be if more than 1/20 or 5% of the target text's
> running words are unknown to them.[i]

Wendy Arnold (2004), a certified teacher of English learners in Hong Kong, China, wrote:

> It has taken me a long time to come around to acknowledging
> that this is what was missing. I'd made assumptions about what
> my learners had been taught and WOW, was I wrong. I think
> everybody can do with a rerun of how to decode.[ii]

Ms. Arnold vividly remembers arriving in the UK from Ecuador as a child when she was ten years old. When the principal gave her a spelling test, she tried to sound out every **ph** in the word. No one told her that decoding English was different from decoding Spanish! Her mother was a Scottish primary teacher, and she assumed that her daughter knew or was able to "figure out" words because she was an avid reader and writer. When the principal told her the *magic* of **ph** sounding like /f/, the young Miss Arnold laughed and was relieved. She knew that she had been getting it all wrong, but didn't know why. Today, Ms. Arnold acknowledges the importance of learning phonics decoding skills.

> It's just like joining a secret club; you must be initiated or taught the rules of the club and not be expected to work them out yourself. I've just finished a 10-hour summer course with 6 groups of English learners, and there is absolutely NO doubt left in my mind that every single one of them benefited by being told the rules to get into "the club," that is, how to decode words: just simple, basic letter-sound correspondences, blending, rhyming, and segmenting; no rocket science. [iii]

Phonics is not just for English learners; it is for everyone who wants to read and speak English successfully. Woven throughout this book are stories about individuals, male and female, young and old, of all races and socio-economic backgrounds, who after much emotional pain, frustration, and embarrassment were able to learn to read. They were finally taught the rules and were able to join what Ms. Arnold so aptly described as the "secret club" of those who can read well, using phonics.

Of course, the principles of phonics must be combined with the other essential components of successful reading: fluency, an expanded vocabulary, and comprehension. This allows the individual to achieve his or her potential in such areas as academic work, test taking, and all of life's reading requirements. This book is about sharing *the secret.*

Assumptions

In the eyes of the public, educators hold a position of trust and respect. Their responsibility to educate youth is an awesome one. The public assumes that new teachers leave their institutes of higher learning armed with intellectually sound, research-based methods of teaching. Additionally, the public assumes that the children, who will be taught by these teachers, will be given the crucial foundations that make progress possible at higher scholastic levels. These assumptions may not always be valid.

Likewise, teachers themselves often make the erroneous assumption that they have been adequately trained. Yet, they are often unprepared to provide for the actual needs of their students. They are surprised when they find their students unable to read the assigned history, science, and math textbooks.[iv]

In contrast, a basic high level of academic achievement was once the norm in the classrooms of the 1950s and earlier. This high level of achievement, however, is much more difficult to accomplish in the contemporary educational environment. In the past, students were equipped with effective reading strategies in the primary grades. Today, innumerable ill-equipped students are *socially promoted* from grade to grade.

Consequently, without a minimal level of phonemic awareness and an inability to figure out the "secret," learners experience frustration much of the time. In some cases, a reading specialist or special education teacher is called in. All too often, the reading specialist or other teachers are overburdened with too many students and responsibilities and, moreover, may not have been trained how to teach phonics skills. As a result, the frustrations and failures continue for teachers and students.

Thus, students struggle to read by using ineffective reading strategies that they have been taught to use. Regularly, they are erroneously assumed to have *learning disabilities, dyslexia, attention deficit disorders,* and various other *emotional problems.* I have tutored adult illiterates who had been in special needs classes most of their school years. These individuals, and often their classmates, assumed that they were *just stupid.* In fact, they merely were taught to use inefficient reading strategies.

Damaged Lives Reflect Consequences

This book alerts the reader to the tragic results of failed instruction in the classroom. The anecdotes in this book shed light on just a few of the innumerable lives that have been negatively affected by failed methods of reading instruction.

It is my hope that these stories inspire the reader, particularly educators, to change the inferior education that plays so significant a role in the lives of too many students. Beyond the anecdotes, there is also rigorous scientific research that confirms that training in phonics is one of the most essential tools for successful reading.

Here are some of the people whose stories are told in *The Secret Club*:

- One boy said, "When I was in high school, I would wait until everyone was in class, before I went to my special education class. I didn't want anyone to know I was in those classes. I always got detention at school when I was late, followed by a whipping at home for getting a detention. But the whippings didn't hurt as much as the humiliation would have if anyone at school found out that I was in special ed."
- An elementary teacher, who was nearing retirement age, told me, "I can't teach your program." When I advised him that I was in his room to assist not evaluate him, he said, "No, you don't understand. I can't read well enough to teach your program. I have been afraid to tell anybody."

- A sweet intermediate-level teacher, who spoke with a pronounced accent, enthusiastically, taught her English-speaking and English-learning students to pronounce *hot* and *mop* instead of *hat* and *map*. Her students dutifully "read" these words back to her as she taught them. She most likely was unaware of the problems in speaking, reading, and spelling that would arise for her students in the future with such instruction.

Reading Deficiencies Affect Everyone

Low literacy skills are ubiquitous in society. Individuals with these deficiencies have difficulty with commonplace activities such as taking tests, applying for jobs, getting appropriate medical attention, making purchases, or doing banking. On the other hand, we all have had frustrating and negative experiences as a result of a store clerk or other entry-level workers making errors in reading and spelling.

For instance, on a trip to the mall, one young, expectant mother went into a store that did custom monogramming. For sale were caps, T-shirts, sweaters, and the like. She told the clerk that she wanted to buy a cap for her seven-year-old daughter. The custom wording was to read, "I'm the big sister." The clerk took the cap to the machine and returned with a cap that read, "Im [sic] the big sister." When the young mother mentioned that it was incorrect, the clerk said, "I got to put in one of those little marks somewhere, don't I?" The clerk then put the cap aside and took a new one on which to write the correct phrase. The cap that had the error was a material loss for the employer. In addition, the customer's added waiting time for another cap to be monogrammed correctly was a loss of time for her. Moreover, it was evident that the employee's low literacy and grammar skills most likely would cost him advancement in the world of work.

It is imperative that all teachers understand the myriad, immediate, and long-term problems caused when individuals cannot read, write, and speak well. Adult students have told me horror stories of their early school years – such as wishing to die instead of going to school. They have described the avoidance games they played, the lies they told, and the fears they had of being found out. Those who were erroneously branded with the dyslexia label have elaborated about pain and humiliation of being in special education classes. As one adult reported, "I could have handled the embarrassment of being a special education student – if they had taught me something." This student is not alone. Students with the same thoughts and feelings are sitting in classrooms today. As the aunt of one of my adult students said, "They labeled her and then they warehoused her until they graduated her when she was twenty-two. They never taught her to read, and I worry about what will happen to her when she is out on her own." The young woman says that because she couldn't read, her regular classroom teachers told her just to "listen and learn" when she returned from her special education classes. The aunt, who lives on a limited and fixed income, pays for reading lessons for her niece to learn what the teachers had been paid to teach but never did. Her niece is now learning how to read, but has to make up for many years of lost learning opportunities.

Scientific Evidence

Based on the extensive failures of the experimental instructional systems, phonics instruction has started to return to the center of reading education. However, obstacles remain. Many teachers have never been taught to read phonetically. As Janet Martin, former president of the Arizona State Board of Education, has stated, "Teachers are not exempt from the fact that we don't know what we don't know." Learning is essential.

An excellent source of information is *The Partnership for Reading: Bringing Scientific Evidence to Learning* at http://www.nifl.gov/partnershipforreading/. The Partnership is a collaborative effort of the National Institute of Child Health and Human Development (NICHD), the U.S. Department of Health and Human Services, and the U.S. Department of Education. Its purpose is to make evidence-based reading research available to educators, parents, and policymakers. According to the Partnership, good reading instruction uses research-based instructional strategies that include the five critical components of reading defined in the National Reading Panel's report, *Teaching Children to Read 2000*. The components that are also named in the *No Child Left Behind Act* are:

- **Phonemic Awareness**
- **Phonics**
- **Fluency**
- **Vocabulary**
- **Comprehension**

Word of Caution

Often, when the teaching of reading using phonics is discussed, someone might be heard to comment, "Children cannot learn to read using phonics; they need exposure to books." Agreed. An inadequate but helpful analogy at this point may provide clarification of phonics as related to reading. Consider the teaching of appropriate phonics strategies as compared with the teaching of appropriate movement of arms, feet, hands, and body necessary for efficient swimming. If a swimming instructor merely had the students stand or lie at the edge of the pool while learning *what* to do, we would say that the instructor was foolish. These strategies need to be applied and practiced in water.

In similar fashion, the teaching of phonics decoding strategies without inclusion of reinforcing decodable materials to develop fluency, vocabulary and comprehension would be foolish. Phonics strategies need to be applied and practiced while reading, and that includes the reading of books. There will be more about this later.

The Correct Approach

No one wants children to serve as guinea pigs in the classroom. Increasingly, concerned educators, researchers, grassroots groups, and politicians have stepped up on behalf of the learners so that they will be taught with proven and non-experimental methods. This book details today's rampant literacy problems, its causes, and the practical solutions that can eradicate illiteracy and improve low literacy skills. Each chapter in the book begins with Focus Points and ends with thought-provoking questions for further consideration.

On another note, you, the reader, are encouraged to become not only an educator, but a scholar as well. Learn as much about reading as you can. For example, after you finish this book, you may want to find an old copy of Constance Weaver's book, *Reading Process and Practice: From Socio-Psycholinguistics to Whole Language.* It is a popular textbook on the whole language philosophy. As you read, critically compare that philosophy of reading instruction to that of phonics instruction. It is prudent to examine *both* sides of any argument. To form opinions based solely on limited approaches or criticisms of adversarial philosophies and methodologies is unwise. Understanding non-phonics approaches, the kind frequently taught in colleges of education and then used in the classroom, may help you to grasp an understanding of why learners may be making so many errors in reading, writing, and spelling. No matter what subject area is involved, if your students and children cannot read well, the best attempts to teach them will most likely fall short.

Frequent references to *Phonics Steps to Reading Success* occur throughout this book. My colleague, Theresa Manriquez, M. Ed., and I have co-authored this fast-paced, phonics-based decoding program for use with older students. This approach was developed as a result of our concerns about the reading deficiencies of our own students. One needs little training in the teaching of phonics to teach the information found in the *Phonics Steps to Reading Success* program. It has been successfully used with individuals of all ages to teach basic phonics concepts. Our company, *Edu-Steps, Inc.,* promotes literacy for all students. There are many others that do the same.

For most of us adults who can read, it is difficult to understand the hardships for upper-grade students and older individuals who have been passed along through the grades without knowledge of essential phonics strategies.

Illiteracy has many facets. For example, E.D. Hirsch (1988) wrote eloquently about *cultural* illiteracy. Here, I paraphrase his words as they relate to the ability to read:

> The fact that we ignore something is because we have been able
> to take it for granted. We ignore the air we breathe until it is thin
> or foul...Literacy [my change] is the oxygen of social
> intercourse.[v]

Knowing this, when we encounter illiteracy and its consequences, it is critical that we must be shocked into action. If we are, there is hope.

We have to look beyond our personal preferences and ideologies to turn student deficiencies into competencies. We have to look to ourselves and get to work. We must educate ourselves about what is effective and become advocates for those whose lives are impaired because they cannot read or read well. We have to make sure that new readers are taught properly. There is much work to do, but it *can* be done.

Once more, it must be noted that when the term "phonics" is used throughout this book, it refers *only* to scientifically research-based, systematic, explicit, direct phonics instruction. Moreover, it refers to phonics as but *one* of the essential elements required for reading. (The essential elements are phonemic awareness, phonics, fluency, vocabulary development, and comprehension.) It is important to know that phonics does *not* mean any of the various forms of non-explicit phonics instruction that may be referred by such terms as "embedded," "implicit" phonics, "combined methods," "eclectic approaches," or "balanced reading approaches," and the like. Only systematic, explicit phonics has been *scientifically proven* to be effective and to lay the foundation for lifelong successful reading, spelling, and writing. Students deserve the best.

Of necessity, there will be discussions in this work of non-phonics methodologies. Nevertheless, the criticisms that are presented concerning whole language instruction dismiss the value neither of its proponents nor their purpose. The information, however, is intended to demonstrate the fact that any enjoyable and meaning-filled experience of the written word must be built on top of a strong foundation of essential skills. That foundation must be provided by structured and sequential instruction of phonics.

Formatting note: The double-spaced format has been used to provide ease of reading and making notations.

References

[i] Locky, J. P. (2004, May 26). *Phonemic Awareness.* [Msg. 441] Message posted to
   ExtensiveReading@yahoogroups.com.

[ii] Arnold, W. (2004, May 25). *Phonemic Awareness.* [Msg. 1942]. Message posted to
   ExtensiveReading@yahoogroups.com.

[iii] Ibid.

[iv] Roe, B., Stoodt-Hill, B., Burns, P. (2004). *Secondary School Literacy Instruction: The Content Areas, 8th
   ed.* New York: Houghton Mifflin Company, p. 4.

[v] Hirsch, E.D. (1988). *Cultural Literacy: What Every American Needs to Know.* New York: Doubleday.

CHAPTER ONE

READING DEFICIENCIES AND NEGATIVE BEHAVIOR

*"Conduct or behavior and the factors which influence conduct or behavior are all of one piece -
all of education has conceivably an influence on conduct...."*

Frank Freeman, *Journal of Educational Psychology*, 1936

FOCUS POINT: A connection exists between reading deficiencies and negative behavior in students. Poor reading produces poor self-esteem that in turn results in poor behavior. Many problems in the classroom can be rectified when students gain foundational skills for independent reading. A teacher can diagnose deficiencies in reading and comprehension by observation and by testing students' reading skills. By attacking the problem(s) and by making sure that students develop a knowledge base, the teacher is then able to build the trust that is essential to students' continued academic success. Systematic phonics is crucial to establishing this foundation.

This chapter discusses the common, yet often overlooked, cause-and-effect relationships that may occur between reading deficiencies and negative behavior. The chapter also explains that laying foundations to enable students to read well can often end these relationships, often reversing negative behaviors. The benefits can be significant.

A Frequent Scenario

Consider this fictitious, but all-to-common, scenario.

Jano's Story: *I am a high school student. My teacher is always well prepared and is good at explaining the lesson and answering questions. The lesson interests me. I* *pay attention. I want to learn. I know I am smart because I know all the answers. When the teacher calls on me, I answer correctly. I feel self-assured. I am confident because I know the material. Then, the teacher assigns homework.*

The Homework: *The homework is a study sheet that contains an illustration and several paragraphs that review the lesson. It includes questions to answer. The teacher says that the questions will be on the test tomorrow. The teacher stresses that if we pay attention in class and complete our homework correctly, we will do well on the test. She says that we may use the textbook to help in answering the questions.*

I fold the homework paper and put it with my textbook inside my backpack. When I get home, I am ready to do my homework. This should be easy enough because I paid attention in class. The teacher explained that this handout is a review of the lesson and will prepare me for the test. I have my textbook. I am all set.

I take out the homework paper and begin reading. Some of the words – maybe two out of every ten – seem to me to be written like they were in a foreign language. I have trouble comprehending the passage because I can't figure out all of the words, even though some of the assignment makes sense to me. I get the gist of the work. I try all the strategies that every teacher has ever told me to use. I try to guess at what the words might be. I substitute words that I think might make sense in the sentences.

I look for little words in bigger words. I look for word parts that I know. I look for context clues. To choose the correct answers, I try matching words in the questions with words in the passages. I try to make smart guesses. I look at the illustration for clues.

I'm confused. I feel so dumb. I'm getting frustrated. Deep down inside, I begin to panic. I try to remember the discussion in class. My frustration mounts. I try to use my textbook, but it seems like some of its words are in a foreign language, too.

Nothing seems to make sense. I want to do well. I want my parents to be proud of me, but the more I try to figure out the words the more I feel frustrated. My level of anxiety is rising. I knew the answers when the teacher asked questions in class. I just can't comprehend my homework with all of the confusing words mixed in. My brain feels like it's in a fog.

I take a break, get a snack, and watch TV. My mom tells me to get back to doing my homework. I tell her that my homework doesn't make sense. She tells me to try harder. I've heard that before.

She says, "Your teacher says that you have comprehension problems when you read." Then she reminds me that I might do better if I paid attention in class.

I snap back that I do pay attention, but that the homework is "stupid."

She says, "Well, if you paid better attention in class, it wouldn't be stupid, now would it?"

I yell at her. I tell her that she doesn't understand. I feel helpless, defeated. I'm a real loser. I go to bed angry. I remind myself how much I hate school.

The Test: *The teacher reviews the homework orally. Just as I did in class yesterday, I know all the answers. It's the reading part that messes me up.*

I hope that I might have a chance to do well on the test, despite what happened last night. As the teacher gives each student a test, she says, "This is going to be easy.

This is the same paper as your homework. If you paid attention in class and did your homework correctly, you will do well on the test."

The teacher walks by. She hands me the test. I know what's coming. I feel defeated already. The tension in my throat and stomach increases. My mom has told me that she read somewhere that these are symptoms of test anxiety. I guess that's what I have. I take a deep breath. I look around. Everyone is working on the test – everyone except me.

I try to read the first paragraph. It's no use. It just doesn't make any sense. I can't read all the words. It's the same as my homework. Let's face it. I accept the fact that I have a problem. I can't comprehend what I read. I know that I must have some kind of learning disability. There's nothing I can do. I scribble down whatever comes to mind. I think, "Tomorrow she's going to pass back the tests. I know already that I got an F." It's frustrating to know all the answers and yet, tomorrow, I am going to be handed a failing grade like always. My anger at my failure builds up.

I ask to be excused to go to the restroom. As I walk down the hallway, I say to myself, "Maybe I won't show up tomorrow. Why bother?"

Even if Jano knew 100% of the answers, but had been able to read only 80% of the words on the test passages or questions, it would have been difficult, if not impossible, for Jano to score 100% on this test. Jano's experience, although fictitious, is quite real for many students. I have heard this story told in many versions by numerous students and adults who lived with the same daily defeat and discouragement. They say that the frustration becomes more painful as they advance in age and move up through the grades.

The Need to Read

Reading is a fundamental requirement in society. The success of a representative government rests on a well educated, reading populace. It is necessary for the formation of well-grounded opinions, the enrichment of family life, success in the world of work, and invaluable throughout life. Essentially, reading is required for innumerable tasks, such as:

    (a)   to experience literary enjoyment;

    (b)   to gain information;

    (c)   to fill out forms and to understand contracts; and

    (d)   to follow directions.

Students must read to gain and communicate information. Students must be able to read independently, read aloud, do homework, perform research, and take tests in preparation for the time when they take their role as responsible adult citizens in society. What they do and how they succeed in the classroom, therefore, affects them throughout their lifetimes. Consequently, the classroom is a critical starting point.

Connecting the Dots

As in the scenario with Jano, if a bright student in a class learns aurally, that student may be able to comprehend 100% of the material presented aloud in class. Some professionals believe that if a reader can read most of the words in a passage – perhaps at least 70% – then the reader can get the *gist* of the passage's meaning. While this may be true, students who *cannot accurately* read what is written *cannot accurately* comprehend an author's meaning, pass tests, or move forward successfully with schoolwork done well.

Dr. John Paul Loucky, who has done extensive research in bilingual and acquisition of English reading strategies, understands this important truth (http://www.4All.US). In 2004, Dr. Loucky wrote the following as part of a message posted to ExtensiveReading@yahoogroups.com. It is cited in the introduction of this book, but worthy of repetition here:

> Without help in reaching a 'minimal phonemic awareness,'
> learners will be at a frustration level virtually all of the time, just
> as they will be if more than 1/20 or 5% of the target text's
> running words are unknown to them.

Students like Jano do not have effective decoding and reading strategies. Therefore, they live at a high frustration level all of the time. Since reading has inherent social value, such individuals fail to read successfully and, therefore, experience an overwhelming sense of defeat, embarrassment, and poor self-esteem. They are unable to achieve academically. The longer that they are in the education system the greater their burden grows. Negative emotions may eventually manifest themselves when students act out in socially unacceptable ways both inside and outside of the classroom.

Accordingly, the angst of teachers in the upper grades grows. Dedicated educators can become discouraged because they are responsible for teaching required curriculum although many of their students cannot read well enough to do the work. Furthermore, teachers must respond to classroom disruptions caused by students' negative behaviors and attitudes. Many of these academically frustrated students may be seeking negative attention since they receive little positive affirmation for educational tasks done well.

However, teachers and administrators may not "connect the dots." Because of their different areas of concern, educators often look for diversified solutions. Consequently, in recent years, educators at all levels have devoted considerable attention to improving classroom behavior by, for example, introducing "character education" programs. These programs undoubtedly are beneficial in themselves. Similarly, but in another area, educators place a strong focus on students' test scores. Tests are important because they evaluate how well the teachers are teaching and how well the learners are learning.

Not surprisingly, educators must understand, as did Frank Freeman, who was quoted at the beginning of this chapter, that character education and all other aspects of education, particularly those aspects involving reading acquisition, are interrelated. Indeed, many behavior problems and literacy deficiencies are definitively *not* unrelated.

Statistics on Behavior Problems and Illiteracy

Each year, a large number of students continue to fail at reading. Individuals of all ages, who are unable to read well, often internalize negative feelings. Without their realizing that the origin of their inability to read well may lie outside of them, they experience an ever-present sense of personal inferiority. While delinquency is an obvious negative outcome, other long-term and widespread negative social effects may occur. Illiteracy puts young people at risk.

One person who has understood this for years is Robert Sweet, a former high school teacher. He also is a former senior official at the U.S. Department of Education, the former White House domestic policy advisor to President Ronald Reagan, and the former head of the Office of Juvenile Justice and Delinquency under President H. W.

Bush. In July 1997, he resigned as president of the Right to Read Foundation that he founded. He then became a professional staff member on the U.S. House Committee on Education and the Workforce. In his essay (1996), "The Century of Miseducation of American Teachers," he wrote:

> Although statistics are always subject to challenge by some, the evidence from such prestigious sources as the National Assessment of Education Progress [NAEP] (which found that '70 percent of fourth graders, 30 percent of eighth graders, and 64 percent of 12th graders did not...attain a proficient level of reading) cannot be ignored. These students have not attained the minimum skill level in reading considered necessary to do the academic work at their grade level. The National Adult Literacy Survey, after a five-year study, confirmed that finding indicating that 42 million adults can't read, and that 50 million more recognize so few printed words they are limited to a 4th and 5th grade level of reading.

> Even more troubling are the findings of The Orton Dyslexia Society, that illiterate [individuals] account for 75 percent of the unemployed, one third of the mothers receiving AFDC, 85 percent of the juveniles who appear in court, 60 percent of prison inmates, and nearly 40 percent of minority youth. Of people in the work force, 15 percent are functionally illiterate, including 11 percent of professional and managerial workers, and 30 percent of semiskilled and unskilled workers. Is it any wonder that a Census Bureau survey released in February of this year found that 'American employers regard the nation's educational system as an irrelevance?' Rather 'businesses ignore a prospective employee's educational credentials in favor of work history and attitude.'[1]

In another essay, "Illiteracy: An Incurable Disease or Education Malpractice," Robert Sweet (1996) wrote:

> One out of every four teenagers drops out of high school, and of those who graduate, one out of every four has the equivalent or less of an eighth grade education. According to current estimates, the number of functionally illiterate adults is increasing by approximately two and one quarter million persons each year. This number includes nearly one million young people who drop out of school before graduation, 400,000 legal immigrants, 100,000 refugees, 800,000 illegal immigrants, and 20 % of all high school graduates. Eighty-four percent of the 23,000 people, who took an exam for entry-level jobs at New York Telephone in 1988, failed. More than half of Fortune 500 companies have become educators of last resort, with the cost of remedial employee training in the three Rs reaching more than 300 million dollars a year. **One estimate places the yearly cost in welfare programs and unemployment compensation due to illiteracy at six billion dollars**. [Emphasis added.] An additional 237 billion dollars a year in unrealized earnings is forfeited by persons who lack basic reading skills, according to Literacy Volunteers of America.[2]

Serious concerns over these numbers have prompted numerous educators, business professionals, the United States Congress, and the Department of Education to make sure that poor readers get help. An admirable, Herculean push is being made to make sure that primary students are taught to read using a systematic, explicit phonics approach. However, if individuals in fourth grade and beyond are unable to decode words efficiently, they will always be at a disadvantage. These students and others have been deprived of the knowledge of word-attack or phonics skills that would enable them to "sound out" unfamiliar words. Most likely, they have been taught by means of various reading methodologies that include the strategies used by Jano. They have been taught to guess at words, to substitute an unfamiliar word with a known word, to get the "gist," or to construct their own meaning of a passage or text.[3] Whole language is one such approach.

What the Experts Say

In 1995, a group of forty reputable Massachusetts professors signed a letter that strongly objected to incorporating "whole language" standards into the *Massachusetts Curriculum Framework for English Language Arts* in the content chapter, "Constructing and Conveying Meaning." This group included linguists and cognitive psychologists from such prestigious universities as Harvard, the Massachusetts Institute of Technology, and Boston University. Three members of the National Academy of Sciences, four presidents of the Linguistic Society of America, three directors of major research training programs and the authors of two significant books on language signed a letter that made the following point:

> The proposed Content Chapter replaces the common-sense view of reading as the decoding of notated speech with a surprising view of reading as directly "constructing meaning." According to the document, "constructing meaning" is a process that can be achieved using many "strategies" (guessing, contextual cues, etc.). In this view, the decoding of written words plays a relatively minor role in reading compared to strategies such as contextual guessing. This treats the alphabetic nature of our writing system as little more than an accident, when in fact it is

the most important property of written English – a linguistic achievement of historic importance.[4]

Social Promotion in the Schools

By using various ineffective reading strategies, students struggle with school assignments. Nevertheless, many poorly prepared, under-performing, and unsuspecting students have been promoted from one grade to the next in a common practice that is often referred to as *social promotion*. Ironically, students with inferior reading skills are socially promoted to protect their "self-esteem." Unfortunately, these students lack a solid educational base to progress to a more advanced grade level academically. Their experience of failure is compounded as they mature into adulthood.

The experience of forty-seven-year-old James S., an African-American gentleman, tells the tragic tale. He was less than functionally literate and had enrolled in a class for remedial readers that I taught at a junior college. The head of the reading department permitted me to use my phonics program to teach basic decoding skills as long as I also followed the assigned course curriculum. James responded very well to the lessons and was thrilled to be reading. He spontaneously declared, "I'm reading for the first time in my life!"

He disparagingly spoke to the class about his former teachers when he said, "They kept passing me on, but I couldn't read. I was nothing but a goat to them. They were worried about my self-esteem. Now, I can't get a good job. It cost me two marriages. What woman is going to stay with a man who can't earn enough money to support her? Where is my 'esteem' now?"

He proudly told the other students in the class that he learned to read more in one hour in our class than he had learned in all of his years in school. It is a refrain that I have heard often from my adult students.

For James, and others like him, the frequency and significance of damages caused by their social promotion is staggering. Educators must consider the lasting consequences when they promote unprepared students to the next level. When educators disregard this lack of preparedness, students fall farther behind. Moreover, the future teachers whom these students will subsequently encounter have a *right* to expect well-prepared students entering their classrooms. When this does not happen, both teachers and students are forced to deal with lowered academic achievement and its related negative consequences. Clearly, social promotion – no matter what immediate benefits there seem to be for the students or the school – does not seem to help anyone's long-term self-esteem. **Below-level reading does <u>not</u> correct itself automatically just because the student moves ahead in the school system or gets older!**

On the other hand, when addressing the necessity of a student's retention, parents and educators at all levels must note that extreme caution is to be taken by all concerned. It is imperative that the student is taught how to use *effective* reading strategies and is not forced to spend another year learning how to use the same *ineffective* strategies more efficiently. You may have heard the insightful saying, "If you always do what you always did, you'll always get what you always got."

If students are not taught the foundational reading strategies essential to be successful in academic work, they will be intellectually handicapped. They are prevented from thriving and being successful in academic subjects. It is fundamental that all learners become skilled at using effective reading strategies. Teachers who do not accept this reality negatively affect their students' futures significantly. It is the educators' responsibility to teach those students so that they learn what they need in order to grow academically and to become successful participants in a decidedly literate society.

Poor Reading ↔ Poor Self-Esteem ↔Poor Behavior

The task is challenging. The law in each state requires a student to attend school approximately seven hours each day for five days each week during much of the year. To a below-level reader, particularly one who has the intelligence to work on or above grade level, the act of stepping inside a classroom is like stepping into a hostile environment. Some individuals, such as James, are more comfortable sharing about their painful experiences after they have learned how to read well or are making significant progress.

Before overcoming their reading problems, students might suppress or redirect a recurring and overwhelming sense of failure. They might attempt to camouflage their stress with negative attitudes or behaviors that seem to provide them with some semblance of personal control. Teachers are often poorly equipped to deal with the resulting layered complexities in the classroom.

I began teaching in the intermediate grades in the mid-1960s. Most of my students had been taught in previous grades to read by using *whole word* or *whole language* strategies. [These strategies are detailed in Chapters Two and Three.] Students also came to class with diverse behavior problems. After I taught all of my students to read using phonics strategies, the behavior problems significantly decreased. Another teacher quizzed me, "How do you get all the good kids?" Most assuredly, effective reading instruction had been a major factor although, quite honestly, not the only one. Nonetheless, when the students could read the work, they could focus their efforts on doing the work.

In contrast, however, many poor readers who are unable to do school work successfully may show one or several of the following symptomatic behaviors, recognized by Monroe and Backus (1937) in their book, *Remedial Reading.*

1. **Aggression:** The child opposes the individuals whom he or she blames for thwarting his or her success.

2. **Withdrawal:** The child withdraws from antagonistic or painful situations.

3. **Compensation:** The child compensates for a reading disability by success in a field that doesn't require reading.

4. **Giving up:** The defeated child gives up.

5. **Hyperactivity or Depression:** The child develops a general hyperactivity, excitability, or depression.[5]

Caveat

Of course, I do not claim, nor do I believe, that reading deficiencies cause *all* manifestations of general hyperactivity, excitability, depression, brain disorders, and the like. Nevertheless, parents and teachers can serve students better by first ensuring that students, who manifest such symptoms with no scientifically determined cause, are capable of using scientifically research-based and effective reading strategies.

In fact, effective reading instruction can significantly correct problems that have been caused by ineffective reading instruction. One observant educator has facetiously, but perhaps accurately, said, "Try reading *before* you try Ritalin."

Symptomatic Behaviors

The following material is drawn from my experiences as an educator and includes anecdotes associated with each behavior listed:

1. **The child opposes the individuals whom he or she blames for thwarting his or her success.**

When Victor (not his real name) entered my upper intermediate classroom on the first day of school, he made it plain that he hated reading, hated school, and hated me. He was reading on a first grade-level. In fact, most of the other students in the class were also reading at various levels below what would be required to do work for their grade. Not surprisingly, they all lacked significant knowledge of phonics principles.

I decided to instruct the class to read and write using phonics decoding skills. The students blossomed academically and personally. This class won the top three awards at a local college and community-supported science competition. A visiting state legislator was impressed with these students from this traditionally under-performing district. Victor had become one of our articulate spokespersons and stunned us all when he spontaneously stood up to share with her the following:

> When I was in first grade, I felt pretty good about myself. When
> I was in second grade, I wanted to kill the teacher. When I was
> in third grade, I wanted to kill my classmates. When I was in
> fourth grade, I wanted to burn down the school. When I was in

fifth grade, I didn't want to live any more. Now that I am in
Mrs. Doran's class, I learned how to read and now I know I can
be somebody!

His story is moving. Over the years, I have learned that many students similarly feel the way he felt before he learned how to read well. I suspect that there are many more. Sadly, not all such stories have happy endings.

2.   The child withdraws from antagonistic or painful situations.

Frustrated and afraid of embarrassment, some students withdraw from the class. This can be an actual, physical escape. Young children, who are unsuccessful in reading, often ask to be excused from class for a restroom break or a drink of water instead of risk being called upon to read.

For older students, truancy is a common form of withdrawal. A young man told me that when he was in junior high school, he skipped school eighty-five days in one school year. When the assistant principal passed him in the cafeteria and commented on the absences, the boy lied by saying that he suffered from bad headaches. Neither the assistant principal nor the boy's teacher ever contacted his parents. His excessive absences were never mentioned at the parent-teacher conferences.

In another fashion, a child might also withdraw by paying attention to some cerebral pastime, often a daydream. When fantasy substitutes too often for authentic and successful experiences, this intensity of mental withdrawal can negatively affect a child's personality.

Joey, one of my former elementary students, told me that in earlier grades he used to sit in class and "make stuff up" in his head; that is, he would daydream. He said, "I never was in trouble. I just used to be dumb."

Most definitely, Joey was not "dumb." After phonics instruction in our class, Joey became actively involved in oral and written work. He continually surprised himself whenever he answered correctly or received a good grade. Afterward, he gleefully commented *every time*, "I used to be dumb!"

At another level for older students, the use of illegal drugs or alcohol can provide other means of withdrawal. One man told me that he used to go to his junior high and high school classes *stoned* on marijuana or alcohol. He said, "Then I sat in class and I didn't care whether I was a loser or not."

Several adult students have told me they had wanted to die instead of having to face another day at school. One young man also said that he knew it was wrong to commit suicide, so, as a young adult, he prayed that he would contract a fatal illness or be killed in a traffic accident. How many students are there like these who are uninvolved, merely occupying seats in classrooms, feeling as though their lives are worthless, when they could be successfully reading and learning by being positively engaged in school?

Despite the extent of the problem, such behaviors can be reversed. One example is John. This young boy had a long history of handling embarrassment and frustration by running out of his classrooms in tears. One day, as my class was diligently taking a state-mandated test, I walked by the desk where he was sitting. I was aware of his test anxiety and his penchant for running out of classrooms when he was frustrated. To provide reassurance for him, I asked how he was doing. With a big smile he said, "This test is fun – now that I can read!" He had entered my sixth grade classroom reading at an early first-grade reading level. This bright boy's reading ability had improved several grade levels and now he had the skills, potential, and desire to advance further.

3. **The child compensates for a reading disability by success in a field that doesn't require reading.**

Martin was twelve-years-old. He was a tall, quiet boy and able to read only on a beginning first-grade level. When I told his mother that he was seriously deficient in reading skills, she said adamantly, "I *thought* he couldn't read! But when I asked his other teachers, they told me not to worry. They said that he was a pleasure to have in class and was a talented artist."

On another occasion, it was the final weeks of a school year. I was the school librarian at the time, when I encountered a tall, withdrawn, teenage boy, Mark, who had just enrolled in the school. He came to the library with his class. He had attended other schools in the district since kindergarten. When I tried to help him find a book, I discovered that he had no reading skills, and he was unable to identify any of the letters or sounds of the alphabet. When I asked him what his teachers had taught him, he said they told him that he was a really talented artist. Then he added, "They let me draw."

When Mark entered the seventh grade after summer vacation, Theresa Manriquez was his teacher and became his advocate. She worked with the special education teacher who agreed to teach phonics skills to Mark. Although he was slow in his learning, by the end of seventh grade, he was able to read simple books independently. Everyone agreed that more hard work lay ahead; however, for the first time in his life he was successful, not only in art, but in using critically important reading skills as well.

Obviously, if a skill that compensates for reading failure is advantageous, such as a skill in art, athletics, or music, it should be encouraged. However, the teacher and the school system maintain an undeniably primary responsibility to their core duties, the basis of which is the teaching of reading. Students can have positive experiences with artistic, athletic, and musical success, but such achievements are not to be considered adequate replacements for essential success in reading. The most talented artist or athlete will fail to achieve his or her highest potential if unable to read successfully.

One such young man, Robbie, was an aspiring professional athlete. His ability to help win championships for the schools he attended blinded his teachers and administrators to the importance of remedying his lack of reading skills. Although barely reading at a beginning primary level, he graduated from a university with a degree in counseling. He was told that because of his exceptional athletic talent, it would be unnecessary for him to know how to read. Many friends and instructors told him that he would have enough money to hire people to do his reading for him.

However, something went terribly wrong for this young man when he injured his back. To this day, the pain keeps him from pursuing his athletic career. Furthermore, his inability to read has kept him from being employed to do any other meaningful work. For a brief period, he was able to get a secure job that did not require reading skills. He quickly rose in the company, but when other employees complained that their supervisor was writing all of Robbie's reports, Robbie quit rather than see his supervisor fired. Despite the fact that his teachers gave him a high school diploma and a college degree, their lowered expectations failed him when he needed to function as an adult. Depressed, he said, "Now I know why guys get guns and rob convenience stores just to get money." His athletic skills, once the keys to his success when he was a student, are of no use to him now. The 2004 movie, *Friday Night Lights,* is a story about a determined high school football team. The tragic experience of an injured, illiterate team member, Boobie Miles played by Derek Luke, sadly bears a similarity to that of Robbie's.

On the other hand, not all students compensate for poor reading skills by pursuing art, music, or athletics. Students might behave in ways that we label class clowns, bullies, or smart alecks. Their behavior may garner attention, albeit negative attention, and ultimately distract from their inability to succeed academically. By gaining such negative attention, these students often discover ways to "succeed" if only in their own minds.

4.   The defeated child gives up.

Repeated failure at tasks that require reading can condition some students into believing that they cannot succeed. Students may become so accustomed to daily failure that they are crushed before they attempt new things. They develop an internal weight of hopelessness and apathy. These feelings are often difficult, if not impossible, to overcome. To restore their self-confidence, they must be provided effective, corrective reading instruction at whatever levels required. Most importantly, such students must be given many experiences of meaningful success. Students know when they are learning. Nevertheless, an ongoing, ingrained feeling of inescapable failure on the part of learners of any age can block the corrective efforts of even the most capable instructors. Patience and perseverance for everyone involved are cardinal qualities needed for success.

Consider Tom, whom I met when he was thirty-five. A friend of his introduced us and offered to pay for his tutoring. The friend was befuddled as to why Tom couldn't read because it was obvious that Tom was bright. When he completed his first reading session with me, the grin on his face said it all. He was learning the fundamental principles of phonics and was actually able to read words instead of guessing at them. Tom said he felt like a new man. He told me that he read more with me in one hour than he had done in all of his years in school. During our first session, he explained that when he was a child, his low-level reading skills qualified him to receive special education services. Throughout his schooling, from first grade through college, all of his teachers had made accommodations for him. For example, they read test questions to him and wrote down his answers. He resented the fact that he couldn't read or complete regular schoolwork. He also resented that these accommodations made him feel "stupid." Nevertheless, his peers liked and respected him. He said that, as a child, he found enjoyment in his life playing with his friends on the playground and in sports activities.

Sadly, however, he returned only once more for tutoring. He told me that, because he couldn't find employment, he had to move in with his mother in another state. He hated the idea of being a grown man and having to move in with his mother. I gave him my phonics program with self-teaching audio CDs, but I never heard from him again. I may never know if he succeeded in learning to read. Perhaps the defeat that he experienced for so many years was a barrier that he could not overcome. If there is no meaningful intervention, defeat can be a forceful internal enemy that causes one to give up. I hold out hope for him.

5.   The child develops a general hyperactivity, excitability, or depression.

Some older students have shared their memories of when they were younger and couldn't read. They relate that they existed with daily tension, worry, depression, and excitability.

Students with reading difficulties might brood over inferior grades on daily assignments, looming deadlines, upcoming tests, and previous failures. Students carry the effects of these memories into their day-to-day activities and expect the same difficulties in the future. Although they may be intelligent enough to recognize they have a problem, they may not feel they can talk to anyone. The habit of worry and dread may result in unhealthy personality traits. Overwhelming depression may lead to thoughts of suicide. Some symptoms seem to mimic behaviors that are associated with what is popularly identified as *Attention Deficit Disorder* (ADD) or *Attention Deficit/Hyperactivity Disorder* (AD/HD).

Should teachers stop giving grades on assignments, setting deadlines, or giving tests to ensure students do not experience reading difficulties? Obviously, this is not the answer. The solution is to *teach what is missing,* so students can experience academic success. If reading deficiency is the reason for this symptomatic behavior, the answer is to eliminate the *cause* of the problem. Often this can reverse symptoms.

Such a reversal happened in the case of Jason. One year, on the first day of school, all of my students – except Jason – were sitting attentively as I took roll. He was nonchalantly strolling about the classroom.   I asked him what he was doing. Immediately, several students volunteered that he was "allowed to do that."

One said, "He's hyperactive."

"He can't pay attention," said another.

One student chimed in, "He's allowed to do what he wants as long as he doesn't bother anybody."

I asked him, "Is it true that your other teachers let your walk around?"

"Uh-huh," he responded.

Respectfully, but firmly, I told him, "Sit down."

Then, I continued. "Let me tell you something," I said. "You may be hyperactive at home. You may be hyperactive on the playground. You may be hyperactive in the principal's office. You may be hyperactive *anywhere* you choose. I don't care. But when you are in *my* classroom, you will sit down and follow the rules. Do you understand?"

A bit surprised, he sat down. I spoke gently to him. I continued, "I bet that I know something about you. I bet that you can't read well."

The students were surprised. "How did you know?"

Call it intuition. Call it what you will. I had known others like him.

I said, "Jason, I'll make a deal with you. I'll teach you how to read and you can stop walking around." He agreed. Whether he believed me or not, he didn't seem to have a choice.

Jason and I kept our agreements with each other. By the end of the school year, Jason became a leader in the classroom. He learned to read. His wandering stopped, and his academic successes increased. We were glad for him when he became our spokesperson at a science fair at a local college where our class won the "Best of the Fair Award." At a public presentation where he presented information about a class project, his mother watched. She had tears in her eyes. Later, she told me that Jason never thought he would be able to do anything like that. She was grateful for the change in him. We all were. It was encouraging, however, to see the dramatic improvement in Jason. Jason was fortunate. Not everyone is as fortunate as Jason.

Reading expert, Diane McGuinness, Ph.D. (1999), writes in her book, *Why Our Children Can't Read and What We Can Do About It:*

> Because teachers are never provided with training and skills to teach reading correctly, their classrooms are filling up with children who are 'dyslexic' because they have a 'brain disorder,' or 'don't pay attention because they have a 'brain disorder,' or 'aren't motivated,' or are 'emotionally handicapped.'[6]

It is imperative that educators gain extensive knowledge and utilize skills to diagnose, analyze, and remedy problems, particularly those related to reading. It is important to reverse a prevalent practice that focuses on labeling students as having a learning disability, and then making instructional accommodations to fit the label.

Although there has been much progress made, without a doubt, countless students in regular classrooms across the country are still reading below their capabilities. This topic is discussed in local, state, and national reports, educational journals, as well as on editorial and opinion pages of newspapers. For example, one K-8 school boasted of a zero-percent retention rate, yet the students were graduated from the eighth grade reading at an average of a fourth-grade reading level.

I do not claim, nor do I believe, that reading deficiencies are the cause of all manifestations of general hyperactivity, excitability, and/or depression, or brain disorders. Nevertheless, students would be better served, if, when confronted with some of the above symptoms and there is no proven cause, parents and teachers focused first making sure that the students have been taught phonics.

Finding a Solution

A few motivated students or adults may recognize and find solutions to their own reading difficulties. Perhaps through hard work and determination, they may succeed. Of course, self-recognition and correction are the most desirable responses to failure in any area. The individual, who is able to take such an attitude, can approach a problem in a constructive way and may handily succeed in overcoming the difficulty. Positive character traits may be innate. On the other hand, one *can* be taught how to develop an "overcoming personality." Whatever the circumstances, most individuals must be explicitly *taught* the skills essential for successful reading.

Therefore, the administration needs to work with the classroom teacher to provide remedial reading strategies in any classroom where there are students who have below-level reading skills. Even good readers who are not reading at their highest potential should be considered to be under-performing readers.

A suggested model for teachers to solve reading deficiencies of limited, as well as capable readers, is to follow a procedure of *determine, attack,* and *build* (DAB):

1. *Determine* the cause(s) of the problems.

2. *Attack* the cause(s) at their roots.

3. *Build* a strong knowledge base.

Teachers can **determine** academic deficiencies in reading and comprehension by testing students' reading skills. Tests that identify levels of phonemic awareness are very helpful. The National Right to Read Foundation (NRRF) offers *The Oral Reading Competency Test*, which is free, easy to use, and may be downloaded from the following address: http://www.nrrf.org/readtest_background.html. According to the NRRF website's explanation of the test, "Part 1 contains phonetically regular one-syllable words that will help you to determine how well the student knows phonics. Part 2 consists of paragraphs taken from the middle part of school readers, grades 1-6 that were in wide use 100 years ago....Keep in mind that grade-level 6 is equivalent to high-school level reading today."

There are also various and excellent diagnostic tests that are commercially developed. One that I have used frequently is the *Reading Level Indicator: A Quick Group Reading Placement Test* by American Guidance Service (http://www.agsnet.com). It is easy to administer to a single student or to a whole class. It usually takes less than twenty minutes and provides information regarding the *instructional* as well as the *independent* reading levels of each student. This information is helpful for the teacher to know because when a student has a high instructional reading level, yet a low independent reading level, inevitably there will be frustrations and complications that arise for both teacher and student.

The earlier story that related the frustration of the fictional student, Jano, is one such example of a student with a high instructional reading level and a low independent reading level. This is a common cause for poor academic performances on the part of learners at all educational levels.

Another approach to determine specific reading problems can be done through informal observations. In short, when listening to a student as he or she reads orally, the instructor can pay attention to the types of errors that are made. For example, if the student (a) skips words, (b) guesses at words, (c) substitutes words, such as *wagon* for *cart*, (d) attempts to use illustrations as clues to read words, (e) reads only parts of words correctly, then the student probably lacks phonemic awareness and skills in phonics. (More specifics will be discussed in Chapter Five.) This may or may not involve the formal recording of such errors, depending on the circumstances. In the case of the regular classroom instruction, for example, the general observation by the teacher will be enough. On the other hand, reading specialists might require more extensive record keeping. Nevertheless, the instructor will be able to see how such strategies negatively affect the reader's fluency while holding the individual back from adequately developing vocabulary and from successfully comprehending what is written. [More about these errors will be discussed in detail in Chapter Five.]

The next step, that of **attacking** a reading problem, means getting rid of the ineffective strategies at their roots, neither making accommodations for them nor ignoring them. It is essential that the instructor make students aware of any of the ineffective strategies that they are using, and then explain why they are using them, and why they are ineffective.

Finally, in conjunction with attacking or tearing down the reading problem is the **building** of a strong knowledge base. This provides students with foundational knowledge in phonics so they can replace ineffective reading strategies with effective ones. It takes a DAB to improve literacy in the classroom.

Developing Trust in Students

In order to accomplish the task of removing and replacing ineffective reading strategies, it is important that teachers develop trust with students who are learning to read. Be cognizant that these students most likely have long histories of repeated failures. As said before, students in any remedial strategies curriculum must honestly be told that it is quite possible that they have been taught to use ineffective reading strategies. They may have been taught to guess at words, skip words, substitute words, and the like because these teaching strategies were what their teachers were taught. If teachers had been taught to view reading as a *guessing game*, they could only give of what they knew. It is imperative not to blame former teachers as it has only been recently that rigorous, scientific research has validated the importance of phonemic awareness and phonics as being essential for successful reading.

It is beneficial to share with older students a brief history of how this came to be. This will be further explored in the following two chapters, but a hint is given in the following quote. Karin Chenoweth (2002) wrote in *The Washington Post*:

> The National Reading Panel bemoaned the paucity of good research on a whole range of topics related to reading. But, it said, enough research exists to begin building knowledge of what constitutes good reading instruction. And one part of that is

phonics instruction, particularly for children in kindergarten and first grade and **older children who are having difficulty reading**. [Emphasis added].

Phonics instruction is by no means all that children need, the panel said. They need to have stories read to them by fluent readers so they can understand the wonder of a good story. They need many conversations using sophisticated vocabulary so they can build their storehouse of words and ideas. They need opportunities to write poems and stories that are fun and interesting for kids. The only really controversial part of the panel's recommendations, as far as I can tell, is that it called for phonics instruction, a conclusion disputed by those who say that phonics instruction is too boring for children and too quirky to rely on because English words don't always follow phonetic rules. **But those dissenters haven't been able to produce research that meets the reading panel's scientific standards.** [Emphasis added.]

What's interesting about the way the National Reading Panel did its work is that if its standards stick and are applied to all of educational research, that would represent a genuine turning point in education – the beginning of a common base of knowledge similar to what has been built in the medical sciences in the last hundred years. [7]

It is good news that improvements are being made. Unlike what has been accepted in the past, increasingly, educational methods are now being held to rigorous scientific standards. [More on educational research is included in Chapter Four.] Help is available to any teacher who wants to *determine* the causes of reading disabilities, *attack* the causes at their roots, and help readers *build* a strong knowledge base. All teachers at any level and in any subject area must make sure that they have the essential training and skills to teach and utilize effective reading strategies. By doing so, reading deficiencies will decrease as will related negative behaviors. Moreover, teachers and students in the classrooms, as well as in society, will benefit exponentially.

Conclusion

This chapter explored the possible connections between reading deficiencies and negative behavior. Concerned educators must examine these relationships. When individuals can read successfully, positive things can happen.

For the reasons presented in this chapter and throughout the rest of this book, it is reaffirmed that phonics instruction is necessary to provide the foundation for reading success. Basic phonics skills are essential for *all individuals* at *all levels* in the educational system and beyond. No student should be allowed to fall through the cracks.

If prior instruction or learning has been inadequate, blaming either the previous instructors or the student does not eradicate the problem. Rectifying the problem, however, is of paramount importance.

Until that happens, however, teachers and classmates will continue to suffer the consequences of the negative behaviors exhibited by angry, depressed, defeated, difficult individuals who act out because they cannot read. The relentless emotional distress and the failures that are experienced by older illiterate students, who are unable to do the work or pass the tests, will follow them into adulthood. On the other hand, educators and parents cannot overlook the fact that average, good, or high-achieving students may also be under-performing readers who are capable of coping well but are using inferior strategies to read. These students will also be at a disadvantage while in school and in the years to come.

There is encouraging news. The strategies that are required for beginning readers to learn how to read effectively are now known and are generally being taught. Moreover, for those older individuals who previously have been taught to use ineffective reading strategies, it is possible to replace the ineffective ones with effective ones. The age of the learner is not a factor. Ultimately, if we *don't* make the change, the costs are too high for everyone.

For Further Consideration

- Consider examples from your own high school experience when you encountered non-readers or below-level readers. How might circumstances have been different if these individuals had been able to read well?

- Can you think of a time when you or someone else was given meaningless approval in an attempt to bolster self-esteem?

- If you were given the *Best Hockey Player of the Year Award*, but knew you were barely able to stand up in skates, would the award be meaningful to you?

- Describe how various individuals, who use different methods in activities such as car repair, cooking, yoga, brain surgery, or house painting, can be successful. How could you identify the *best method*?

- How would one be able to identify the best method in any of the various aspects of education?

- Describe a fictional incident when on-going personal, emotional failure could influence negative affect on one's behavior.

References

[1] Sweet, R. Jr. (1996). *The Century of Miseducation of Teachers.* National Right to Read Foundation, Washington, D.C. Retrieved November 24, 2004 from http://www.nrrf.org/essay_Century_of_Miseducation.html, para. 5-6.

[2] Sweet, R. Jr. (1996) *Illiteracy: An Incurable Disease or Education Malpractice?* National Right to Read Foundation. Retrieved October 29, 2004 from http://nrrf.org/essay_Illiteracy.html.

[3] Weaver, C. (1994). *Reading Process and Practice: From Socio-psycholinguistics to Whole Language.* Portsmouth, NH: Heinemann, 230.

[4] Bach, E., Calabrese, A., Caplan, D., et al. (1996). *Letter From Massachusetts Linguists on WLL by David Klein.* Retrieved December 2, 2004 from http://mathforum.org/epigone/amte/swiraxkhay.

[5] Monroe, M. and Backus, B. (1937). Remedial Reading: A Monograph in Character Education. Cambridge, Massachusetts, 8-9.

[6] McGuinness, D. (1997). *Why Our Children Can't Read and What We Can Do About It.* New York: Touchtone Simon and Schuster, 9-10.

[7] Chenoweth, K. (2002, March 28). "Phonics Debate Linked to Nature of Educational Research." *The Washington Post*, GZ05. Retrieved November 24, 2004 from http://www.nrrf.org/article_chenoweth_3-28-02.htm.

CHAPTER TWO

EARLY HISTORY OF READING INSTRUCTION

"For the letter is the first and simplest impression in the trade of teaching, and nothing before it."
Richard Mulcaster, *The Training of Children*, 1581

> **FOCUS POINT:** Many adults today were taught to read with one or a combination of the following methods: *look-say*, *sight-word*, *sight-reading*, *whole language*, or *phonics* methods. Current theories regarding the teaching of reading have arisen as the result of historical developments; they have evolved as models, variations, and expansions of theories developed through history.

This chapter explores the history of the teaching of reading in the Western world from ancient times to the turn of the last century, and looks at the controversy between the look-say, sight-word, whole language, and phonics methods of teaching reading. It is necessary for educators, parents, and those who have a stake in the educational system to understand how these methods evolved. If *ineffective* method(s) are used to teach an individual how to read, one would be safe to say that the net result would be that the reader reads *ineffectively*. We may know bright individuals in our families, those with whom we work, or upon whom we depend, who are at a reading disadvantage. Most of us don't seem to understand why or how that is possible.

It is, therefore, necessary for all of us to understand causes, problems, and solutions in areas associated with reading instruction. One question that needs to be explored is that of how we got to a point when so many individuals who have passed through the school system, nevertheless, still struggle with literacy.

Much of the information used in this book regarding the history of reading has been adopted from Robert McCole Wilson's informative works. Wilson is a student of the history of education and author of *A Study of Attitudes Towards Corporal Punishment as an Educational Procedure From the Earliest Times to the Present* and *Teaching Reading - a History, Parts I and II.* He said, "...I do have some knowledge of the history of education and I knew that this debate was not new. I hoped that an historical view would assist those in the debate to be clearer and more accurate in their arguments."[8] It is for reasons similar to that of Mr. Wilson's, that this information was included in *The Secret Club.*

Another source that was extensively used in this work is the challenging and informative book, *The Underground History of American Education,* by John Taylor Gatto. Mr. Gatto has been honored as a New York State and New York City *Teacher of the Year.*[9]

Beginning with Early Written Languages

Archaeologist Panikos Chrysostomos in 2002 identified what he believes are traces of a writing system in northern Greece dating back to 5300 BC. He compares the simple forms and patterns to the contemporary way we use the drawing of a slash through a word or a picture to mean that something is prohibited. He called the collection a *protoscript.*[10]

Evidence of an early Egyptian alphabet that dates to 1600 BC has been found near turquoise mines in modern Egypt. Although ancient Egyptians had to memorize hundreds of hieroglyphics, it is now believed that they may have also used letters with separate sound values.

Some archaeologists believe that around 1300 BC, the ancient **Phoenicians** had an alphabetic language; they attributed a sound to each symbol and connected the sounds into words. The Phoenicians kept written records of their commerce and trade. The **Greeks** understood that untold political and civil power could be gained by using such a means of communication. They used written language as a means of **(a) analysis, (b) study, (c) inquiry, (d) exhortation,** and **(e) development of ideas**. They understood that using pictures, such as *hieroglyphs*, strictly limits development of thought and communication; while, on the other hand, using an alphabetic language bore the capacity to develop and communicate limitless ideas.

The Romans

Rome's foremost writer on educational practice, Quintilian (circa 35-95 A.D.), wrote extensively on Roman education. In his work, *Institutes of Oratore*, he writes about the method he observed saying, "It will be best for children, therefore, to be taught the appearances of the letters at once."[11] While he also emphasized the interaction of reading, writing, and speaking, because the art of rhetoric was so important in the public life of the empire, it is clear in *Book X* that he viewed reading and writing as supports for speaking.[12]

During the days of the Roman Empire, Latin, an Indo-European language, was widely spoken and written. The Roman alphabet was derived from the Greek alphabet with some changes. With the addition of letters *j*, **u** and **w**, the Roman alphabet is, fundamentally, what is used to write English today.

As Roman armies advanced in Europe, the conquered peoples were influenced to write their languages using the Roman alphabet. French, Italian, Portuguese, Rumanian, and Spanish are but a few of the languages that emerged because of the Latin influence. Many peoples had spoken sounds in their languages and dialects that did not fit into the limited Latin sound/symbol structure developed by the Romans. Digraphs (two letters that combine to form a unique sound such as *sh* or *th*), for example, arose as a solution to aid individuals in coping with the deficiencies in the Latin alphabet when they attempted to write unique sounds of their language.

> **COMMENT:** It is helpful to briefly explain to students the historical reasons why the letter symbols *c* and *h*, when written together as *ch*, say /*ch*/ as in **choo-choo**, and the letter symbols *s* and *h*, when written together as *sh*, say /*sh* / as in **shin**. Moreover, throughout the passage of time, poor copying and handwriting also caused shifts in how words were spelled and, therefore, pronounced. For example, a *skiff* (boat) most likely was sometimes written as *skipp* or *shipp*. That may explain why we have a *skipper* in charge of a *ship*.

Charlemagne

Charlemagne, 742-814 AD, a European king and emperor, ruled from 768 to 814 AD and had a major influence on European education. Charlemagne could read and speak Latin, the language of educated people of the time. However, he never learned to write. He could not write his name despite his practicing with a stylus and wax tablet that he kept near his bed.

> **COMMENT:** Both reading and writing should be taught specifically, directly, and systematically. It cannot be assumed that if one can read, one can automatically write.

Most people during Charlemagne's time lived in small villages, farmed, and had no education. Charlemagne elevated education for those in academic, religious, or elite social classes by setting up a school at his Aachen Palace. That became a magnet for the finest teachers and students in Europe. The palace school also educated individuals to teach throughout the empire. Scholars at the school collected and copied ancient Roman manuscripts which otherwise might have been lost forever.

Accuracy in the transcribing was critical to Charlemagne who insisted that scribes replicate every letter exactly. He was concerned that those scribes who were unable to read would just copy meaningless shapes of letters. If the illiterate scribes were inattentive, inaccurate, or lazy, then doctrinal errors could occur when religious documents were copied. Therefore, Charlemagne required that all monks and priests were to be thoroughly educated in *both reading and writing*.[13]

> **COMMENT:** Charlemagne understood that the copying of letters does not naturally impart reading knowledge. Notwithstanding, some activities in today's classroom often involve *word searches* or *filling in boxes* with words that are copied by the students. Students may successfully complete these word-search activities, and teachers may readily correct them; however, such assignments do not enhance reading instruction. They are often used based on the faulty premise that if students are exposed to and can copy enough words, then they will naturally become familiar with words. Charlemagne experienced first-hand the problematic aspects of this reasoning. So, too, did Jim Janssen who, although illiterate, said he became adept at successfully completing word searches by matching shapes of words. He related that the only help that word-search skills were to him when he

was an adult was when he would attempt to match the shapes of the words on street signs with the words on a page of directions. He adds that people in other cars must have hated to be driving behind him.

The Middle Ages

In 1440, **Gutenberg** invented the printing press using movable type. He published his now famous Gutenberg Bible. The invention of the printing press was a monumental advancement in written communication since it made written materials commonly available and, therefore, fostered a desire to read among all classes.

In 1527, Ickelsamer wrote *The Shortest Way to Reading* in an effort to simplify the teaching of the German language. His primer stressed that speech sounds were to be learned first; letter names were secondary.

COMMENT: It may be that the knowing of the names of letters is not the essential first step of learning to read. An effective, but not the only, method to teach reading is to teach the *sounds* of the letter symbols *first* before the names of the letters are taught.

This can be demonstrated by use of an anecdote about an incident that occurred when I was having lunch with a friend. A young woman approached our table. She said, "I want to thank you." She explained that we had met at a gathering a few years earlier and she had been telling me how proud she was to be teaching her two-year-old son his alphabet. I pointed out that she might do well to teach him the sounds associated with letters first so that he would be able to blend the letters' sounds together to read words. Afterward, he would then be able to learn the letter names. She proudly explained that, because of her using this approach, her child was an avid reader at age four.

Learning the alphabet names first may not always be the most effective approach. For instance, the saying of the letter **names** of *m, a, p* in sequence does not result in reading the word *map*. However, pronouncing the **sounds** assigned to the letters /m/ /a/ /p/ in sequence does result in reading the word *map*. Associating sounds with letter symbols also makes spelling easier by saying sounds as one writes /m/ /a/ /p/ rather than repeating a list of memorized letters in a particular order, *m, a, p*.

Equally important to remember is that when it comes to consonant pronunciation, it is probably a good idea to avoid teaching the consonant sounds as /m**uh**/, /p**uh**/, and so on. Otherwise, students might erroneously believe that the letters *m* and *p* have the short /*u*/ sound attached and they will read the word *map* as m*uh-ah-puh* or *muhapuh*. This can inhibit fluency, requiring students to unlearn these erroneous pronunciation strategies in the future.

Variations and Dialects

Languages like English and German are not pure languages. The fluid intermingling of Latin, French, Greek, and Germanic languages with those of the various peoples of the British Isles created many regional variations. As a result, we see the influences in the spellings and pronunciations throughout the development of the English language. In the 1560s in England, Sir Thomas Smith and John Hart attempted to alleviate confusions in spelling by expanding the alphabet to reflect the English sounds. John Hart settled on **34 letters in his expanded alphabet**. Other creative minds, Benjamin Franklin, for example, also toyed with the idea, however unsuccessfully.

COMMENT: This might have been a great idea but it failed to take hold. If *you* expanded the alphabet to alleviate confusions in spelling, what might your alphabet look like?

Richard Mulcaster became the first headmaster of the English Merchant Taylor's School in 1561. In 1581, his work, *The Training Up of Children,* published in London, Mulcaster wrote:

> For the letter is the first and simplest impression in the trade of teaching, and nothing before it. The knitting and jointing wherof groweth on verie infinitely, as it appeareth most plainely by daily spelling, and continuall reading, till partly by use, and partely by argument, the child get the habit, and cunning to read well, which being once goten, what a cluster of commodities doth it bring with all?[14]

The Age of Reason, the Enlightenment, and "Natural" Approaches to Reading

Comenius is sometimes referred to as the *grandfather of modern educational methodology.* Starting in 1658, Comenius published illustrated textbooks on many topics. He stressed the importance of following the order of **natural** development of a child's education, appealing to the senses, the gradual uncovering of ideas, or the discovery of information of interest to the child instead of adult-devised and directed learning. He believed that instruction should focus on life functions and not on the acquisition of abstract knowledge.

In 1693, **John Locke** reacted negatively to the severe treatment of children that was a common practice of the time. He attempted to eradicate the harsh, often cruel and extremely humiliating punishments used by some parents and educators of his day. Children who did poorly in their lessons and rote recitations were sometimes beaten, denied nourishment, or made to accept the jeers and taunts of their peers. For example, a student may have been punished by being made to wear a "dunce cap" – a tall, cone-shaped hat often made of paper – and be required to sit in the corner for an extended period of the school day.

Locke advocated non-forced, pragmatic, and interesting instruction. Although he did understand that the acquisition of reading must begin with letter recognition, he wrote in his work, *Some Thoughts Concerning Education*, that "...it must never be imposed as a task or made a trouble to them.... Children may be cozened into a knowledge; be taught to read without perceiving it to be anything but a sport, and play themselves into what others are whipped for."[15]

COMMENT: Harsh, cruel punishment is always unacceptable. It is *not*, however, the same as prudent, humane, and structured *discipline* that leads to and reinforces necessary **self**-discipline and meaningful self-esteem.

When psychologists, educators, and the like became appalled at the idea that children were being roughly punished for not knowing the specific rules, dates, and data presented in lessons, some associated the harsh discipline with instruction methods such as rote memorization, and so forth. Therefore, some people erroneously concluded that the severity of corporal punishments or food deprivation would be eliminated if there were no rules to learn and if the children were able to construct their own learning experiences.

John Jacques Rousseau supported the growth of *philosophic humanism* in the 1750s. This later developed as an educational theory supporting natural learning. He believed that humans were, by nature, good and that education is a gradual and unhurried process in natural development. He felt that a human's understanding was acquired through the senses and that learners should be in charge of their own destinies. Rousseau gave his own five children away to a foundling home.

COMMENT: Natural learning is not to be confused with *passive* learning. Passive education requires less effort than active, natural education. For example, as Marie Winn says in *The Plug-In Drug*, "The television experience does not further...verbal development because it does not require any verbal participation...merely passive intake."[16]

She adds, "The increase in the number of low [College Board] scores may reflect the influence of television...since it is known that television viewing increases reading difficulties."[17]

Friedrich Gedike (1754-1803), a German, influenced by the philosophers of his day, promoted what he called the *natural approach* to learning to read. He believed:

- Learning letters by **rote** leads to slow pronunciation and no comprehension.

- An **imagination** stimulated by songs, stories, and drawings is **ideal for learning.**

- Children at around **age ten** can learn easily by going from **wholes to parts.**

Gedike's *natural approach* was one of the various *whole-to-part* approaches to reading that were pitted against the systematic, direct phonics approach that taught parts first leading to the reading of the whole.

In 1783, ***Webster's American Spelling Book*** was published. It employed the phonics method of teaching reading in English. It was a milestone in American education.

COMMENT: This phonics method was a systematic, orderly, direct instruction approach. It was historically and undeniably effective, but lost favor.

The Advent of Sight-Word and Whole-Word Reading

Jean-Jacotot (1790-1840), while teaching Dutch students to speak French, developed a *whole-to-parts* method whereby his students first memorized a long passage by hearing it. Once they had acquired it aurally, they attempted to "read" by following along during an oral recitation of the passage. Students would try to mentally connect the words they *saw* as the words were being *recited.* Their independent reading of that passage was expected to follow. Once the words were known, it was thought that students would identify the individual sounds within the words.

By using this method, students' attempts at becoming fluent readers of other texts were slow and tedious. Some German teachers also used an aspect of this approach; however, they often had students memorize whole paragraphs instead of the longer passages.

At the same time, in the United States, Reverend **Thomas Gallaudet** (1787-1851) invented a picture-word approach to teach his deaf students how to read. Students associated pictures or objects with written words, but obviously, not with the sounds of letters. The theory was effective.

For example, a picture of hands was shown next to a card.

A reader could associate the *picture* of the hands with the written word, "hands." Several words learned from pictures, therefore, could be connected. A deaf reader could then begin to know some of the words in a written sentence that may appear in a book as in:

"The **boy** has **two dirty hands**."

Although learning to read the English language by using this approach was like learning a pictograph language, the deaf reader could get the concept or *gist* of what was written. Of course, memorizing thousands of these picture/word partners was a daunting task. Nevertheless, it was an important beginning step toward literacy for the non-hearing person who, up until then, had no opportunity for literacy at all.

Horace Mann (1796-1859) and other educators were intrigued by the sight-word and picture-word approach developed by Gallaudet. They promoted it to teach not only non-hearing individuals but hearing people as well. Mann attacked the alphabetic and syllabic methods of teaching reading, calling them "meaningless repetition of skeleton-shaped ghosts." He supported the using of a combination of picture-word and sight-word associations. By using such associations, students **learned letters** through **repetition of the same letter in many words** until the student became familiar with its **sight, sound,** and **use**. He believed that the teaching of each isolated letter and its sound should be avoided.

In 1830, Gallaudet published *The Child's Picture Defining and Reading Book*. The book universalized the picture-word approach used in teaching the deaf to read. Gallaudet also promoted it as a book to be used for children who were able to hear. In the book's preface, he introduced for the first time basic **whole-word standards** of instruction. In the 1830s, Mann encouraged his second wife, Mary Tyler Peabody, to write a book compiling the sight-word ideas including those of Gallaudet.

In 1840, John Bumstead of Boston published *My Little Primer* to teach children to read by the whole-word method. The book had students first memorize the whole name of an item and then learn its letters and memorize its spelling.

Horace Mann, assisted by lawyer friend, George Combe, wrote the *Seventh Report to the Boston School Committee of 1844* that stated, **"I am satisfied that our greatest error in teaching children to read lies in beginning with the alphabet."**[18] The report was Mann's effort to promote Gallaudet's picture-word system.

COMMENT: Gallaudet and Mann were well liked and highly influential in educational circles. They developed theories that became the basis for whole-word reading instruction that expanded throughout educational systems. In other words, Mann proposed to teach a nation of hearing students as though they were deaf. None of their theories had ever been subjected to rigorous, scientifically based research. Nonetheless, these theories flourished at the university level, in colleges of education, and, subsequently, in the elementary classrooms.

The Reading Wars Begin

Not all agreed. **Samuel Green,** of the Philips School, **opposed Horace Mann** by pointing out the following weaknesses in Mann's theories:

- Reading English using the sight method means English loses its advantage over languages that are based on pictographs.

- Learning only some words does not lead to mastery of other words.

- Spelling becomes increasingly difficult for students learning the sight-word method of reading, as words and written material become long and complex.

- Eventually, letters must be learned.

- While a student must be happy in learning in the classroom, it is also extremely important that the educator **establish a firm and permanent foundation** for the student's future learning and advancement.

COMMENT: Mann's methodologies focused on the success and happiness of the **child in the classroom.** Green, however, understood that students must be prepared to enter the world outside of the secure and supportive environment of the school.

Around the 1840s, **most grammar school teachers discredited the sight method,** saying it was ineffective. They and other opponents of the whole-word methods became more vocal in their disagreement. They complained that students were required to learn thousands of words before they learned to spell; the disastrous consequence was very **poor spelling.** They observed that the variety of methodologies was inconsistent with the traditional, effective methods. They objected to:

- Relating pictures to word shapes, and

- Requiring words to be learned *without* learning letters.

Public awareness of the problem led to what became known as the **"reading wars."** These so-called *wars* found their battlefields in the public press as represented by the following opinion of a reader:

> Education is a great concern; it has often been tampered with by vain theorists; it has suffered from the stupid folly and the delusive wisdom of its treacherous friends; we hardly know which have injured it most. Our conviction is that it has much more to hope from the collected wisdom and common prudence of the community than from the suggestions of the individual. Locke injured it by his theories, and so did Rousseau…All their plans were too splendid to be true…We are in favor of advancement, provided it be towards usefulness…We love the secretary [Horace Mann, Secretary of the State Board of Education in Massachusetts, 1837] but we hate his theories. They stand in the way of substantial education. It is impossible for a sound mind not to hate them.[19]

Progressive Education

G. Stanley Hall (1844-1924) studied psychology in Germany. Then, in 1877, he organized a psychology lab at John Hopkins University in Baltimore, Maryland. He channeled his philosophical and psychological theories into educational methodologies. He believed that children below the age of eight years should be able to experience life in a non-restrictive stage similar to that of apes. He believed that in this simian stage, when the child grows rapidly and when energy levels are high, the child should be able to express his/her animal nature. According to Hall, the child at age eight is finally able to use reasoning, show religious sensitivity, and social discernment. Then, formal learning can begin. Hall believed that if a child were forced to learn before this, long-term negative effects would result.

In 1911, Hall wrote a book that supported the word method and, at the same time, **minimized the value of reading in instruction.** He became one of the chief proponents of the *look-say* philosophy. John Dewey, the man considered to be the *father of progressive education*, endorsed Hall's theories.

In 1898, John Dewey wrote in his essay, "The Primary-Education Fetish," that "the pleas for the predominance of learning to read in early school life because of the great importance attaching to literature seems to be a perversion." He stated that the instruction of phonics as part of reading was so laborious that children would turn their backs on genuine learning. John Dewey noted that a child acquires spoken language naturally and pointed out that a child speaks whole words like *mama* and *dada* without being taught each sound separately. He believed that learning to **read whole words** in like manner comes naturally.[20]

COMMENT: Dewey thought phonics was an obstruction to learning. Quite the opposite is true. Without the effective strategies of phonics, students find that guessing at unfamiliar words limits their comprehension and, ultimately, their true enjoyment of reading. Many individuals say that they can read but do not like to read. Most of these individuals also do not have phonics skills.

In fact, opponents of Dewey's Progressive Movement said that Dewey failed to recognize that the sound's written symbol, that is, a letter of the alphabet, is a contrived, fabricated encoded tool of communication developed only in the past few thousand years, whereas voice communication is innate in humans. Teachers, therefore, must systematically and directly instruct students how to decode letters. That is, they must teach students to read by (a) identifying the contrived shape or *letter*, (b) using the sound assigned to that letter shape, and finally, (c) connecting or *blending* the assigned letter sounds in the order that they appear in the word.

It happened that many classroom teachers who had seen the decline in academic achievement and classroom discipline considered Dewey's approach as **too permissive**. The self-discipline of students declined at the same time.

COMMENT: When administrators, teachers, and parents place high expectations on students for their self-discipline and academic achievement, *and* when students are simultaneously given the tools for successful learning, classrooms can be places of inquiry and enthusiasm for learning. In classrooms that are too permissive and the students do not have effective strategies for learning and self-discipline, the experience for teacher and students can often be disastrous.

Despite the challenges to these natural approaches, publishers, college educators, and the academic elite of the 1930s enthusiastically were promoting the whole-word method. Publishing companies introduced expensive, attractive products for teachers to use in advancing the "new and improved" reading methods in their classrooms. College professors advocated novel ideas to survive in the publish-or-perish academic world. Colleges of education adopted the whole-word methods training and eliminated the phonics approaches that were considered old-fashioned methodologies. Thus, several generations of educators, themselves taught to read by the whole-word approaches in their own primary education, assumed that they were being prepared in college to teach reading using the most effective methods.

COMMENT: Perhaps the phrase, "little did they know," takes on a dual and thought-provoking meaning, considering the lack in the education of these unsuspecting, future teachers.

Conclusion

So far, this survey of the history of teaching reading has examined the earliest indications of a written language in hieroglyphics, then a phonetic alphabetic. The trends in teaching reading have evolved from a purely phonetic approach to less structured so-called natural methods. Progressive education, as well as several other experimental systems, launched the modern reading wars. The chief value of this historical overview is a practical one: educators who want to be truly knowledgeable in their craft can bring to the table a historical perspective that can contribute to the promotion of effective discussion and debate regarding current issues in the teaching of reading.

For Further Consideration

- What is the importance of being aware of the experiences of the past, and how does knowledge of these experiences help us to understand the present and to plan for the future?

- Think about an instance when a poor reader or a poorly educated individual negatively caused problems for himself or herself, you, or society.

- If you developed your own language, how would it be communicated in written form?

- How would the words be pronounced? How would you teach others to use it?

References

[8] Wilson, R. M. (1970). *Teaching Reading – A History.* Retrieved October 29, 2004 from http://www.socsci.kun.nl/ped/whp/histeduc/wilson/wilson10.html.

[9] Gatto, J.T. (2001). *The Underground History of American Education.* New York: Oxford Village Press.

[10] Atlantis Rising Online. (2004). *Carvings Spark Debate Over Alphabet:When Did Civilization Move Toward Its First Alphabet?* Retrieved October 30, 2004 from http://www.atlantisrising.com/xnews.html.

[11] Wilson, 1970. (Watson's Translation, 1856, I, 1, 25).

[12] Ibid.

[13] CTVC-Independent Television Productions. (1999). London Weekend TV.

[14] Mulcaster, R. (1581). *Positions Concerning the Training Up of Children, Chapter 5.* Retrieved October 29, 2004 from http://www.ucs.mun.ca/~wbarker/positions-txt.html.

[15] Locke, J. (1693). "Some Thoughts Concerning Education." *The History of Education and Childhood.* Retrieved October 27, 2004 from http://www.socsci.kun.nl/ped/whp/histeduc/locke/, Sections 148 and 149.

[16] Winn, M. (1977). *The Plug in Drug.* New York: Bantam Books/Viking Press, 7.

[17] Ibid,107.

[18] Gatto, 2001, 68.

[19] Ibid, 69.

[20] Sweet, R. (1997 May-June). "Don't Read, Don't Tell," *Policy Review*, Number 83. *The Century of Miseducation of Teachers.* National Right to Read Foundation, Washington, D.C. Retrieved November 24, 2004 from http://www.nrrf.org/essay_Century_of_Miseducation.html.

CHAPTER THREE

THE READING WARS OF THE 20TH CENTURY

"There are three ways to go through life. First, the easy way is to learn from the mistakes of others and not copy them. Second, the hard way is to make your own mistakes and learn from them. Finally, the totally miserable way is to copy others' mistakes and never learn from your own." Pat Doran, *My Steps Journal*, 2002.

FOCUS POINT: Phonics was once the staple of reading education. It fell out of favor in some academic circles and has recently been rediscovered as an essential component of successful reading. The pendulum is swinging back.

This chapter covers the most recent developments and controversies in strategies used to teach reading in the United States and elsewhere. During its initial stages, the American education system placed a premium on the study of the arts, literature, science, history, and mathematics. Foundational literacy skills helped to make this possible.

For the past several generations, however, classrooms across America have been saturated in diluted curricula, an over-abundance of peer tutoring, and poorly applied cooperative-learning techniques to accommodate a large-scale shift in education philosophies. Meanwhile, the emphasis on foundational literacy skills (phonics and phonemic awareness) went by the wayside. Many educators became more child-centered and less knowledge-centered. While they admirably attempted to focus on the short-term, they often failed to address what students would need beyond the classroom.

Sight Reading and Other Approaches Take Hold

At the start of the 20th Century, **Francis W. Parker**, a teacher with little academic training – as was often the case in the early days of education – originated the **Quincy Movement**.

The Quincy Movement:

- Used **group activities** and promoted the group over the individual.

- Emphasized the use of the "scientific method" and knowledge acquisition through **discovery**, instead of the traditional classical studies of history, philosophy, logic, and literature.

- Promoted informal methods of instruction and allowed **casual dress** of students and teachers as well as **informality in conversation**. For example, students and teachers called each other by their first names.

- **Eliminated rigid discipline** as being psychologically damaging to children.[1]

COMMENT: Francis Parker's philosophy predominates today in many schools; however, his and other similar philosophies are being reevaluated. Successful schools today demand mutual respect between teachers and students, have structured curricula emphasizing personal success, and accept no excuses for failure from administrators, teachers, or students. Rod Paige, when he was U.S. Secretary of Education, referred to these successful schools as "islands of excellence in a sea of under-achievement."[2]

Also at the beginning of the 20th Century, A.J. Demarest, Superintendent of Public Instruction in Hoboken, New Jersey, and an associate, William M. Van Sickle, encountered the problems caused by teaching reading using sight words. In the preface to their book, *New*

Education Readers: A Synthetic and Phonic Word Method that was published in 1900, they wrote words to which today's teachers might relate:

> Many of the methods in vogue to-day [sic] lack definiteness of purpose and require a specially trained teacher in order to present them successfully. These methods, instead of serving as an aid to good teaching, become a stumbling block and thus many a willing teacher in her earnest endeavors to keep abreast of the times, has been confronted with a dismal failure at the close of the reading period.[3]

They attempted to correct the problems by melding elements of systematic phonics with the teaching of 183 *stock* words. Students memorized the stock words by sight, accomplishing what they termed *word building* or the *synthetic phonic word method*. Their reference to stock words is comparable to what may be considered *sight words* in today's educational parlance. Children were not to have books until the foundation was laid.

COMMENT: Many of the stock words listed by Demarest and Van Sickle, such as "apple," "an," "it," and "is" (Demarist, 1900, p. 19) were unnecessary to learn by "sight" because these, and many so-called sight words, could have been decoded easily through the application of rules of phonics.

The typical daily procedure for Demarest and Van Sickle's *synthetic phonic word method* can be summarized and presented in the order named as follows:

Step 1. **PHONIC METHOD:** Drill on consonants, such as *g*.

Step 2. **WORD METHOD:** Drill on the stock words or memorized words, such as *sin*.

Step 3. **SYNTHETIC METHOD:** Drill on the *blend words*. For example, $\boxed{f}$ + $\boxed{an}$ is read $\boxed{fan}$, or the stock word $\boxed{sin}$ plus the consonant $\boxed{g}$ make a blended word, $\boxed{sing}$. (*Perception –* or *flash-* cards are used for fluency.)

Step 4.   **SENTENCE METHOD:** Drill on reading complete thoughts and reading for expression so the blend words become part of the vocabulary.

Can the little birds **sing**?
Can the big bird in the tree **sing**?
Will the pretty birds **sing** for me?

Demarist and Van Sickle developed lessons that were free of "diacritical marks so that words would be presented in the form in which they are found in any book or paper."

COMMENT: This one approach is, indeed, valuable. Instruction in the use of diacritical marks is a required dictionary skill to be used when one has difficulty with pronouncing a word and as an aid in reading. After all, diacritical marks are not found in common reading material. Therefore, students must be taught word-attack skills to be used when no dictionary is available. Forms of *synthetic* strategies are being taught today.

Using the synthetic phonic word method, students were not permitted to blend consonants until the forty-sixth day. The authors wrote, "In teaching blended consonants like /bl/, sound the /b/ first, then /l/ and then blend the two as /bl/."

COMMENT: Teaching consonant blends with a separate emphasis may be unnecessary. It is also time-consuming and can be confusing for some readers in subsequent reading tasks. Students should *not* have to memorize pl, bl, sl, fl, br, pr, sr, tr, dr, cr, st ,fr, gr, gl, sl, spr, str and so on, "by sight." The letters, *s, t,* and *r*, for example, do not change sounds when they are together. Blending or sliding individual consonants in left-to-right reading is a simple, efficient way to teach students to decode *any* consonant sound that is not one of the digraphs such as *ch, sh, th,* or *wh*.

In my experience, older individuals who were drilled to memorize consonant blends often make common errors, assuming the presence of a blend when only a single letter is written. Actual mistakes made by my students include reading *drip* not *dip, slip* not *sip,* and *truck* not *tuck*.

Maria Montessori, a psychologist and a philosopher, added insights and adaptations that seemed reflective of the natural movement. In 1912, she wrote in her much-acclaimed treatise, *The Montessori Method: Scientific Pedagogy as Applied to Child Education*:

Maria Montessori wanted teachers in her programs to:

> ...understand that her [the teacher's] new task is apparently passive, like that of the astronomer who sits immovable before the telescope while the worlds whirl through space....That...little ones would, from us, be able to learn to read and write without fatigue, made a great impression upon me. Thinking upon the results I had obtained in the school for [the learning disabled], I decided...to make a trial upon the reopening of [another] school....It has for too long been virtually her [teacher's] duty to suffocate the activity of her pupils.[4]

Maria Montessori explained her approach to reading instruction by writing:

> We present the cards bearing vowels painted in red. The child sees irregular figures painted in red. We give him the vowels in wood, painted red, and have him superimpose these upon the letters painted on the card. It was discovered that some students made mistakes in the letters if they only looked at the letter, but could discern by touching it, revealing learning preferences of visual and motor.
>
> The consonants are painted in blue, and are arranged upon the cards according to analogy of form. To these cards are annexed a movable alphabet in blue wood, the letters of which are to be placed upon the consonants as they were upon the vowels....The teacher, naming the consonant according to the phonetic method, indicates the letter, and then the card, pronouncing the names of the objects painted there, and emphasizing the first letter, as for example, 'p-pear: give me the consonant p—put it in its place, touch it,' etc. I had thus, about the year 1899, initiated my method for reading and writing upon the fundamental lines it still follows.[5]

Controlled Vocabulary

Hanna T. McManus, public school principal, and **John H. Haaren,** Associate Superintendent, both of New York City, decided to tackle the problem of reading difficulties in the area schools. In the preface of their 1914 book, *The Natural Method Readers: A Primer*, they state that instruction in reading should use nursery rhymes so the "rhyme thus becomes a part of the child's mental equipment, and is made to serve as a key to the recognition of words. It takes but a little practice to enable the pupil to **pick out the words of the rhyme.**"[6] This resembles the philosophy of Jean-Jacocot (1790-1840). The McManus-Haaren philosophy claimed that by reciting nursery rhymes, the child would want to read the memorized rhyme and would, therefore, enjoy the experience of reading.

McManus and Haaren also promoted controlled-vocabulary materials. "It has been the aim to so limit the number of words to be taught in a lesson that the task set before the teacher and pupil may not be beyond the ability of little children in the first year of school."[7]

COMMENT: Only knowing limited, controlled, sight-word vocabulary might be sufficient for students in the lower grades, but it is limiting, handicapping the older reader. Teachers often complain that students' standardized reading test scores drop in fourth grade and that the students are impeded when reading materials independently. Clearly, controlled vocabulary does not provide a sufficient foundation.

The rejection of the idea of supporting limited and controlled vocabulary materials is not the same as rejecting the use of graded materials. Without a doubt, the readability of materials is essential. It is well established that we read smoothly when we know at least 95% of the surrounding context for instructional reading and 99% for independent reading. Moreover, the beginning reader should have a comfortable level of knowledge of the topic. It would be irresponsible to ask students to read materials at a level of readability that is significantly higher than their skill level. Thus, the importance of using decodable text, particularly for new readers, is essential.

Clearly, however, students with phonics skills are able to read the many words that they have in their aural and oral vocabularies – approximately 20,000 – by the time they are in second grade.

Older students should know significantly more words. Thus, the readability levels of materials for phonics-trained individuals should be considerably higher than those who have only a limited, controlled reading vocabulary that they have been required to learn. In any event, education's purpose is not to limit artificially the reader's reading level, but to provide knowledge and materials that will allow the reader to soar academically.

William S. Gray, of the University of Chicago, was hired by Scott, Foresman and Company to write a new whole-word pre-primer and primer. In 1930, Gray's *Dick and Jane* primers that utilized the look-say or see-say approaches were introduced to American schoolchildren. These primers used controlled vocabulary and became successful in that they experienced longevity in the public schools.

As you look at the chart on the following page referencing the changes in the *Dick and Jane Pre-Primer* between 1930 and 1951, note the decrease in the number of sight words and the increase in the amount of repetitions. Also keep in mind the historical roots of the look-say and sight-reading methods, contrasting the limited amount of sight-words learned with the *thousands* of words that phonics-trained students would be able to read. Nevertheless, Gray, like McManus and Haaren, sincerely believed that children at the primary level should be comfortable in reading tasks and "not challenged beyond their abilities." Their intentions were admirable, but perhaps a bit errant.

Consequently, by 1951 the publishers significantly increased the number of times a new sight-word was used in the *Dick and Jane Pre-Primer.* Note the increase in the number of pages in the teacher's guide. Moreover, illustrations were increased.

1930 Edition	1951 Edition
Teacher's Guidebook - **87** pages	Teacher's Guidebook - **182** pages
68 sight words	**58** sight words
• *"Look"* was repeated **8** times • *"Oh"* was repeated **12** times • *"See* was repeated **27** times	• *"Look* " was repeated **110** times • *"Oh"* was repeated **138** times • *"See* " was repeated **178** times
39 pages of story **39** illustrations **565** words	**172** pages of story **184** illustrations **2,603** words

(Adapted from John Gatto, 2000, p. 72)

In any event, it seemed that developers of the materials became aware after the 1930s that sight-reading with controlled vocabulary was not as effective as they had originally thought. They had to make adjustments by increasing the number of times the students would be exposed to a new word in order to memorize it by sight.

In 1936, Edward Dolch published his **Dolch List** of sight words. A typical lesson of commonly used words from the Dolch List would introduce specific words, have students speak the word aloud, study, and memorize it, and then review the word in a controlled-vocabulary reading exercise. Students would be drilled on these words.

COMMENT: To be fluent means to be able to read smoothly, quickly, and with expression. If the reader can quickly identify frequently used words, fluency increases. Although the Dolch List has the most frequently used words, only some of them might be considered troublemakers that need to be memorized for quick identification. Words such as ***although, some,*** and ***come*** can be treated as "sight words." However, other words on the list such as ***on, no,*** and ***here*** follow specific phonetic rules and would not need to be memorized. Flashcards and word lists should be used as drill only for (a) reinforcing words or names that are clearly exceptions to the rules, such as *through, Chicago,* and (b) increasing the speed and fluency at which the reader <u>decodes</u> words that follow the rules, such as *stand, fast, flap*. Flashcards should never be used as a sight-word memorization substitute for explicit phonics instruction.

It may be that some students who have been drilled on words with similar beginnings such as ***this, that, these, those,*** and ***then*** may frequently confuse or incorrectly guess at the word beginning with *th*, saying the first "*th* word" that comes to their mind rather than reading from left to right.

Periodically, one of my adult students encounters small words that he memorized by sight. Often, he falls back into his "recitation habit" from his former sight-word training. Although he can read complex words correctly, he often confuses and misreads the little words such as *an, on, is, it, our,* and *out*. These are his "sight words." He explains that during sight-word recitation time, he never really "read" the words on the word lists. Often, he got lost. Instead, for whatever reason, he just chimed in with his classmates as they recited the word lists. He says, "I became a great mimic." He admits that he subsequently guessed frequently when asked to read the words. He was diagnosed as being a *dyslexic*.

He now uses phonetic rules, not relying on the sight-word strategies that he learned as a child. The only time he reverses letters is when he quickly reads little words like *on/no* and *was/saw*. He now understands why he makes the mistakes he does. Moreover, he catches his errors and self-corrects by using phonetic principles. He has made the observation from his own experience that if educators spent less time drilling sight words and more time teaching decoding skills, they would be offering their students opportunities to read better and would most likely have fewer dyslexic students.

In 1952, the Reverend John A. O'Brien produced a revision of Gray's *The New Our New Friends*. Following are samples from the story, "The New House," in *The New Our New Friends*.

Page 6

"See Spot run," said Jean.

"See Spot run to the new house."

"Come home, Spot," said John.

"Come, Spot, come. Come home."

Page 7

Spot did not come home.

So John and Jean went to the new house.

"Spot is not here," said Jean.

"He went that way."

"He went this way," said John.

"Run, Jean! Run this way."

According to the vocabulary information at the end of the primary reader, *The New Our New Friends*, the only new word on these pages is *way*. The students in the pre-primer supposedly had previously mastered the other words. The author's comments noted that variations of words are not counted as new words. For example, *like* is counted, but *likes* is not; *surprise* is counted, but *surprised* is not.

Such limiting and controlled vocabulary by the authors was in contrast to youngsters' abilities to learn. Through normal development, students enter first grade speaking and knowing 10,000-25,000 words. Second-grade phonics students generally should be able to *read* any of these words. Students using the reader, *The New Our New Friends*, mastered only the limited, publisher-selected 346 words by the end of first grade. As students advanced to the upper grades, they were unable readily to read non-vocabulary-controlled materials. They had no tools to attack new words. By comparison, fifty-years earlier, the synthetic word method of Demarist and Van Sickle in 1900 that used both phonics and sight words, contained 426 sight and blended words and gave students some word-attack skills.

The national reading levels were plummeting. Consequently, a giant remedial-reading industry was born. Universities and book companies collaborated to develop remedial basal readers, graded readers, and support materials. They developed remedial reading programs that provided students with more practice of the look-say strategies in an effort to fix the problem that these same methods had created.

COMMENT: An educational theory that purports to reduce dependency on rules and, thus, to make reading a *natural* discovery or learning experience, does not take into consideration the fact that reading requires the mastery of unique skills. These are skills required to decode an *unnatural*, humanly devised sound/symbol system. Clearly, then, remediation of the ineffective method and *not* of the student would seem to be more logical.

The Reading Wars Take on New Dimensions

In 1955, **Rudolf Flesch** wrote *Why Johnny Can't Read*, laying blame at the feet of the education establishment's abandonment of phonics. In what may have been seen by some as a countermove in 1956, the **International Reading Association (IRA)** was formed.

The IRA published three journals supporting its viewpoints:

- *The Reading Teacher*
- *The Journal of Reading*
- *The Reading Research Quarterly*

In the early 1960s, **Frank Smith** recast the look-say philosophy into what is now termed *psycholinguistics*. **Ken and Yetta Goodman** promoted the *whole language* philosophy, stating that readers should figure out a word by using the "least amount of information [pictures, context, print] possible to make the best **guess** possible." In other words, the Goodmans believed that readers should guess at a word by its context and by what makes sense. This turned reading into a *guessing game*. The best readers would become the best guessers in a *psycholinguistic guessing game.*[8]

To facilitate the guessing, three *cueing systems* were used. It was believed that children could easily acquire an understanding of the written code for their language using the following cueing systems that are now found in many whole language instructional formats:

1. **Context** to determine meaning
2. **Grammatical structure** to anticipate which word is most likely to follow
3. **Patterns of sounds** in speech

Subsequently, children were not considered to be making *mistakes* in their reading. Instead, they had *miscues*. These theorists also believed children did not spell words *incorrectly*; they used *inventive spelling*. As implausible as this may seem to the average person, it did make, and still makes, perfectly good sense to some educators and theorists.

COMMENT: Several years ago, I heard a whole language proponent, a college professor, being interviewed by a radio talk-show host. I have forgotten some of the details, but I recall the general discussion and the disbelief of the show's host at what he was hearing.

The conversation began with a discussion of how children learn to read. It then flowed into the related topic of spelling. When the host asked how children would be taught to spell *correctly* using the psycholinguistic approach, the guest retorted, "Correct according to whom?"

When the host challenged that employees in businesses and the like needed to spell correctly, the guest went on to add that if the individual actually had to spell according to some conventionally accepted system, "There is always someone around who is good at spelling. Ask them." The host was at odds with the guest, frustrated by an accomplished educator whose approach would create dependent individuals rather than independent, life-long learners.

Diane McGuinness, Ph.D., in her 1997 book, *Why Our Children Can't Read and What We Can Do About It,* addresses these concerns. She explains that while reporting on errors that children made when reading stories, the [whole language proponents] were intrigued with why children failed to rely more on context and grammar to avoid making mistakes in reading. The proponents did not use scientific methods to determine the cause of errors; instead, they blamed phonics. These experts used subjective language, identifying possible causes for miscues, for example, by saying that the student may have been preoccupied or trying to do two things at once. They disregarded the importance of getting the words right.

> **COMMENT:** In 2004, Janet Martin, the former president of the Arizona State Board of Education, eloquently stated the problems of guessing when she said, "Here we are with the self-limiting failure of anticipatory reading strategies. It keeps one forever in the loop of his or her own limitations. Individuals cannot anticipate what they don't already know."

Example of the Problem

Guessing or depending on picture clues can lead to errors. Suppose an illustration depicts children diving into water. The words of the sentence read, "The children are diving into the ocean." Yet, the student without decoding skills might look at the picture and read, "The children are jumping into the *lake*." Such a student may have been instructed to use the *picture* to make an educated guess. It might seem that perhaps a student may be able to construct his or her own meaning, or *get the gist*, from the text. Perhaps it might be thought that the student would be able to gain *confidence*, but, in reality, the individual is unable to read what the author has written. Such a student, for example, may erroneously think the answer to the following comprehension question is *lake*.

> According to what you read above, choose the correct answer to complete the following sentence:
>
> *The children are jumping into the ___.*
>
> a. lake **b. ocean** c. pool d. river

Perhaps the student matches the shapes of words in both passage and question segments to get the "correct" answer of *ocean*. How is the student to be graded? Is the student to be graded on appropriately using learned guessing strategies in order to get the gist or on accurately comprehending what the author has written? The answer is obvious.

Although a teacher may have advised the student that guessing and constructing one's own meaning are acceptable strategies, such attempts can mean failure on a standardized test or transfer of knowledge. When the stakes are high for passing a state-mandated test for high school graduation, acceptance into a university, or on-the-job requirements, such guessing, construction of one's own meaning, or getting the gist of the passage, can cause serious problems. C. Bradley Thompson stated the problem with whole language in a forceful way:

> How would you like to be flown by a pilot or cared for by a nurse taught that reading is 'a psycholinguistic guessing game'? A pilot who looks at his instruments and confuses the similarly shaped words 'attitude' and 'altitude' will crash. Or consider the nurse who is told to give a patient a life-saving drug for dangerously high blood pressure. She looks on the shelf and sees two bottles side-by-side. One is marked 'hydralazine' (for high blood pressure) and the other 'hydroxyzine' (for itchy rashes). She looks at the shape of the two words and then follows Goodman's advice to guess. Whoops, she guessed wrong![9]

COMMENT: Do mistakes like this really happen? Betty Price, Director of *Professional Reading Services* in Roanoke, Virginia and author of the *See Me Read* reading program, reports that she was hired to tutor a fully-licensed pharmacist who was unable to discern the difference between the written names of "Chlorpromamide" (blood sugar medication) and "Chlorpromazine" (an anti-psychotic drug).[10]

A college student told me of a discussion she had with another student who is majoring in biology. He is having difficulty pronouncing long or scientific words. Moreover, he has difficulty trying to remember how to spell them correctly. Should his professors or future employers accept his constructing his own meanings or inventive spellings if that is what he has been previously taught?

Experimental Surge

Despite obvious problems, the whole language philosophy expanded into an experimental tidal wave. Colleges of education, without question or rigorous scientific scrutiny, adopted, and enthusiastically promoted, what we now know to be theories lacking scientifically research-based evidence of their effectiveness. As a result, most colleges of education, training grounds for future educators, entirely abandoned effective, explicit decoding and encoding instruction, despite the fact that there was no significant scientifically based proof to support the non-phonics approaches. One idea will become credible if one reads and learns all that can be said in its support, and excludes all that can be said against it.

Charles Sykes wrote the following in 1996 in *Dumbing Down Our Kids: Why American Children Feel Good About Themselves But Can't Read, Write, Or Add*:

> 'So dynamic is the whole language movement,' Kenneth Goodman [said] in 1989, 'that innovative practice is leaping ahead of research and rapidly expanding and explicating the fine points of theory.' In other words, educationists are adopting whole language programs without waiting for any indication that they work and insist that the lack of research to support what they are doing is not a sign of recklessness or wishful thinking, but rather an indication of their dynamism.[11]

Scientific Studies of Reading Techniques

The National Institute of Child Health and Human Development (NICHD) was formed in 1965 to conduct research on educational strategies. The Health Research Extension Act of 1985 gave the NICHD the power to apply scientifically rigorous research to focus on reading difficulties and the effectiveness of the teaching of reading. The NICHD, headed by **Reid Lyon,** conducted exacting and objective studies. These studies did not embrace any *a priori* theory. The average length of the studies was eight years with some studies covering from three to thirty-one years. The benefit of a longer-term design is that it allows evaluation of effects of different instructional variables on later reading performance.

A significant conclusion of the studies was that **lack of phonemic awareness seems to be a major obstacle in reading acquisition.**[12] However, the studies from the 1980s and later, found that phonemic awareness alone is insufficient for reading well. Explicit, systematic instruction in common sound-spelling correspondences is also required. The findings emphasize the value of systematic instruction in phonological skills and alphabetic principles, but they recommend no specific program. It was found that key features of systematic instruction are (1) the lessons are logically organized (systematic) and planned; and, (2) the lessons allow for extensive practice in applying phonological skills in decodable text. The importance of the application of skills through reading is essential. The reports are available on http://www.nichd.nih.gov/publications/nrp/findings.htm.

The Pendulum Swings Slowly

The pendulum has been slowly swinging back toward phonics since the end of the 20th Century. Opponents of the whole language approach have challenged it as scientifically unproven. Others have criticized it as being ineffective.

Theodor Seuss Geisel, whose pseudonym was Dr. Seuss, at a public interview in 1981, criticized the "killing of phonics" in the following comments:

> I …[wrote *Cat in the Hat*] for a textbook house and they sent me a wordlist. That was due to the Dewey revolt in the twenties in which they threw out phonics reading and went to word recognition as if you're reading a Chinese pictograph instead of blending sounds or different letters. I think killing phonics was one of the greatest causes of illiteracy in the country.
>
> Anyway, they had it all worked out that a healthy child at the age of four can only learn so many words in a week. So there were two hundred and twenty-three words to use in this book. I read the list three times and I almost went out of my head. I said, "I'll

read it once more and if I can find two words that rhyme, that'll be the title of my book. I found 'cat' and 'hat' and said, the title of my book will be The Cat In the Hat."[13]

Long before Theodor Geisel spoke these words, it was becoming obvious that there were problems in our schools. Numbers of students exhibiting reading problems had been on the rise. Between January of 1929 and June of 1932, there were only 88 articles written in various journals of pedagogy on reading deficiencies and remedial reading instruction. However, by December of 1938, this became a hotter topic as the number rose to 239.

Moreover, Gatto points out a conundrum that existed for whole language advocates. He says, "From 1911 to 1981, there were 124 legitimate studies attempting to prove...whole-word advocates right. Not a single one confirmed whole-word reading as effective."[14] Nevertheless, most colleges of education continued to teach whole-word strategies to future teachers who in turn taught these faulty strategies to millions of unsuspecting students.

Advocates of whole language continued to maintain that instruction should be child-centered and child-directed. They explained whole language was a philosophy, not merely a method of teaching reading. They claimed no connection with the philosophy and methods of Progressive Education of the early 1900s, although there appeared to be numerous threads connecting the philosophies and the methods of both. Universities and book companies continued to promote whole language; explicit phonics programs were scarce.

Meanwhile, the number of students who were being labeled as *learning disabled* increased. The medical diagnosis of *dyslexia* initially had pertained to people who at one time could read, but due to a severe trauma to the head or brain, could no longer read. Then, there came a time, coinciding with increasing numbers of students unable to read well, that the popular culture noted the increased discussion and diagnoses of dyslexia apart from medical studies. Untrained teachers and administrators began broadly to identify students as being dyslexic if the students could read but sometimes reversed letters or misread words. At the same time, many of these so-called dyslexic students were also being taught to guess at words, to construct their own meanings, and invent their own spellings. [There is more on this topic in Chapter Eleven.]

Consequently, increasingly varied and numerous remedial-instruction programs were instituted to service students with reading/learning disabilities. Moreover, with so many students unable to read words, the practice of oral reading all but disappeared from classrooms.

COMMENT: One year, I taught all of my inner-city and "at-risk" students to use decoding instead of guessing and substitution strategies. They were prepared to read our excellent social studies text by Harcourt Brace and Company, 1997. Because students were decoding at widely disparate levels, the traditional oral, "round-robin" approach was still difficult. Nevertheless, my students *read* the entire world history text in one academic year, in addition to reading outside materials independently.

First, we would analyze and discuss the new vocabulary words listed for each section of the text to be read. Second, students would read aloud the questions that were at the end of each passage or section. After that, we discussed key words and concepts included in each question. This helped students to be active readers who learned to focus on important information.

Third, we listened to the word-for-word audio that accompanied the textbook. Students were required to read along, not just to listen. I would walk around the class, making sure that students' eyes were focused on the correct passage. If any students lost their places, they would raise their hands, and I would redirect them. There were no slackers because they all had adequate decoding skills, were eager to learn, and were able to answer questions when called upon.

Last, we would have a Q/A session at the end of each section during which I would randomly select students' names from a bowl. Questions asked were (a) those in the text, (b) some of my own and (c) some developed by the students to challenge their classmates. For objective questions based on what was read, students would have to find a specific passage in the text that answered their question and would have to read it orally. These were tasks that all of the students were prepared to undertake.

During the school year, a docent from the art museum brought a traveling exhibit of the Egyptian King Tutenkhamen's artifacts. She told me that in all of her travels to schools, she had never met a group of students so knowledgeable and so inquisitive. She asked, "How did you prepare your students so well?" I responded, "They read their textbook."

On the last day of the school year, my students opted not to have an end-of-the year party. Rather, they wanted to finish the final pages in their world history text, which they did. They wanted to be the "first kids to read the entire world history textbook, cover-to-cover."

In a discussion with several other teachers, I was told that because their students could not read well enough to read the history text, they had their students dress up in historical dress or make dioramas and talk about what life was like in ancient days. Educational films filled in the information gaps. Although these activities do have educational value, they are not substitutes for reading.

Adapting

Sometimes, we are going in the wrong direction and despite warning indications, we are hard pressed to recognize or admit the error of our ways. Permit me to share an analogy, a personal, embarrassing story about something I did that could have ended in tragedy but, fortunately, did not. It was, however, a lesson learned.

When I was much younger, new in town, and on my way to a party, I was unwittingly following inaccurate directions that I had been given. I followed these directions faithfully. As a result, I took a turn and unknowingly was driving the wrong way on a one-way street. Several oncoming drivers honked at me. Because I was foolish, young, single, and all dressed up for the party, I thought they were flirting with me. After the third driver honked, I began to reevaluate my first impressions. First, I concluded that since it was dusk, they couldn't have seen me clearly. Next, I concluded that they must have been honking for some other reason. Finally, I analyzed the situation, noticed a partially hidden wrong-way road sign, and immediately realized what I had done. I turned around.

I had initially misinterpreted the drivers' warnings because I assumed that I was on the right road. The fact that I could be going in the wrong direction initially didn't occur to me. I felt foolish and somewhat pleased that no one who knew me was around to witness this *faux pas*.

I share this story because it may help explain why some educators may be unwilling to recognize a problem. Just as I was depending on those whom I thought to be more knowledgeable, educators also rely on what experts have presented to them as their road map to reading instruction.

It is for that reason that some educators continue to dismiss the necessity of changing or adapting instruction methods. For example, they may not see the need to require students to read words exactly, as long as students get the gist of or preserve the essential meaning. Perhaps these educators may have been taught and are acting upon the following directives in their own classrooms:

> The miscues...may be considered good miscues [otherwise known as mistakes] because they preserve the essential meaning, or at least partially good miscues because they reflect the use of important reading strategies, like using prior knowledge and context to predict what's coming next. From the perspective of miscue analysis and the supporting body of miscue research, it is inappropriate – even counterproductive – to have the reader try again to get the exact word if the reader's miscue preserves the essential meaning. That is why some miscue forms have had a category of 'overcorrection'.[15]

COMMENT: In other words, is it acceptable to make mistakes if the "essential meaning" of a text is preserved? Would this concept be acceptable in medical reports, legal briefs, contracts, and the like?

Keep in mind that your work as educators is to prepare individuals to achieve the highest life-long goals possible. It is, therefore, essential to *listen to the warnings* and look *for the signs* that will have both you and your students going in the right direction.

Scientific Evidence

Dr. Barbara Foorman is a professor of Pediatrics and the Director of the Center for Academic and Reading Skills at the University of Texas-Houston Health Science Center. She also served on National Academy of Science committees on the "Prevention of Reading Difficulties in Young Children." She was on the learning and instruction panel of the "Strategic Educational Research Plan" that reported that phonics-taught students outperformed whole language students. They also outperformed students taught with a mixed or embedded phonics technique in which phonics skills are introduced along with whole words. As you may recall, this is similar to the synthetic method of Demarist and Van Sickle of the early 1900s. At the 1997 annual meeting of the American Association for the Advancement of Science, she said we now have the first scientific comparison of whole language vs. the phonics method of learning to read.

Stephan Strauss, scientific reporter for the Globe and Mail in Toronto wrote about this as follows:

> The study, which involved 57 teachers, showed that the pure-phonics approach was also better than a mixed – so-called embedded phonics – technique. This is a technique in which phonics are introduced along with whole words. One example, Professor Foorman said, might be a story that featured the word cat in which children were asked to make other words that ended with an "at" sound. A quarter of these children read 2.5 words or fewer.[16]

At the end of the year, the phonics students were, on average, at 43 percent of U.S. national norms in terms of ability to identify and understand words. The whole-language and embedded-phonics groups were at the 30 percent level.

'These percentiles are quite startling and you usually don't find these effects in social science research very often,' Prof. Foorman said."[17]

David Pesetsky (2002), a linguist at the Massachusetts Institute of Technology and co-author of *How Language Should be Taught*, stated that the view that "learning to read and learning to write are a lot like learning to talk" is wrong.[18]

No Child Left Behind

So-called *back-to-basics* private, charter, and other public schools with an emphasis on traditional, classical education began to emerge in the late 1990s. Around the same time, commercial interests started advertising and selling home versions of phonics programs to parents who were frustrated and concerned when their children were not able to read at school.

> **COMMENT:** One parent who was also a teacher told me, "Parents, like me, are eagerly purchasing programs to help their children learn how to read. There are programs like *Hooked on Phonics* and *The Phonics Game,* but there's nothing resembling *Hooked on Whole Language* or *The Whole Language Game.* Parents often understand what we educators don't. Phonics is essential."

The **No Child Left Behind Act (NCLB)** of 2001 was approved by the 107th Congress of the United States in its first session, December 13, 2001, under President George

W. Bush, Secretary of Education Rod Paige, Senator Ted Kennedy, and others. This bi-partisan legislation ensures that taxpayer money is spent to teach reading using research-based reading strategies. Congress determined that no longer would federal funds support the teaching of students using scientifically unproven and ineffective reading-instruction methods. Incorporated in the *No Child Left Behind Act* are various accountability measures for local schools and districts.

There are varying opinions regarding the effectiveness of the NCLB. You may or may not agree with its authors. Nevertheless, one cannot deny the need for states, schools, teachers, and parents to (a) make sure that students are learning to read using scientifically proven, effective, efficient methods and (b) assure that the districts, administrators, and teachers are held to accountability standards as any employee would be held accountable in the business world. Students deserve nothing less than the best, most-effective instruction by the most well-prepared and successful teachers.

Conclusion

For decades, explicit phonics instruction was not taught in American classrooms. Phonics was replaced by unproven, experimental reading philosophies developed by individuals who believed that learning to read phonetically was too boring, unnatural, and difficult. They considered that phonics had too many rules or too many words that "broke" the rules. In the last few years, the trend promoted by some educators and parents has been back-to-basic, traditional education with the goal of increasing literacy for students, teachers, and society.

For Further Consideration

- Pronounce this sentence without vowels: *Prnnc ths sntnc wtht vwls.* Could or should our English language be written without vowels? Can you get the gist of the sentence? Could new readers? What might be the effect if this became the standard for English?

- What in your experience has made you aware of lowered academic standards?

- What changes would you make in education?

- Consider the unintended consequences that might occur if you unknowingly bought ineffective, experimental medicines from your local grocery store.

References

[1] Columbia Encyclopedia. 6th ed. (2004*). Parker, Francis Wayland..* New York: Columbia University Press. Retrieved October 29, 2004 from http://www.bartleby.com/65/pa/Parker-F.html.

[2] Paige,R. (2003, March 13). *Fund for Colorado Event: Remarks of Secretary Rod Paige.* Retrieved November 24, 2004 from http://www.ed.gov/news/speeches/2002/03/20020313.html.

[3] Demarest, A. J. (1900). *New Education Readers: A Synthetic and Phonic Word Method.*, New York: American Book Company, 6.

[4] Ibid, 88.

[5] Ibid, 265-266.

[6] McManus, H. T., and Haaren, J. H. (1914). *The Natural Method Readers: A Primer.* New York: Charles Scribner's Sons.

[7] Ibid, iv.

[8] Thompson, C. B. (2004). *Is Phonics-rich Instruction, as Pushed by the White House, Needed in U.S. Classrooms?* Insight on the News. Retrieved October 27, 2004 from http://www.insightmag.com/main.cfm?include=detail&storyid=634442.

[9] Ibid.

[10] Hiskes, D. (1998, February). "Explicit or Implicit Phonics: Therein Lies the Rub." Right to Read Report. Retrieved October 31, 2004 from http://www.nrrf.org/essay_Explicit_or_Implicit_Phonics.html.

[11] Sykes, C. J. (1995). *Dumbing Down Our Kids: Why American Children Feel Good About Themselves But Can't Read, Write, or Add.* New York. St. Martin's Griffin. 109.

[12] Grossen, B. (1998, November). *A Synthesis of Research of Reading From the National Institute of Child Health.* University of Oregon. Retrieved November 24, 2004 from http://www.nrrf.org/synthesis_research.html.

[13] Gatto, J.T. (2001). *The Underground History of American Education.* New York: Oxford Village Press, 7.

[14] Ibid, 73.

[15] Weaver, C. (1994). *Reading Process and Practice: From Socio-psycholinguistics to Whole Language.* Portsmouth, NH: Heinemann, 230.

[16] Strauss, S. (1997). *Phonics Reading Method Best, Study Finds Whole Language Approach Significantly Less Effective, Houston Research Shows.* Globe and Mail in Toronto, Canada. Retrieved November 18, 2004 from http://www.aci.on.ca/lighthouse/globe.html.

[17] Ibid.

[18] *Sound It Out: Phonics Works Better.* (1997, February 19). The Arizona Republic, 1.

CHAPTER FOUR

ANALYZING RESEARCH CLAIMS

"Don't expect happiness to come from doing the work that requires the least effort. Happiness comes from the satisfaction of accomplishing a demanding task that exacts excellence."

Pat Doran, M.Ed., *My Steps Journal*, 2002

FOCUS POINT: Often, educational research is not held to the fundamental scientific rigorous standards that are required for other scientific research. Three aspects of valid research are: (1) the project procedure contains controls; (2) the results can be replicated by other researchers; and (3) the project has undergone meticulous peer review. For educational research, additional factors that contribute to the validity of the research are its breadth of sampling and duration longer than just a few years.

Defining Research-based Studies

Research-based is the watchword today, particularly in the educational system, regarding studies on methods for the teaching of reading. Educators and administrators must acquaint themselves with qualities of rigorous research practices, so they can intelligently question and judge the value of the many products or ideas that they encounter in their reading, classes, and discussions.

To assure excellence in teaching, educators can no longer use methods unsupported by valid scientific study. Literacy education must employ *true, scientific, research-based* methods, proven effective in the classroom and in the world outside of the classroom.

Often, teachers are introduced to new methods and materials that are *cited* as being effective. The checklist in this chapter provides general, cursory guidelines to help educators evaluate the basic, scientific soundness of contemporary educational research and products.

In the past, various information about research data has been presented to educators as valid. In some cases, the so-called research data was offered to promote a product or advance a theory, philosophy, or idea. Teachers had been unprepared to question the validity of the research. How data was gathered and for whom, however, are important factors for educators in determining bias in any research. For example, data acquired using dubious methods, such as the application of inequitable standards for completion, as well as data that cannot be independently verified, should be disregarded.

In 1965, the NICHD started conducting educational research that contrasted sharply with previous unscientific research. NICHD studies were long-term, that is, longitudinal, averaging eight years in length and ranging from three to thirty-one years. Some studies followed children from preschool to adulthood. The samplings represented the general population by ethnic group, IQ level, and so on. Research bias was minimized as research took place in an average of fourteen different research centers. The results of these studies are summarized by the NICHD at http://www.nichd.nih.gov/publications/nrp/findings.htm.

Questions to Ask Regarding Research Claims

The following questions may not yield definitive answers. Rather, they serve as broad guidelines that educators can use to analyze or question the validity of research claims. These are but elements of background knowledge provided to better equip the wise teacher.

1. **Who conducted the research?**
    - Independent entities, such as the government, schools, universities or foundations?
    - Private companies using *internal* research to validate or promote their product?

- Private companies using *external* research to validate or promote their product?
- Groups advocating a specific agenda?

---

2.   What is the researcher's interest in obtaining positive or negative results?

- Will the research results be used to sell products?
- Will the research results be used to validate or discredit methodologies?
- What is the purpose of the research?

---

3.   Was the research scrutinized by peer review?

- Did the peer review hold the research up to rigorous scientific standards?
- Valid research is replicable. Can results be replicated by outside entities?
- What review articles have opponents and proponents written?

---

4.   What testing instrument was used?

- Did the researchers create their own testing instruments to validate the research?
- Did an independent body create the testing instrument?
- Does the evaluation system align itself with the instructional program, in effect, creating a bias in the results of the evaluation?
- Does the instructional program align itself with the evaluation system, in effect, creating a bias in the results of the evaluation?

---

5.   What teacher training methods did the research use?

- Did the training actively teach to the measurement instrument or test?
- Did the training directly teach content of measurement instrument or test?
- Did instructors know they were part of an experimental project?

---

6.   How many students and instructors were involved in the study?

- What was the total number of students involved in the research?
- Did the study use a realistic teacher-to-student ratio, for example, one-to-one, one-to-five, or one to twenty-five?

7. **What students were included in the program or results?**

- What were the ages, grade levels, and ethnicities of students involved in the study?

- Did it include school-wide, class-wide samplings, or a selected sampling of participants?

- A control group is necessary in scientific research. Did the study include test results of students who received no instruction in the program, that is, the control group?

- Did the study report the success rate of the research group compared to that of the control group?

- Did the study include only those who successfully completed the program?

- Did the study exclude students who scored below a minimum level or drop low-achieving students before final testing

- Did it exclude students who would otherwise have demonstrated that the program was less effective?

8. **Does the research include data on student achievement beyond the instructional period?**

- Were results based on a pre- or post-test?

- Were results gathered to determine the ability of participants to transfer strategies obtained through the reading program?

- Did results report transferability of knowledge, such as in other classes or home?

9. **Was research longitudinal (three or more years in duration) or short-term (two years or less in duration)?**

- For reading programs, longitudinal studies are best. Primary programs that teach reading using picture clues, limited or controlled vocabulary, and acceptable word substitutions might seem effective in the primary grades, but do not prepare students to read text-intensive, vocabulary-rich subject matter in the upper levels.

- Did the study follow students into advanced grades? Adulthood?

10. **Is the quantifiable data replicable?**
- How much of the research reporting is anecdotal and unaccompanied by quantifiable data? Anecdotes and success stories can support with real life experiences what has been demonstrated by quantifiable data, but fail to serve as stand-alone research proofs.
- Can independent researchers get the same results using their own samplings?

Analyzing Research Results

Consider the questions in the guidelines to determine the validity of each of the following two fictitious research projects.

Theoretical Research Project 1

- The purpose of the studies was to compare training methods for teaching reading and identify the most effective way to teach reading.
- The average length of the studies was ten years; studies ranged from four years to twenty years.
- Studies were conducted on the reading skills of more than 50,000 students over thirty-three years at 40 sites in the United States.
- In the decades-long studies, the literacy levels of individuals from preschool through adulthood were evaluated.
- The research used double-blind studies.
- Samplings included all ethnic groups and a full range of IQ levels.
- Children who did not speak English at all were excluded.
- The studies were submitted to extensive peer review.

Theoretical Research Project 2

- The purpose of the studies was to compare training methods for teaching reading and identify the most-effective way to teach reading.
- The average length of the studies was two years.
- Those who collected and collated data had high stakes in the project's success.
- The teachers in the study were paid for instructional work and reports.
- The teachers' supervisors used the teachers' success data to evaluate those teachers.
- The supervisors submitted the data to an evaluation center that used the data to evaluate their own performances.

- Students, whom the teachers believed would be unsuccessful in the project, were not taken into the program or were eliminated from the program as the program progressed.

- Repeated reductions of the number of students in the sampling were unreported.

- Final data appeared in unpublished reports produced by research initiators.

- The reports underwent no peer reviews required for publication in scientific journals, although the articles written by the developers citing the success of the program were printed in various educational journals and popular magazines.

- Independent researchers using standard research procedures were unable to replicate results.

The methods used in Project 1 are consistent with scientific research standards; whereas, the methods used in Project 2 are inconsistent with scientific research standards. Educational products described with phrases such as *studies show* or *research demonstrates* must be approached with caution. *Caveat emptor.* Let the buyer beware.

Today's Studies on Reading Instruction

The Partnership for Reading is a collaborative effort of the National Institute of Child Health and Human Development (NICHD), the U.S. Department of Health and Human Services, and the U.S. Department of Education. Its purpose, as stated on its website, is to offer "information about the effective teaching of reading for children, adolescents, and adults, based on the evidence from quality research." The Partnership makes reading research available to educators, parents, policymakers, and others who have an interest in helping all individuals learn to read well. According to the Partnership, "Good reading instruction utilizes research-based instructional strategies and skills that include the five critical components of reading as defined in the National Reading Panel's report: Teaching Children to Read (2000)." The five critical components are:

1. **Phonemic Awareness:** the ability to hear, identify, and piece together individual sounds (phonemes) in spoken words.

2. **Phonics:** the recognition of the relationship between the letters of written language and the sounds of the spoken language.

3. **Fluency:** the capacity to read text accurately and quickly.

4. **Vocabulary:** the repertoire of words and their meanings necessary to communicate effectively in a language.

5. **Comprehension:** the ability to understand and gain meaning from what has been read.

These components are also named in the *No Child Left Behind Act*. To access the Partnership's website, go to http://www.nifl.gov/partnershipforreading/.

Conclusion

Educational studies should be held to the same standards required for scientific research, including representative sampling, longitudinality, a high degree of replicability, use of control groups, and critical peer review. Teachers must also be alert and able to discuss at a professional level about such standards with reading experts and specialists who are promoting experimental philosophies at the expense of scientifically proven methods.

For Further Consideration

- If you were a sales person attempting to sell the importance of competency in reading, what would you say?

- Who is the most critical sales person for education? Why?

- Can you think of a situation when a good idea was thrown out for the wrong reason?

- How important is it for teachers to be scholars regarding their profession, relying on more than college instructors and teacher's manuals?

- What do you think is the educator's most important responsibility to his or her students?

CHAPTER FIVE

TEACHING POST-PRIMARY STUDENTS TO READ

"If at first you don't succeed, try again, and then try something else." Mason Cooley, b. 1927

FOCUS POINT: Some modern educators have recognized the crucial role of explicit instruction in the use of phonics to teach reading. Universities and publishing companies have started to redevelop effective phonics-based reading programs for the primary grades. However, post-primary students, who have reading deficiencies and who lacked training in phonics in primary school, generally have been overlooked. Additionally, many teachers of post-primary students are unable to determine precisely what reading skills their students lack, because the teachers themselves lack efficient reading skills.

How We Got to Where We Are

Let's take a moment to recap the history chapters. By the middle of the 20th Century, explicit instruction in phonics was disappearing from the primary curriculum in public schools and was replaced with approaches such as *sight-reading, whole-word, look-say,* or *whole language.* These techniques were considered child-friendly or *natural* and based on the premise that since children learn to speak naturally and without formal instruction, they should learn to read in the same manner. Sight-reading was modeled after the methods used to teach deaf people how to read. Supporters of the natural methods overlooked the fact that the skills to master reading are not the same as the skills needed to master speaking. Influential educational professionals, sincerely wanting to offer their students the most beneficial learning experiences, opted to introduce these new approaches as replacements for phonics. Many teachers today have only a passing familiarity with phonics strategies, and, therefore, they are unequipped to help their students with basic word attack skills. Some teachers today, although they might be capable readers, might not have the essential skills necessary to be truly successful readers themselves. Moreover, many sincere, dedicated teachers do not understand why their students cannot read well.

An illustration demonstrating this concept occurred after a presentation I gave to a group of teachers. One individual shared that she had instructed her students to attempt to read only the first couple letters of names when they came across names that seemed long or looked too difficult to pronounce. She explained, "Names are so hard to read. If names are too difficult for me to pronounce, how can I expect my students to be able to read them? Besides, that's how I was taught to read, and I do just fine." It is critical for everyone to understand that many adults, including teachers like this young woman, might not understand what it is to read well. It may be that their own reading education lacked essential information, and they simply don't know it.

Teachers Can Give Only What They Have

The reality that teachers can give only what they have was demonstrated when I was a visitor at a gathering of teachers and administrators. There, I encountered some teachers who were very poor readers. The coordinator directed attendees to break into groups of about six people each. Each group was given specific assignments to complete. In my group, each member was to read some of the assigned materials. I was merely an observer.

The first teacher gave a reason for refusing to read. "I hate to read aloud. I was never any good at it."

Another complained, "This is too childish. I am not going to do it."

The third one said to a fourth teacher, "You do it. You're a good reader. I'm not."

Finally, one frustrated teacher impatiently quipped, "I will read *everything*." Throughout the meeting, these same teachers avoided reading aloud.

Several months later, my company was hired to work with some of these teachers and others at a local school in that same city. My colleague and I conducted workshops, instructing the teachers on the use of our *Phonics Steps to Reading Success* program. The principal asked us to visit, observe, and critique each teacher as he or she taught one of the program's lessons.

On the observation days, the principal had distributed a visitation schedule so that each teacher knew when to expect a visit. The first teacher I visited was nearing retirement. He was teaching an intermediate grade that he had taught for many years. He immediately came to the door when he saw me and in hushed tones, with his back to the class, whispered, "I can't teach your program."

I told him that I wasn't there to spy on him but to encourage and support him.

He insisted, "No, you don't understand. I can't teach your program, because I can't read well enough to teach it. I've been really worried. I couldn't think of a way to teach the material, so you wouldn't find out. Very few people know. My friends told me not to tell you, but I didn't know how to get out of it. I *can't* do it! I don't know how to read that well."

I felt badly for him, but he is not alone. John Corcoran (1994), author of *The Teacher Who Couldn't Read*, had slipped through the system, but graduated from college to become a secondary teacher. He, too, hid his illiteracy from his colleagues and even his wife.[1]

Not wanting to embarrass the teacher, of course, I volunteered to teach the introductory lesson. He took a seat at the back of the room. As I taught the lesson step-by-step, two students stood out who appeared to have good reading skills. I selected the two students to help me teach the program. In fact, I was preparing them to continue the instruction of the program, if necessary.

Later, I notified the principal about what I had learned and the instructional accommodations that I had made with the two students. The principal was not surprised at the situation. She said that she identified with those teachers who do not have effective reading and phonics skills. She confessed that she was a poor speller and wished that she could improve her reading. She realized how essential phonics skills are for everyone to have. She hoped that teachers who had similar problems would learn by teaching the program.

Some teachers and administrators are embarrassed by their lack of reading and spelling skills, assuming their intellectual limitations are to blame. Others believe that reading is supposed to be difficult and prone to frequent errors. As has been discussed earlier, some have been taught to believe that errors in reading are actually *miscues* and not real mistakes. Low expectations and mediocrity, therefore, become the norm.

Nevertheless, questions arise. Even if they recognize the reading problems, and want to take the necessary steps to correct them, do teachers have the time to learn effective phonics strategies? Do they have the time to teach these skills in the midst of their increasing classroom responsibilities? The answer to both questions is, "Yes." Teachers can learn and teach effective reading skills.

The Challenge for Teachers

At a time when many teachers must raise student achievement, they are also expected to instruct an increasing number of students with diverse needs. In a single classroom, a teacher might be responsible for English-language learners, students with learning difficulties, students with above and below grade-level academic abilities, and those with emotional or physical disabilities. Any or all of these students might have deficient, below grade-level reading skills; yet educators are responsible for teaching them using grade-level curriculum.

To be successful, teachers must be grounded in both subject matter and pedagogy. Teachers must present subject matter in such a way that all their students can understand it. If students are not learning one way, then teachers must find another way for them to learn. It is, obviously, not enough to present information.

Teachers' responsibilities are wide-ranging and complex. Teachers must be proficient in human relations as well as in classroom management. They must be aware of the many-faceted emotional, social, and physical needs of each student. Taken together, such awareness allows educators to exert a positive influence on all their students and to raise every student's achievement level. This task seems overwhelming, yet teachers attempt to tackle it everyday. While many are successful, some fail. Notwithstanding the problems, the excellent teacher accepts the struggle while remaining determined to improve for the betterment of the students.

Undoubtedly, as we have seen, the teaching of reading skills and comprehension is an essential responsibility of all educators. When students read proficiently, they can be academically successful. When students are unable to read well, their time in the classroom becomes burdensome to themselves, their classmates, and their teachers. Instead of being active participants in their classrooms, they sit passively for 1,400 hours each year. Failing students frequently demonstrate negative or disruptive behavior as was discussed in Chapter One.

Literacy is the solution that goes to the heart of many problems currently facing educators. Fortunately, effective programs and techniques do exist to help older illiterate or functionally illiterate individuals. One of the techniques is that of identifying error-causing reading strategies.

Identifying Error-Causing Strategies

The types of errors older students make while reading aloud can give teachers insight into how the students were taught to read. Common error-causing strategies include skipping words, substituting words, relying on picture clues, using only the first letter(s) to guess a word and reading only small, frequently used words.

Following are a few examples of what happens to reading and comprehension when a student uses ineffective strategies.

1. **Skipping Words:** A student who skips words while reading aloud might say "whatever" or "something" instead of reading the actual words.

Consider the following sentence:

The man lived an outrageous and grandiose lifestyle.

A student who has been taught to skip difficult or unfamiliar words may read the sentence in the following way:

"The man lived an...*something*...and...*something*...lifestyle."

The student might have been taught to skip a troublesome word and return to it in order to figure it out by using context clues after finishing the sentence or paragraph.

Usually, the student fails to return to the unfamiliar word. Fluency and comprehension suffer.

2. **Substituting Words:** A student might substitute a word that is similar in meaning for the unknown word: for example, *street* for *road*, *house* for *home*, *kid* for *child*. The student might have been taught that single words are unimportant. So, he or she should concentrate on getting the essential meaning or gist of a passage. The student might even have been praised for substituting a word that made sense even if it wasn't the correct word.

By substituting words, the student may seem to be reading rapidly; however, ultimately the substitution of words will lead to inaccuracies and poor understanding of what the author had intended, namely, poor comprehension.

3. **Depending on Picture Clues:** A student might look for picture clues to help identify text because he or she was taught to do so in the primary grades. Older students are often still dependent on "reading" pictures, instead of actually reading what the written words say.

Suppose an illustration shows a cowboy rounding up cattle and the text says, "The cowboy rode his *feisty mustang* into the herd." Relying, in part, on the illustration, the student might read, "The cowboy rode his *horse* into the herd." In primary school, the student might not have been corrected because, again, the student has the essential meaning by relying on the illustration. Consequently, elementary as well as some high school texts increasingly are now containing more pictures and fewer words. They are, in essence, robbing the student of opportunities to build vocabulary and enjoy the richness of the written word.

4. **Using the First Letter(s) or General Appearance of a Word to Guess a Word:** In attempting to read a word, a student might substitute another word that contains or starts with the same letters. In this case, the student might be using *some* phonics clues. In trying to read fluently, the student will read the first letter(s) phonetically,

then insert the rest of another known word. Or, the student will complete the word using substitution or picture clues, for example, saying *pond* instead of *pool*. Note that the first two letters are identical and each word refers to a small body of water.

In one instance, a student read about a group of children who heard sneezes. She read, "The *noses* confused them," instead of "The *noises* confused them."

Another student read about a young native boy shown in an illustration wearing primitive, tribal garb. The student relied on the structure of the word as well as the illustration about the native boy. He read aloud, "The boy didn't have his *pants* with him." The actual word was *paints*, an easily decodable word. This is an example of how comprehension problems arise by use of ineffective strategies when the reader relies on the first few letters of a word, the general appearance of a word, and an illustration to guess at words. It also demonstrates that one vowel can make a *significant* difference in meaning, thereby, inhibiting comprehension. This student was humiliated when classmates laughed at the silly picture this misreading brought to their minds.

5. **Reading Only Small, Frequently Used Words:** If a student appears able to read only small or frequently used words, the student has probably been taught to read using the sight method and has visually memorized words such as those on the high-frequency lists. Such a student finds difficulty in "sounding out" bigger words and is intimidated by long, polysyllabic words. Before I taught my students practical decoding skills, one boy, David, emphatically told me, "I don't read big words, and you don't make me!" If I had followed his directions, I would have kept him in poverty, namely, not being able to access the richness of the English language.

To illustrate this further, imagine for a moment that polysyllabic words are the "high-dollar value" words of language. The poverty of the "poor" reader's word bank would be obvious when he or she reads only "low-dollar value" words of the high-frequency lists. In reality, the ability of anyone to use phonics to easily, readily, and fluently unlock big words as they read is a key to word wealth and rich comprehension.

Cumbersome Chunking (Anatomy of an Ineffective Reading Strategy)

You may encounter students who have been taught to use a reading strategy called *chunking*. Proponents of the use of chunking strategies have written extensively about this strategy.

For example, the authors of *Reading in Elementary Classrooms: Strategies and Observations* direct the instructor to teach chunking to decode polysyllabic words, such as *entertainment, international,* and *boutonniere*. The instructor is directed to say, "If you looked at them [the words] letter by letter and tried to apply vowel rules that work for short words, you probably could not decode them."[2]

Actually, this statement may indicate a lack of understanding of left-to-right phonemic strategies and phonics rules. In fact, each of these words can be pronounced using basic phonics rules. The only troublemaker may be the last part of the word, *boutonniere,* because it comes to us from Old French. Nevertheless, this originally "foreign" word can still be pronounced using English phonics rules, although perhaps with a Standard English regional or dialect variation. The phonics reader will not be deterred by its length.

Using basic phonics vowel rules, the vowel sounds in the word *entertainment* can easily be decoded and the word pronounced.

---

en·ter·tain·ment

1. *en* - The vowel is alone, so it says its *short* sound.
2. *ter* - Use the *er, ir, ur* rule.
3. *tain* - The first vowel says its name; the second is silent.
4. *ment* - Read the single vowel, short sound.

Thus, reading phonemic sounds from left to right across the word, while applying basic phonics rules, enables the student to read *e·n·t·er·t·ai·n·m·e·nt* fluently. Presumably, new readers may do so slowly at first, but they would have the necessary word-attack tools to read the word accurately. Moreover, the vowel rules that are effective for reading short words ordinarily are effective for polysyllabic words when reading from left to right.

On the other hand, consider the following imaginary lesson plan, based on suggestions found in *Reading in Elementary Classrooms,* directing a teacher to teach students to attack the word *entertainment.* Compare the complicated chunking steps with the phonics strategies.

Sample Lesson Using Chunking Strategies

Subject: ***Learning to read a word using familiar chunks.***

Type: ***Teacher directed.***

Objective: ***Students will learn strategies for decoding polysyllabic words.***

Materials: ***Small strip of paper, approximately 3"x 5"***

Procedure:

1. **Say:** This is a long word, but it is not very difficult to figure out if you use other words you know.

2. **Do***:* Write the word on the board and then cover up all but *enter.*

3. **Say:** This first chunk is a word you know. [This assumes the students can read *enter* which many cannot.]

4. **Say:** The second chunk you know from words like *maintain* and *contain.*

5. **Do**: Write *main<u>tain</u>* and *con<u>tain</u>* on the board, underlining the *tain.*

6. **Say:** Finally, you know the last chunk, if you know *argument* or *moment.*

7. **Do:** Write *argu<u>ment</u>* and *mo<u>ment</u>* on the board, underlining the *ment.*

8. **Do and say:** Since English is not a language in which letters or chunks have only one sound, you might also write the word *moun<u>tain</u>* on the board, underlining the *tain* and pointing out to students that the letters *tain* also commonly have the sound you hear at the end of *mountain.*
9. **Do:** Have students try to pronounce *entertainment* with the different sounds for the *tain* chunk.

10. **Say:** When it sounds right, you know it makes a word. So now you know to use the sound of *tain* from *maintain* and *contain* (adapted from Cunningham, et. al. 1989, p.70).

Let the reader understand, as explained in the introduction, that it is not my intention to disparage any proponent of whole language. Again, "Teachers don't know what they don't know, and they don't know that they don't know it." To be fair to the authors of *Reading in Elementary Classrooms*, we must note that much has been researched and learned about the teaching of reading since the book was written in 1989. But, many new and experienced teachers had once been and are, even today, being taught this way in classrooms and seminars. Notice the mental gymnastics required for the reading of a single word. It is no wonder that teachers of post-primary grades feel that they lack the time to teach reading. For struggling and even good readers, this method is cumbersome.

If students use chunking to pronounce words, imagine the time it would take them to read this passage that contains many polysyllabic words:

> The mayor added a blue boutonniere to his suit as he prepared to encounter the flamboyant entertainment coordinator at the international conference. When they were introduced, the conductor of the magnificent symphony postulated that the inadequate skills of the flautist ruined the performance.

Reading this passage by using chunking would be nothing less than confusing, extremely tedious, and limiting. While this may be true, you may find that for students who attempt to look for chunks or familiar word patterns, you will have to remind them repeatedly to read from left to right. **It takes patience and perseverance to change old habits**. Warning: Students may have heard that different individuals learn differently and may not want to learn new strategies. While the statement cannot be denied, you must patiently explain that all students read better when using scientifically proven strategies. But again, be patient! Ineffective strategies that were learned and bad habits that were developed in the primary grades have been practiced and reinforced over a long time. Effective strategies and good habits will be developed only through practice and reinforcement over time as well.

Replacing Old Habits

To teach correct strategies to older students, teachers and students must identify which strategies are ineffective and why they must be replaced. It is beneficial to explain to students that they are not *bad* readers. They are simply *good* at using the *ineffective* strategies they were taught. The following analogy may clarify this concept.

Imagine that when you learned to ride a bicycle, the person who taught you only knew how to ride facing *backward*. Therefore, *you* also learned how to ride a bike facing backward. You sometimes failed and fell, but you never gave up. It was difficult, but, eventually, you became adept at riding a bike backward and it became comfortable for you. The problem is that riding a bike backward is not only inefficient, it is dangerous.

Suppose that now you want to ride correctly, by going forward, but your brain has pathways already developed for riding backward. Riding forward feels awkward to you. You make mistakes. You might fail and fall several times. You might want to revert to the old, familiar ways. With effort and support, however, you can develop a new habit of going forward. It is the same with reading.

Correcting Students' Mistakes

Some teachers have been trained to avoid correcting their students as long as they get close to reading the actual word. As one young teacher told me, "One of my college instructors said that it is bad for a child's self-esteem to be corrected." This is true if done inappropriately, but correction is necessary. It must be done, but done well to be effective and not embarrassing or cause damage to the student's self-esteem.

On the other hand, as mentioned before, the following statement may have been taught to you or to those teachers who have previously taught your students: "Non-meaning-changing errors made by readers who are reading orally with expression are a sign of good reading."[3] While it may be valid, this assumption, if accepted too broadly while students are learning, can lead to problems for the student in the future if it is not addressed and reversed.

Correcting Errors Effectively

The classroom is intended to be a place of learning and that includes having mistakes corrected. It is much better for a student to be corrected in the classroom today and not in the workplace in the future. Thus, the pursuit of excellence should be a paramount endeavor for teacher and students. It is possible to make correction a positive, valuable experience for both teacher and student. When making a correction, you may want to use a version of what I call the *1-and-5 Approach*. The 1 is the *correction* and the 5 represents *praise* as on a scale from 1 to 5. It is reflective of the types of rating scales that one might find on a restaurant comment card, for example.

To illustrate using the 1-5 Approach, consider what might be said when a student reads *house* instead of *horse* or *house* instead of *home*. The teacher may make corrections in the following manner. Either the 1 or the 5 comment can be first; both must be used together.

Positive comment (5):	"I like the way you are trying to read quickly."
Correction of error (1):	"However, slow down and use your left-to-right decoding for accuracy."

Correction of error (1):	"Go back and use phonics rules to read left-to-right without guessing."
Positive comment (5):	"You have done well; learning new strategies doesn't always come easily, does it?"

Correction of error (1):	"Try again."
Positive comment (5):	"It takes practice to improve."

COMMENT: I tutored a thirteen-year-old boy who told me that he hated it when the students in his class corrected him and told him the words as he was reading. He said that he was always angry, and felt humiliated and "stupid" in class. During tutoring sessions, he accepted the meaningful 1 and 5 corrections and learned from them. He later wrote me saying, "I want to thank you for teaching me the proper way to read, write, and sound out words and spell. I know your…program will help me through the rest of my life."

It is imperative for the teacher to explain at the beginning of the school year – and reinforce it frequently throughout the year – that some students may not be able to read well because they have been ineffectively taught. When I taught classes, I would explain that the whole class would learn phonics concepts and that each student was expected to be respectful in helping the others to achieve success. Students were able to assist by *respectfully* offering phonics rule suggestions, if appropriate.

Conversely, the teacher should create a classroom environment of security and respect where students can feel free to "take risks." This concept can be enforced with what I refer to as the "one-clap compliment." For example, when a student attempts a difficult word, give a one-clap compliment and encourage the students to compliment each other in the same manner. (Note of caution: If the teacher permits lengthy and spontaneous "applause," problems may arise when students applaud excessively just to get negative attention. What is intended to reward a successful student with positive attention actually draws the attention away from that student, and the attention is focused on the poorly mannered student. More about this later.)

Finally, no one should be permitted to laugh at anyone in a disrespectful manner. The following was an effective classroom motto that we used to guide the behavior of teacher and students alike in our classroom:

At Every Moment Do What Respect Requires.

Review of Recommendations for Teaching Older Students

Students who have been explicitly taught the rules of phonics are able to read virtually anything in their spoken vocabularies. Foreign words might offer challenges, but phonics-trained readers have the skills to attack even these words.

A review of recommendations for teaching post-primary students phonics strategies should include the following:

1. **Explain to students** that they might have been taught to use inefficient reading strategies.

2. Explain; do not affix blame. Rather, **fix the problem** by systematically and explicitly teaching phonics to your students, whatever their age.

3. When students substitute words, guess, or skip words, **correct** them.

4. Remind students that they can simply apply phonics rules to decode most words.

5. **Be patient, positive, and consistent.**

It Is Never Too Late

A fifth-grade teacher was sincere when she said, "I have more non-readers in my classroom this year than last year, but what can I do? If they can't read by third grade, they can't be helped. I certainly don't have the time to try to teach reading to students who can't learn. Besides, phonics instruction is not part of my curriculum."

Perhaps the statement about children who do not read by third grade is a self-fulfilling prophecy. Perhaps older individuals don't learn to read because teachers assume these individuals cannot learn or, perhaps, no one actually takes the time to teach them.

To be fair, most post-primary teachers feel unprepared or truly are not comfortable at the thought of teaching basic reading skills in their classrooms. For obvious reasons, phonics instruction was not considered necessary at the high school level. On the other hand, time constraints are of legitimate concern. For example, trying to compress the teaching of about 5,000 years of world history events into 188 fifty-minute classes in one year is challenging at best. Certainly, all teachers realize that there is too much to teach and too little time to teach it. Where is the time to teach basic skills?

Phonics Steps to Reading Success does not take an entire year to teach and could be squeezed into 5-minute or 10-minute sessions. Older students may not need complete phonics-based *reading* programs. They may just need to be taught basic decoding concepts that they can utilize across the curriculum. The time spent in teaching all students how to decode will ultimately make the entire teaching/learning process more time efficient.

For example, all of the adult illiterate or functionally illiterate individuals that I have met have high school diplomas. One had been on the honor roll four years in a row, although he couldn't even read the words *honor* and *roll*. A few have completed college. All of them had twenty or more teachers who failed to diagnose or correct reading deficiencies. All of these adult students, without exception, had been taught to memorize words, guess at words, skip words and return to them later, or to read the first few letters of a word and then think of a word that would "make sense" in the sentence. For most of these individuals, reading was not enjoyable and did not lead to academic success.

Good Students Get Better

Besides focusing on poor or non-readers, equally important is the teaching of phonics strategies to all capable and even good readers. An example of this statement is Corrie (not her real name). When I met her, I was assigned to teach a sixth grade class. The district psychologist identified Corrie, an incoming sixth grader, as being *gifted* because of her exceptionally high analytical and verbal abilities. Her fifth-grade standardized reading test scores, however, indicated that her reading skills were average; she scored a 5.9 R.L. at the end of the fifth year and ninth month of school. She was, however, reading at a level higher than most of her classmates whose abilities were far below those required of new sixth graders. Many were reading on a first-grade level.

Up to that point, the school district had neither required, nor supported, systematic, explicit phonics instruction for students in the primary grades. In fact, the district officials explicitly preferred non-phonics, whole language programs. That year, with my principal's approval, I used my homemade phonics materials to teach all my students basic phonics strategies. At the end of the school year, Corrie tested at a level indicated to be post-high school. In other words, she had improved more than six grade levels in one year. The other students improved significantly as well.

Another student in this class was Alex for whom English was a second language. He was extremely bright, spoke English well, and enthusiastically participated in class discussions. Although his spoken language was proficient, his ability to read and write in English was found to be more than two years below grade level. His previous teacher had identified him as one who needed to be tested because his ability to read in English was inadequate for on-level work in sixth grade. I asked Alex how his other teachers had taught him to read unfamiliar words. He said, "They told me to guess." He added, "I had trouble guessing because I didn't know what to guess." He was not familiar with many phonics strategies. Despite my voiced concerns that he was not "learning disabled," Alex was approved for special education services for a total of approximately two-and-a-half hours per week. To the best of my knowledge, phonics was not taught there. The rest of the time, however, he was in our phonics-focused classroom.

At the end of our school year, he tested at almost an eleventh-grade reading level. He had gained approximately seven grade levels in his reading ability in one year. Math scores also increased since he could comprehend word problems. He was a bright boy who had been lacking knowledge of efficient reading strategies to help him attain his fullest potential.

No matter the age of the learners or the deficiency in reading or spelling skills they may have, it is never too late for anyone to learn to read efficiently. A few programs, including *Phonics Steps to Reading Success* (http://www.edu-steps.com), are written specifically for post-primary students. As mentioned earlier, we developed *Phonics Steps* to take approximately twenty to thirty hours for instruction. Instruction time is flexible and lessons can be squeezed into sessions from five minutes to an hour or more. It has been successfully used with older English-speaking students as well as English language learners, ranging in age from 7 to 72 years. Students in elementary schools, high schools, and junior college have benefited. It is a word-attack program that lays the foundations of phonemic awareness and phonics strategies to help students to develop vocabulary and increase fluency and comprehension. Other resources provide valuable information in the teaching of reading. One is the National Right to Reading Foundation at http://www.nrff.org. No matter what program you choose, it is important that you find and use a phonics program that works for you and your students.

Conclusion

As stated in various ways throughout this book, post-primary students who are struggling with reading in all areas were most likely taught to read improperly. Today's post-primary students with ineffective reading skills use cumbersome reading strategies. Many are bright, capable, upper-level students who can comprehend instructional material and orally participate in class. Sadly, these students fall short when it comes to taking a test or working independently.

Because most schools opted to concentrate on unproven approaches and generally did not teach explicit phonics for several generations, unknown numbers of teachers from ages 20 to 70 may not have learned to read using explicit phonics strategies. Therefore, many sincere, dedicated teachers do not understand their students' reading problems. Teachers can learn to help their older students by learning how to teach effective phonics skills, even if those teachers work in the upper grades. It is never too late for the dedicated teacher to teach, and never too late for the reluctant student to learn – provided that both teacher and student are given the appropriate tools. Virtually all illiterate students and adults can learn to read using explicit, systematic, direct-instruction phonics. Identifying the problem and developing phonics skills can effectively remedy most reading difficulties.

For Further Consideration

- How were you taught to read?

- In your own pursuit of excellence, what do you wish you had more time to learn?

- What academic skills do you wish that all of your students had?

- If you were granted the ability to make one permanent change to improve education, what would that be and why?

- How do the poor reading skills of students affect the way core curriculum work is taught?

- When is getting just the gist of a passage good enough? When is getting the gist of a passage not acceptable?

- How might substitution of words in reading school texts and tests hinder students' success?

- What strategies do *you* use when you encounter a long, unusual or unfamiliar word such as *tintinnabulation, mulligatawny, xeranthemum* or *szygomygicotatonosy*?

THE NEXT STEPS INTO THE CLUB

You now have the background knowledge of the history, possible causes of ubiquitous reading deficiencies and of ineffective strategies used by struggling readers. The following chapters of this book will provide you with practical strategies to correct the reading deficiencies that have been caused by failed reading instruction. The following chapters are by no means exhaustive in scope; however, they will provide you with a foundation on which you can build.

It is essential to remember that once basic phonics skills are acquired, they can always be utilized to pronounce new words, no matter the age or experience of the reader. Moreover, fluency, vocabulary development, and comprehension strategies will continue to increase along with academic advancement.

References

[1] Corcoran, J. (1994). *The Teacher Who Couldn't Read:* Focus on the Family, Colorado Springs, Colorado.

[2] Cunningham, P.M., Moore, S.A., Cunningham, J.W., and Moore, D.W. (1989). *Reading and Writing in Elementary Classrooms: Strategies and Observations.* New York: Longman, 70.

[3] Ibid, 77.

CHAPTER SIX

PHONICS STEPS: THE BASIC PRINCIPLES

"The first principles of reading are based on the encoding/decoding system of symbols and sounds. This system requires the brain to utilize specific analytical pathways." Ladner, 2003

FOCUS POINT: While teaching phonics had been the only accepted way to teach reading for generations, it fell out of favor in some academic circles in the United States. With the results of scientific studies on the effectiveness of reading methods, the pendulum has swung back. To become effective, fully independent readers, all learners must be directly, systematically, and explicitly taught to decode (sound out) individual letters and words.

Basic English Phonology

The English language is a competent instrument for communicating sounds as symbols. English has grown with its many and varied foreign influences to a universal language of communication. So widespread is its usage that a German airline pilot landing at a German airport will speak to German air controllers in Modern English.

Phonemes and Phonemic Awareness

A **phoneme** represents the smallest basic unit of speech. There are forty-four phonemes in the English language. Modern English is a language based on *phonemes*. *"Phoneme"* is from the Greek word, *phone,* meaning *sound* or *voice*. For example, there are three phonemes in the word fan: /f/ /a/ /n/. The *sound* /f/ is one phoneme. Thus, when the word, *fan,* is spoken, three sounds or phonemes can be heard as follows: /f/ /a/ /n/.

Graphemes are the written symbols of the phonemes. The first phoneme, /f/, is represented by the written letter *f*, a grapheme. "Grapheme" is from the Latin word, *graphium*, meaning *to write*. A grapheme is a term for all of the letters that can be written to represent that sound. For example, the various graphemes of /f/ are written in bold in the following words: *fan, phone,* and *rough*. In another example, the word, *head,* is composed of the three pronounced sounds or phonemes, /h/ /e/ /d/, and of three written representations of the sounds or graphemes, 'h', 'ea', 'd'.

A **digraph** is a pair of letters representing a single speech sound or phoneme, such as *ch* in *chain, ph* in *pheasant,* and the *ea* in *heat*. "Di"– comes from the Greek word meaning *two* and "grapheme" (above) meaning *to write*. A digraph is one sound that is represented in writing by two letters. In other words, two letters written together to represent one pronounced sound are called a *digraph.*

Phonemic awareness is the ability to detect and manipulate sounds in spoken words. It is generally accepted that *phonemic awareness* must be taught as preparation for *phonics*, namely, the teaching of elementary sound-symbol relationships. More information is available in many books and at various Internet sites such as www.educationnews.org.

Consonants and Vowels

Written English words consist of symbol (letter) combinations that represent phonemes. They are identified as letters representing sounds assigned as consonants and vowels, consecutively written one after the other. A **consonant** is a speech sound produced in one of three ways:

1. **Occluding**, that is, stopping or shutting off the flow of air with or without releasing the air as with /p/, /b/, /t/, /d/, /k/, /g/.

2. **Diverting** the flow of air as with /m/, /n/, /ng/.

3. **Obstructing** the flow of air from the lungs as with /f/, /v/, /s/, /z/.

The lips, teeth, and tongue of the mouth assist in occluding, diverting, or obstructing the flow of air.

A **vowel**, on the other hand, is a speech sound produced without occluding, diverting, or obstructing the flow of air from the lungs. The mouth remains open and its muscles are almost imperceptibly utilized to create different vowel sounds. In producing the short vowel sounds of /a/ (**cat**), /e/ (**bed**), /i/ (**in**), /o/ (**ox**), and /u/ (**up**), parts of the mouth and throat are variously involved. Further information can be found about the speech anatomy or anatomy of the vocal tract involved in vowel pronunciation in various linguistics courses and other academic sources.

Phonics

Manuscript symbols used for the English language alphabet letters are written using circles, straight lines, and curves. For example, a circle attached to the upper right of a straight line becomes the letter *p*. A small circle by itself is the letter *o*. When the letter *o* appears alone between two consonants, the speaker pronounces the sound of *o* with an open mouth.

Phonics is the method of teaching the predictable sound-symbol relationships required for reading. By itself, phonics is not "reading." Phonics is but one aspect required in the teaching of reading. It is, however, essential for instructors to explicitly teach the way in which symbols (letters) are used to represent speech sounds.

There is a basic body of Standard English phonics information. It consists of twenty-six letters of the English alphabet used to symbolize forty-four phonemes (sounds of speech) that can be used to read and spell approximately seventy of the most common spelling sequences.

In English grammar, the printed letters appear as "upper case" (capitals) written as *A, B, C, D, E,* and so forth; and "lower case" (small letters) written as *a, b, c, d, e,* and so on.

COMMENT: The terms "upper case" and "lower case" originated at the time when printed texts were typeset letter by letter. Every capital letter, lower case letter, and punctuation mark was raised on its own piece of metal. These metal tiles were kept in large, open cases from which the printer could select the required letters' tiles to be set in order on an iron ruler that was called a composing stick. The capitals were commonly kept in the "upper case" while the non-capital letters were kept in the "lower case." If the printer wanted to write the name, *Tom,* he would direct the apprentice to give him an *"upper case T," "lower case o," "lower case m."* Thus, we still refer to upper and lower case letters.

Encoding

Encoding consists of translating sounds into the conventionally accepted, pre-determined letter symbols (graphemes). By writing the graphemes from left to right as they are pronounced, one can write words, sentences, and so forth. Encoding is used in writing. **Encoding is spelling.**

Decoding

Decoding is the reverse of encoding. Decoding means "breaking the code" or translating written symbols--pronouncing each of the assigned sounds as they appear in a word--starting at the left and reading to the right, all the way to the end. This is where we get the phrase, "sounding it out." Decoding, therefore, is the act of translating written symbols into sounds, across a word from left to right. **Decoding is reading.**

The Recipe: An Allegory

Sally is a terrible cook, but she wanted to bake a cake. Sally attempted to bake a chocolate cake using an old recipe, enjoyed by her family for generations. She decided that the cake recipe required too many ingredients and too many exact measurements. So, she took a less regulated and more natural approach to cooking. She put in some flour, tossed in an egg, and added a few bitter chocolate squares. She added some water and stirred as she had seen her mother and grandmothers do when they had baked cakes. While she expected to produce the same cake that her family had always enjoyed, the finished product came out bitter and flat. What had gone wrong? She thought it might be her old oven, so she went out and bought a new one. She tried again. The cake was worse than before. She thought that perhaps she needed a more expensive mixer, better mixing bowls, and, possibly, a new spoon. Repeatedly, she tried to make the cake with her new hardware. Each time, she failed to get the same results that her mother and grandmothers had produced.

Sally had a problem. She did not consider the fact that she had unsuccessfully departed from a successful recipe. Nothing was wrong with the recipe or her baking equipment. Obviously, she did not follow the specific *rules* of the recipe.

Think about the process of learning to read. If past generations learned to read phonetically and comprehend well and, if today's students are not reading and comprehending well, we might ask, "What is missing from the recipe for successful reading by today's students?"

Take Exception to the Rule

Readers are familiar with words that are *exceptions to the rules* of phonics. There are reasons for those exceptions. The meanings, spellings, and pronunciation of English words reflect the history of the development of spoken and written English, as explained in Chapter Two.

North American regional or dialectical variations exist sometimes as the result of the influence of early settlers in the area. For example, in certain parts of the United States, spoken English has many similarities to British English. On the other hand, in areas that were settled primarily by people from France, one might encounter more words with French spellings or pronunciations. A well-known regional variation is that of the *Pennsylvania Dutch* because of the Germans who settled the area. The *Dutch* part of the name is akin to the word *deutsch*, which is German for "German." Nevertheless, despite the variations reflecting historical origins or local dialects, Standard English pronunciations based on standard phonics rules for speaking, reading, and spelling are nonetheless essential.

The following section explores these basic principles of pronunciation and spelling. In a systematic, explicit phonics program, these rules are taught directly and systematically. Moreover, students must be given practice to allow them to be able to directly apply the rules in the reading of decodable text.

Rules of Phonics

The following is included as a basic introduction to phonics principles taken from *Phonics Steps to Reading Success (PSRS)*. Presented compactly in a single chapter, these principles are intended only as an overview. (See Theresa's story, Chapter 13, Story 14.)

1. Read and spell from left to right. *(p. B-G)*

2. Be aware of the shape of your mouth as you pronounce sounds. *(p.1)*

3. When a vowel in a word stands alone, the vowel says its **short sound** and not its name, as in:

Vowel	Sound	Example
a	/a/	**A**nn's **a**pple
e	/e/	**E**d's **e**gg
i	/i/	**I**n the **i**gloo
o	/o/	The **o**x says "Aaah." Open wide!
u	/u/	**U**p, **up**, **u**mbrella

   (p.1)

4. Most words with a short vowel sound that end with the /k/ sound are spelled with *ck* at the end:
   tack
   neck
   pick
   clock
   duck *(p. 4)*

   [–ck Spelling tip]

   (a) Say the sounds as in the silly word, **smick**, left to right: /s/ /m/ /i/ /k/.

   (b) Say the sound /s/ as you write *s*.

   (c) Say the sound /m/ as you write m.

   (d) Then, say to yourself, "I hear a short i (igloo) sound and the /k/ sound."

   (e) Therefore, I must write *ick.*] *(p. 5)*

5. If a word contains any vowel <u>and</u> ends with the letter *e*, the final *e* is always silent. *(p. 8)*

6. If a word ends in *le*, pronounce the /l/ sound as in bund**le**; the *e* is silent and makes no sound. *(p. 8)*

7. Vowels that appear together are called *vowel teams*. Generally, when two vowels are next to each other in a word, the first one says its *name* while the second one is *silent*. Thus, the old saying, "When two vowels go walking, the first one does the talking." *(pp. 12-21)*

Vowel team	Examples
ae	m<u>ae</u>lstrom, G<u>ae</u>lic
ai	p<u>ai</u>l, m<u>ai</u>n, gr<u>ai</u>n
ay	p<u>ay</u>, st<u>ay</u>, M<u>ay</u>
ea	s<u>ea</u>m, l<u>ea</u>f, sp<u>ea</u>k
ee	m<u>ee</u>t, sl<u>ee</u>p, str<u>ee</u>t
ie	p<u>ie</u>, t<u>ie</u>d, sp<u>ie</u>d
oa	g<u>oa</u>t, t<u>oa</u>st, m<u>oa</u>n
oe	h<u>oe</u>, t<u>oe</u>, J<u>oe</u>
ue	bl<u>ue</u>, tr<u>ue</u>, contin<u>ue</u>
ui	s<u>ui</u>t, fr<u>ui</u>t, recr<u>ui</u>t *
ew	f<u>ew</u>, n<u>ew</u>, bl<u>ew</u> **

   * In the United States, **ui** is generally read with an /oo/ sound as in *moon*.

  ** **ew** is generally pronounced <u>e</u>u or ***long u***; the letter *w* was once a *double u*.   *(pp. 10-21)*

8.   When a consonant is between a vowel and its silent, shadow teammate *e* – as in *ape* or *kite* – the consonant is called a *blocker*. In such a positioning, (a) the first vowel says its name, and (b) the *e* is silent.   *(p. 22)*

     The following general rules apply:
- The *e* is the only vowel whose influence can "pass through" the consonant blocker to make the vowel say its name.   *(p. 23)*

- The *e* can send its influence through only one consonant blocker, not two. In the word āpe the *a* says its name, but in *gaffe* or *appetite,* the *a* is pronounced as its short sound. Similarly, in kīte the *i* says its name, but in *kitten* the *i* says its short sound.   *(pp. 22-25)*

9.   A single *e* at the end of a word or syllable says its name:
   (a)   when it is the single vowel in an entire word (*he, she, we, me*); and

   (b)   when it is the last letter in a single-vowel syllable (*maybe*).   *(p. 22)*

10.   When reading unfamiliar words, change the form of your mouth to pronounce each phoneme as it appears in the word.   *(p. 26)*

11.   If a word with a vowel ends in *y*, then the *y* says /ee/ as in *funn<u>y</u>*.

     [**Spelling tip:** If you hear an /ee/ sound at the end of a word and there is another vowel in the word write *y* at the end. The word *s-o-r-e* does not say *sorry*.]   *(p. 27)*

12.   If a word with a vowel ends in *y*, the effect of *y* on the vowel is the same as that of a silent *e*. That is, the vowel is "forced" to say its name. Two blocker consonants between a vowel and final *y* keep the vowel short.
- *Kitty* is not *kity*.
- *Bunny* is not *buny*.   *(p. 27)*

13. If **y** is the only vowel in a word, it is pronounced as long *i* as in *my, dry, cry,* and *fly.* *(p. 28)*

14. When **o** ends a word, the *o* it says its name as in *go, so, ego,* and *no.* *(p. 28)*

15. When **y** is between consonants, it "acts like" the vowel *i*. It is either *long* or *short*. It is pronounced as short /i/ as in *myth, gypsy,* and *physical*. It is pronounced as *long i* in the words, *type, typist,* and *cypress.*

    [**Tip:** Words with y often have regional variations. When in doubt, use a dictionary.] *(p. 29)*

16. *Psych* is pronounced /sike/ as in *psychic, psychology,* and *psychiatry.* *(p. 29)*

17. Some words break the rules, because the English language developed over several centuries. Other languages and a variety of dialects have influenced English and spelling. *(p.30)*

    [**Tip:** When in doubt of how to pronounce a word, first follow the rules. Then, if you are able, adapt the pronunciation of the word as it is commonly pronounced or use a dictionary. The "worst" that will happen is that you may pronounce the word with a slight variation from commonly accepted pronunciation or with a British, Scottish accent, and the like. Moreover, at least you will be able to make a reasonable attempt to pronounce the word that will neither impede fluency nor significantly digress from correct Standard English.] *(pp. 30-32)*

18. The sounds of **aw** and **au** are pronounced with the mouth shaped like an oval or an egg. *(pp. 36-38)*

19. When **i** is followed by **a** or **u**, it is **not** a vowel team. The **i** is pronounced /ē/ as in *Maria, Austria, lithium.* (It seems easier to pronounce than ĭ/ă.) *(p. 37)*

20. The **oo vowel digraph** has either a long sound as in *moon,* or a short sound as in *foot.* When decoding, try using the long sound first. Generally, more words have the long sound than have the short sound. Other principles may apply. *(p. 39)*

21. The letter **r** affects the sound of the vowel that comes before it. Therefore, the vowel is called an **r-controlled** vowel.

ar	pronounced	/âr/	as in	*car, arm, bar, farm**
or	pronounced	with a *long o* /or/	as in	*for, torn, born*
er	pronounced	/ûr/	as in	*verb, fern, herd*
ir	pronounced	/ûr/	as in	*girl, birth, fir*
ur	pronounced	/ûr/	as in	*fur, turn, spur*

    *[**Spelling tip**: When you are encoding sounds into symbols (spelling) and you hear what sounds like the *name* of the letter r, write "ar," as in *car*.]

    However, when a ***vowel team with a consonant blocker r (vc-e) occurs***, then the first vowel says its name and the final *e* is silent as in *fire, store, cure,* and *here.* *(pp. 40-42)*

22. The **digraph *ch*** is usually pronounced /ch/ as in *choo-choo* or *chip*. When ***ch*** follows a short vowel, a consonant blocker must be present as in *ditch, French,* and *match.* *(pp. 43-45)*

23. The **digraph *sh*** is pronounced /sh/ as in *ship, sheet, fish,* and *cash.* *(p. 46)*

24. The **digraph *th*** is pronounced /th/ by softly sticking the tongue behind the teeth and blowing out, as in *Thanksgiving, thick,* and *bath.*

    The **digraph *th*** can also be pronounced with a "harder" sound, by putting the tongue between the top and bottom teeth, blowing, and vibrating the tongue slightly as in *this, that,* and *those.* *(p. 47)*

25. The **digraph *ph*** is pronounced /f/ as in *phone, dolphin,* and *photo.* *(p. 48)*

26. The ***digraph wh*** can be pronounced /h̲w/ with a slight puff of air expelled as in *whale, when,* and *whim.* *(p. 49)*

27. The single vowel ***i*** is pronounced as *long i* as in the following exceptions:
    - *ild* words as *wild, mild, child;*
    - *ind* words as in *find, kind, blind;*
    - *ign* words as in *sign, design, resign*; and*
    - *igh* words as in *sigh, high, flight*.*

    *Note that in *-igh-* and *-ign- words,* the *g* is silent. *(p. 50)*

28. The ***eu*** and ***ew*** teams are pronounced as long u, as in *dew, grew, deuce,* and *feud.* Say *long e* and *long u* <u>very quickly</u> together to say /eu/. You will hear *long u.* *(p. 54)*

29. The **dipthongs *ow*** and ***ou*** are pronounced as in "Ow! Ouch!" and words, such as *flower, wow, loud,* and *mouth.*
    - ***Ow*** can also stand for the *long o* sound as in *snow, show,* and *tow.*
    - The dipthong ***ou*** can also stand for the /oo/ sound as in *through.*
    - The dipthong ***ou*** is also pronounced as a *short u* when followed by the letter ***s*** as in *famous, momentous,* and *disastrous.* *(p. 56)*

30. The vowels in **alt, alk, aught, all, ought** have the *aw* sound as in *saw, walk,* and *taught.* *(p. 59)*

31. The letter ***c*** sounds like:
    - /s/ when followed by ***e, i,*** or ***y*** as in *center, citizen,* and *cymbal;*
    - /k/ when followed by ***a, o,*** or ***u*** as in *cash, coffee,* and *cup;* or
    - /k/ when it is the last letter of a word as in *picnic.* *(pp. 60-65)*

32. The letter ***g*** generally sounds like:

- /j/ when followed by *e, i,* or *y* as in *gem, gin* and *gym* (with some exceptions such as *target, girl, gift);*
- *hard g* when followed by *a, o,* or *u* as in *gash, go,* and *gush;* or
- *hard g* when it is the last letter of a word as in *dog, dig* and *dug.*

(pp. 66-70)

33. If a *ti, ci,* or *si* is followed by a vowel, it makes the /sh/ sound as in *option, cautious,* and *conscious.* *(pp. 73-75)*

34. Syllabication basics:

(a) When two consonants are between vowels, the syllable ends with the first consonant as in *rab·bit, mur·mur,* and *mag·net.* The syllable is called *closed.*

(b) An "open syllable" often occurs when one consonant is between two vowels. The syllable is divided before the consonant as in *so·lo, spi·ral* and *ve·to.*

(c) A vowel may say its name when it is at the end of a syllable as in *fi-nance.*

[**Tip:** If this is a new word to the reader and the reader pronounces as *fin-ance* by following the short-vowel rules, he/she would be equally correct with perhaps a slight accent as may be heard in parts of England. See note at #18.]

(d) With words ending in a **consonant + le**, the **consonant + le** pattern is considered to be a separate syllable, as in *han·dle, wrin·kle* or *pad·dle.*

(e) The following are usually separate syllables:
- Vowel teams with **blockers** as in *con·crete* and *in·side;*
- Vowel teams **without blockers** as in *de·feat, team·mate;* and
- R-controlled teams as in hard·en, herd, fir, port·ly, and curt·ly.

(p. 76)

35. Diphthongs *oy* and *oi* are sounded by changing the mouth position first, to pronounce the sound of the first vowel (*long o*) and then, to slide **quickly** into the sound of the second vowel (*short i*). The result, *oi*, seems to make one unique phoneme as in *oil, point, toy,* and *joy.* *(p. 78)*

36. If *–ed* follows the letters *t* or *d*, it is pronounced *–ted* or *–ded*.
- However, *-ed* is considered to be a separate syllable as in *plant·ed* and *raid·ed.*
- If *–ed* follows any other letter, it is pronounced simply as /d/ or /t/ as in *harmed* (harmd) or *ripped* (ript) and the *–ed* is not a separate syllable. *(pp. 80-82)*

37. The diphthong of *qu-* is usually pronounced /qw/ as in *queen, quit,* and *quest.* It is pronounced infrequently as /k/ in words with a French influence such as:
- *-qu*et as in *croquet;*.
- *-qu*ette as in *croquette, etiquette,* and *briquette; and*
- *-qu*e as in *antique, oblique,* and *catafalque.* *(pp. 83-83A)*

38. Prefixes are syllables at the beginning of a word that modify or change the word.
   - Not all letter combinations that look like prefixes are actually prefixes.
   - One way to determine if a combination of letters *is* or *is not* a prefix is to remove the combination that resembles a prefix.
   - Sometimes (but not always), if a word remains, then the combination is a true prefix as in the words, *undone* and *supernatural*. However, if a word does not remain, it is not a true prefix as in *uncle*. When in doubt, use a dictionary.

The most common prefixes and their meanings are:

ad-	to	per-	through
ante-	before	pro-	before, for
anti-	against	re-	again, back
circum-	around	se-	aside
con-	with	sub-	under
de-	down, opposite, from	super- (sur)	above
dis-	apart, not, opposite	trans-	across
ex-	out	un-	not
in-	in	uni-	one
inter-	between, among	bi-	two
intra-, intro-	within	tri-	three
mis-	wrong		*(pp. 84-102)*

39. A troublemaking vowel team is *ie*. When this team is found in a word, it **sometimes** breaks the vowel-team rule. Namely, the *i* is silent and the *e* says its name, as in *piece, believe, achieve*, and *field*

Summary

In summary, explicit phonics teach that letter symbols represent corresponding sounds. For example, *a* represents the sound /a/ and the letter symbol *t* is the sound /t/. These letters written together represent the sounds /a/ /t/, that is, the word, ***at***. After learning the phonemes represented by the consonant graphemes, reading the sounds from left to right across the word, students can read words such as the following:

/b/ /a/ /t/	bat	/c/ /a/ /t/	cat
/h/ /a/ /t/	hat	/m/ /a/ /t/	mat

With very few rules of phonics, students can also read words like *matador* and *catapult*. With the addition of the rule governing silent *e* and long vowels, students can easily decipher words like *entertainment, platitude,* and *gratitude*. Armed with phonics concepts, students gain the confidence to attack most words, even words that contain exceptions to the rules. When encountering an unfamiliar word, it is best for the reader to use phonics rules rather than skipping, substituting, or guessing. A dictionary is always a helpful tool to use when possible.

Phony Phonics

Phonics instruction is based on the understanding that letters are symbols that represent sounds. Explicit phonics builds up words from part to whole, working from left to right. Some approaches, such as the whole-to-part, whole language, embedded or implicit phonics approaches, may expect students to implicitly *figure out* phonics concepts as they are encountered in words. In such approaches, phonics instruction is not systematic and explicit. Rather, it is haphazard or occurs by chance. It is often assumed that the student will figure it out at some point and, therefore, not all students are expected to learn how to read well early on. Phonics concepts also may be casually addressed in random instruction or as an incidental instructional element in whole-to-part or whole-word approaches. Other approaches break down the whole into parts, as the chunking procedure explained earlier. Consequently, students gain few explicit phonics strategies and are unable to read fluently and efficiently. Moreover, some educators may incorrectly regard decoding as a method that teaches readers to break a polysyllabic word down by using a set of syllabication and accent rules.[1] In fact, phonics decoding is the orderly utilization of the sound/symbol relationships as one reads from left to right. Syllabication and the use of accent rules are but simply support strategies.

The extensive results of solid research overwhelmingly demonstrate the effectiveness of explicit phonics instruction. Despite the fact that the demand for phonics instruction is rising, many proponents of whole language philosophies remain convinced of the validity of their approach. As mentioned earlier, most of us understand how difficult it is to admit errors and to change or adapt to new ways even in the face of strong evidence. As a result, you may discover whole-word and whole language strategies being repackaged with a dusting of phonics concepts, then renamed, advertised, and promoted as *phonics* programs. Such programs continue to fall short of offering the research-proven strategies that result in excellent reading skills.

Phony phonics, as various critics of these renamed-methodologies refer to them, are not the same as the rigorous, research-based methodologies and do not have the same effective results. The only real and effective phonics programs are the ones that utilize scientifically proven approaches. As stated before, effective programs teach sound-symbol relationships (1) explicitly, (2) directly, (3) systematically, (4) working from part to whole, and (5) providing practice with decodable text. Be alert.

While real phonics-trained students are able to read a broad range of outside material, students trained to read with non-explicit phonics programs favor books specially tailored to their limited vocabulary. School librarians are able to have a broad view of what is going on in an entire school based on students' choices of books and reading habits. In my experience as school librarian, I saw students who were not phonics trained, and who were drawn to reading materials significantly below their grade levels. However, students who had strong phonics skills sought out a variety of materials and were not as self-limiting with their selections as were their non-phonics trained schoolmates.

Phonics is a Beginning Step to Reading

As noted, the rules of phonics cannot be taught in isolation, apart from reading. The reader must be able to apply the rules to develop reading skills. The teaching of reading is not rocket science. However, if one cannot read, one cannot hope to be a rocket scientist!

Readers must have the following skills:

- **Phonemic awareness**: *the ability to hear, identify, and manipulate sounds in words.*

- **Phonics**: *the knowledge of the relationships between phonemes and graphemes.*

- **Vocabulary**: *the knowledge and ability to use information about meanings and pronunciations of words.*

- **Fluency**: *the ability to read text accurately and quickly.*

- **Comprehension**: *the ability to understand, remember, and communicate what was read from the written text.*

In the following chapters, you will find practical steps to develop vocabulary and elements of reading comprehension.

Conclusion

A reading program that claims to be phonics based might, in reality, be a less-effective, implicit phonics program. Programs that attempt to teach phonics concepts in context use so-called balanced approaches, embedded phonics, and combination methods. They attempt to teach phonics implicitly. This has been proven not to be the most effective method by which to develop successful reading skills.

Explicit phonics, on the other hand, has been demonstrated by rigorous, scientific-based research to be effective. By learning few rules, students are able to fluently read tens or hundreds of thousands of words instead of merely hundreds of words. Ineffective strategies impede fluency and comprehension and must be replaced with effective ones.

For Further Consideration

- To what project or relationship in your life would you choose to apply the *second-most* effective strategy instead of the *most* effective strategy?

- What problems face the teacher when his or her students cannot read well?

- What does it mean to *sound it out*?

- How did you learn about the rules of phonics?

- How would you answer these comments?

  → We don't have a literacy problem; we just need to find out what interests our students and then they will read.

  → We do teach phonics, but not everyone learns the same way. No one method for teaching reading is best.

  → We use a combination of methods, because some people have different learning styles; some take longer to "catch on."

  → At-risk students aren't interested in academics.

  → The student has ADD, ADHD, dyslexia and needs medication or lowered expectations.

  → It's the parents' fault; schools can't work miracles.

  → Students watch too much TV; schools cannot compete.

  → English has too many exceptions to teach phonics.

[1] Cunningham, et al. (1989). *Reading and Writing in Elementary Classrooms: Strategies and Observations.* New York: Longman, 70.

CHAPTER SEVEN

BUILDING VOCABULARY

"Without knowing the force of words, it is impossible to know more."

Confucius (551 – 479 B.C.)

> **FOCUS POINT:** An extensive vocabulary is a critical element required for successful reading and comprehension. A few ways that can help students develop skills that build vocabulary are as follows: (a) by teaching and promoting the use of the dictionary, glossaries, and the thesaurus; (b) by making connections with prior knowledge; (c) by using context to ascertain meanings; (d) by applying prefixes, suffixes, and word variations or origins; and (e) by modeling vocabulary-rich, quality speech. Vocabulary can develop naturally through exposure to vocabulary-rich materials. Of paramount importance, of course, is the reader's ability to use decoding skills to read fluently.
>
> An exhaustive treatment of vocabulary acquisition is not within the scope of this work. There are many excellent sources and means available. Ultimately, however, the very best way for anyone, young or old, to extend vocabulary knowledge is to read extensively and, when possible, use a dictionary.

Vocabulary is an Element of Comprehension

Consider this vocabulary-rich sentence:

One faces a conundrum of positive and negative conceptual dilemmas tangent to one another and effectively present, albeit implicitly, when one does not comprehend vocabulary innuendoes and minutia of meanings.

The sentence says that the sense of a passage is confusing when the reader fails to understand shades of meanings of even a few individual words. In other words, sentences and paragraphs with big words, such as the one above, may be challenging for some readers to comprehend. Teachers and parents may assume erroneously that such readers have *processing deficiencies*. Moreover, the reader may be considered to have difficulty with *abstract conceptualization*. Thus, it may be that even a reader who can efficiently decode the text might find it void of meaning if the meanings of some words are unknown. In other words, the vocabulary-rich sentence is true: A good vocabulary *is* required for comprehension.

The ability to imagine and to communicate is enhanced by one's knowledge of the specific and general meanings of words, as well as abstruse nuances. Members of a healthy society must be able to compose or comprehend ideas by interacting with the intellects of others. Vocabulary development in speech and in the written word ubiquitously enhances communication of ideas.

Teachers must be aware that guided, direct instruction helps build a foundation of vocabulary in their students. In summary, for individuals to be able to comprehend any text, they must be able to do the following:

1.   Decode all words with accuracy;

2.   Master the meaning(s) of individual words, identify the things, ideas or concepts that the words specifically represent; and

3.   Comprehend the words as they are used in relationship to other words in the text.

A Lesson from History

A limited vocabulary reflects a restricted range of ideas. As vocabulary increased, early primitive cultures had vocabularies with only a limited number of words. Often, the individuals in tribes or groups never developed the means to communicate beyond what was required for their daily survival needs. In some cases, although they knew other groups were around, there was no oral communication. When the tribes and groups did intermingle, they generally adopted new words or word forms to expand their vocabularies. Because of the ebb and flow of human encounters throughout the centuries, the English language continued to gather in words of other peoples. It grew to include hundreds of thousands of words and their variations. With such increased communication capabilities, individuals were able to expand their ability to manipulate ideas or abstract thought and to process increasingly complex concepts.

As stated in previous chapters, the history of teaching reading shows how education became less academically and intellectually challenging for students. Some of today's philosophies of education rely on a child's *natural* acquisition of vocabulary, which is, without a doubt, limited. Other philosophies concentrate on learning vocabulary that is primarily limited to various assigned word lists. These instructional methods ultimately suppress vocabulary acquisition of students. This, in turn, hinders literacy development. Too many students are poorly prepared for life's chores and challenges when they leave school.

Moreover, one may question how it came to be that the common language of communication in society today is limited, often replete with emotionally charged "four letter words" and common vulgarities. Has society deprived its youth of the tools to use language beyond emotional response? Linguistics and literacy are acutely intertwined.

As William Lutz states in his book *The New Doublespeak: Why No One Knows What Anyone's Saying Anymore*:

> Language is relevant to the foundations of an ordered society; it is essential. The irresponsible use of language leads to the destruction of the social, moral, and political structure that is our society, our culture, and our nations.[1]

Another aspect of this theory would seem to assert that when educators do not use students' time in the classrooms in meaningful and academically challenging work, it is wasteful and leads to negative impacts on society and on individuals.

In contrast to contemporary curriculum, in the late 1880s students entering Bridgewater-Daleville College in Virginia were required to study Anglo-Saxon, Middle English, College Rhetoric, Composition, and several courses in English and American Literature. In the early 1900s, courses were added to include astronomy, biology, chemistry, English, English Bible, French, geology, German, Greek, history, social sciences, and political sciences, Latin, mathematics, pedagogy, philosophy, physics, and Spanish.[2] Certainly, with such challenging work, vocabularies were enriched.

Sadly, contemporary students are not so challenged. In 2003, Elizabeth, a student at the junior college level, reported about her experience:

> *When the instructor calls for a volunteer to read, no one raises a hand. At the beginning of the semester, the instructor called on students randomly, but so many of them were hesitant and faltering in their reading that the teacher just rolled her eyes. Now she usually just calls on me, reads the material herself, or we don't read at all. I don't understand how these students graduated from high school.*

> *The class discussions are limited and are usually based on how we feel about something. However, my teacher now also demands that we learn vocabulary, so I am making an 'endeavor' to 'enhance' mine! I know I have a larger vocabulary than most of my peers, but I want to learn more. I realize that I have to read more on my own because I am realizing how little I know.*

Most students are not like Elizabeth. Because she can read well, she most likely reads more than her peers do. Nonetheless, one could comfortably assume that she has not read any of the lengthy, vocabulary-rich, original classics penned by the likes of Edgar Allen Poe, Charles Dickens, and Sir Arthur Conan Doyle. For the most part, these original works, once read by the commoner, are generally now beyond the purview of all but literary scholars. Some classics are translated into diluted imitations with controlled vocabulary for individuals with low reading levels.

Today, because students do not have the necessary skills to read an original work, the "dumbing down" of the quality of the materials accommodates to their levels. With what is known now of reading research, it is impossible to justify or ignore failed reading instruction and to merely substitute modified reading matter by saying, "At least they are reading." Of course, the challenge for educators is to raise the students' reading skills. Many dedicated educators successfully are doing just that. It can be accomplished by all.

The Challenge

Because many students have not been exposed to the challenge of critical vocabulary development in their early education, content area teachers in post-primary grades must be responsible for teaching extensive and meaningful vocabulary. Furthermore, advanced disciplines require appropriate understanding of terminology specific to those disciplines. The importance of one's vocabulary knowledge and vocabulary-building skills that are critical to attain real academic success cannot be overemphasized. The designers of the college entrance exams understand clearly the importance of enhanced vocabulary being critical for success in college. This can be seen by the great emphasis placed on vocabulary knowledge. Teachers must be up to the challenge.

COMMENT: It is extremely *imperative* that educators value having and *using* an extensive vocabulary themselves. When the teacher models excellence in speech and written communication, such excellence can be an effective tool to inspire students. Conversely, poor attention to excellence in speech and written communication can serve as a poor model.

It would seem logical that the decoding (reading) of a word correctly is the first step toward knowing what that word means. Following that, knowing the precise meaning of the word that the author has written leads to comprehending what the author is intending to communicate via that specifically chosen word. Some, however, have another point of view. Constance Weaver (1994), for example, in *Reading Process and Practice: From Socio-Psycholinguistics to Whole Language*, writes:

> Unfortunately, we may deny children [such] satisfying experiences with books if we assume that first and foremost, reading means identifying the words and getting their meaning. It is all too common to assume that word identification precedes comprehension, whereas in fact, it is clear that in large part language comprehension works the other way around: because, or if, we are getting the meaning of the whole, we can then grasp the meaning of the individual words. The words have meaning **only** as they transact with one another, within the context of the emerging whole.[3]

Most assuredly, it is important that educators do not deny students satisfying experiences with books. Constance Weaver is certainly correct on that point. However, readers cannot get the meaning of the *whole* if they initially do not know the significance of the parts. If students do not identify words and get their meaning, they may be getting the gist of the written word, but, ultimately, books become locked banks of nuanced ideas inaccessible to the reader. Repeated failed attempts to discover the richness inside various forms of literature usually result in the reader discontinuing any significant attempt at reading because it offers little or no satisfactory results. Even if the unprepared reader were to attempt to read a popular fiction or non-fiction book, he or she may only be able to get the gist of what the author had written.

However, once decoding skills are established, students should be able to use context clues, a dictionary, or thesaurus to distinguish various shades of meanings of unfamiliar words. Without the reader being able to determine such subtleties, books will forever contain riches beyond students' imagining and total grasp. It is troubling to hear so many individuals of all ages and ilk say: "I can read; I just don't like to read." For them, reading, sadly, is not a satisfying experience. Therefore, they don't read. It is human nature, common to all of us, to avoid pursuing unsatisfying undertakings.

However, once students can decode readily, vocabulary development is a next easy step. With adequate preparation and with standards held high, students can advance significantly. An example of this can be seen in one small elementary school that adopted the *Phonics Steps to Reading Steps* program for its grades four through six only. Shortly after the teachers began using it at the beginning of the year, the first-grade teacher received permission from the principal to tailor the decoding program as a supplement to her primary reading curriculum. Near the end of the first grade, national standardized tests were given to the students. These *first*-grade students scored at the *fifth*-grade level on the vocabulary section. The principal, Mary Lou Rogers, enthusiastically said, "We were all very surprised and thrilled with the outcome." If continued, these students will be able to pursue even further vocabulary development.

Using Language Responsibly

To this same end, educators at all levels must continue to promote vocabulary acquisition and usage. Notwithstanding their consistent efforts, teachers, however, become frustrated when students repeatedly use inappropriate language or "four-letter words." Schools will continue to have an ongoing and uphill battle against such language, particularly while students have a limited stock of words upon which to draw. So-called *rough* language is also popular in songs, movies, and other media. It may not be surprising that the usual language of emotional expression is replete with "four letter words" and common vulgarities when students, who are products of our educational system and contemporary society, also have limited vocabularies. One's significantly finite vocabulary limits the individual's ability to adequately analyze or communicate feelings such as fear, anger, or rage through words. Individuals often resort to "physical" communication. In other words, they may essentially say, "I can't express my frustration or my anger in words, so I'll show you with my fists, my spray-paint can, or my gun."

COMMENT: The practice of students frequently using four-letter words to punctuate their conversations can be ameliorated, but only with consistency and modeling by responsible adults and peers. It takes effort, particularly in a society when we have become so accustomed to what may be termed *street slang*. When I taught students at any level, I neither tolerated the use of the "inappropriate" language nor got upset when it was used. Rather, with composure and a heavy dose of humor, I sometimes required students to give a literal definition of the slang they used, depending on the circumstances, of course. At the same time, students were to find an alternate, "intelligent" way to express the meaning they wished to convey. Words referencing common slang comments can appear silly in context when one puts their meanings into perspective. This

---

can be observed in the following anecdote about an incident that occurred when a young man in my junior college class told me that he saw one of our students "kickin' it."

I responded, "Was she hurting *it*?"

He explained that she was just "hanging around."

I asked if she needed to be cut down.

Finally, a bit exacerbated, he explained that the student was sitting outside the room, waiting for the class to start.

He got the point of my comments, but initially complained that my way of thinking was "old fashioned." He told me that it was the way people talk these days. I couldn't disagree; he was right. Many people do talk this way.

However, the class and I discussed the various circumstances under which street slang would and would not be appropriate. We determined that the classroom would be one place where the highest academic standards of language should be required. Also, the language standards in the home and workplace should be higher than "street standards." Some suggested the responsibility for adults to model appropriate language when around children.

To be honest, the young man initially was not very pleased with such expectations, but two weeks later, he told me that he had thought about what we had discussed. He said, "When I was at work, I decided that I wouldn't use any street slang anymore." He told me that within a short time, his boss had noticed this and commented on his improved speaking skills. As a result, the boss had promoted this bright young man to a position that meant not only greater responsibilities, but also increased pay. Furthermore, this student thanked me for inspiring him and encouraging him to raise his standards. Although not all students will respond in such a positive manner, all students are worth the effort. It is up to the student to accept the challenge.

Unquestionably, it is critical for teachers to hold standards high. Such efforts are important not only for students' success, but for teachers' success as well. Words like *miscreants*, *maelstrom* and *motley* are more likely to be heard in the classroom or found in students' written work if words like these are modeled by the teacher and expected to be used by the students.

When educators teach rigorous expansion of vocabularies, they can also expect students to express themselves with higher-level panache. Language is a powerful tool, and the more vocabulary words at one's command, the greater one's personal and intellectual strength. The ability of our fellow citizens to read, comprehend, and communicate strengthens every one of us in society.

Ways to Increase Vocabulary Knowledge

The teacher can and must assist students to become life-long, independent learners and active in building their own vocabularies. Suggestions for helping students to build vocabularies include the following:

1. The teacher can model the importance of building vocabulary by personally using a dictionary or vocabulary building aids throughout the class period.

2. The teacher can capitalize on the many opportunities for introducing vocabulary to students, regardless of the subject matter.

3. The teacher can explicitly and directly teach the use of the **dictionary, glossary,** and **thesaurus**.

4. The teacher can be prepared to make interventions, suggestions, or corrections, when necessary.

5. The teacher can teach vocabulary by making connections with students' prior experiential knowledge, using etymologies, reading good literature, using context, and the like.

6. The teacher can help students utilize prefixes, suffixes, and word variations to expand vocabulary knowledge.

7. The teacher can use commercially published vocabulary-developing materials. (There are many fine ones, but one excellent series that I have used, and can highly recommend, is the *Townsend Press Vocabulary Series*, published by Townsend Press, West Berlin, New Jersey.)*

*Suggestion: If you are looking for materials for older readers, you may consider exploring the vocabulary and reading sequenced series for older students by Townsend Press (www.townsendpress.com). I have used their excellent materials with junior college classes and in private tutoring and remedial instruction. These workbooks are well explained and present many opportunities for practice and feedback. They provide a high interest level and ease of use. When used after systematic, explicit decoding instruction, such as presented in *Phonics Steps to Reading Success*, Townsend materials can increase fluency, vocabulary, and comprehension skills. The authors of the materials understand the necessity of providing students with the definitions, review/reinforcement, vocabulary in context, in addition to personal writing and evaluation experiences that are necessary for effective instructional vocabulary development, etc.

Building vocabulary is a fun and exciting challenge that follows clues to uncover the mystery of the hidden meanings of words. The inclusion of new, fresh words into classroom discussions can be invigorating. The goal is to build confidence in students in their utilization of an advanced vocabulary by increasing their self-assurance in the use of the dictionary, thesaurus, glossaries, and other vocabulary-building tools.

Dictionary Skills

The dictionary is a primary tool for building vocabulary. Of course, students must first be able to decode words independently before they can read word definitions. When students can decode well, they will use dictionaries less for pronunciation assistance and more for definition assistance.

It is too often the case that teachers approach the dictionary in class only to teach dictionary skills in an isolated curriculum unit. Dictionaries often sit untouched on the shelf. One teacher called it "the big blue paperweight." Although he was being sarcastic, he expressed a common opinion of a book whose richness many do not appreciate.

Often, students do not use the dictionary because readers with inferior decoding skills cannot read the definitions. Therefore, students as well as teachers generally avoid dictionary use altogether.

Since not all teachers value or effectively focus on vocabulary development, it is a critical responsibility of knowledgeable teachers to demand the highest academic and verbal standards for themselves and for their students. A teacher must model the very same dictionary skills and high-quality vocabulary usage that should be required of all students in the classroom.

COMMENT: When I taught the middle grades in the inner city, it was obvious that my students' dictionary usage and subsequent vocabulary development had been limited. As noted earlier, whole language and whole-word strategies that encourage guessing at words and substituting words do not lend themselves to extensive vocabulary development. Therefore, to counteract this deficiency, after I taught my students essential phonics or word-attack skills, I also provided each student with a paperback dictionary that was required to be on the students' desks at all times. Then, because the students could readily decode not only the words being defined but also the words of the definition itself, the practice of their looking up the meanings of unknown words became fun for them. The confident use of these skills remained with my students as noted by their subsequent teachers. These teachers said that my former students could be identified because they quickly reached for their dictionaries when they came across an unfamiliar word.

Recently, two students whom I had taught through the phonics training were recipients of college scholarships. I had been invited to attend the ceremony where they were to be awarded. Of the thirty-five top seniors from around the city who qualified for this particular scholarship, these two had the highest grade point averages (GPA). The young woman had a 4.4 GPA and the young man had a 4.47 GPA. Although there are obviously multiple reasons why these two did so well, I would allow that their knowledge of phonics strategies and dictionary skills positively contributed to their successes.

To Bridge or Unabridge?

Dictionaries that not only define words but also provide sentences using the word in context, are exceptionally helpful for students. *Abridged* dictionaries provide short, basic, and most commonly used definitions of the most frequently used words. An inexpensive paperback offers ease of use. An example of a good abridged dictionary is *The New Concise Webster's Dictionary*, ISBN 0-87449-703-5. Since many students get the terms confused, remind them that **a _bridge_** is the **short** path across the river just as an abridged dictionary is relatively short.

In contrast to an easy-to-use, concise or abridged dictionary, an *unabridged* dictionary is often very large and can be intimidating to students. By way of instruction, tell the students that if the path across the river is **not** bridged (***unabridged***), then the traveler must take the **long** way around. An unabridged dictionary has more words and long definitions, including more extensive information, such as parts of speech, etymologies, and nuances of meaning.

Stumbling Over *Neuropterous*: A Sample Lesson

On the following pages, you will explore a sample lesson that demonstrates the decoding of a word and discovering its meaning. For instructional purposes, it is obviously belabored, but it illustrates how the teacher and student can utilize a dictionary to discern a meaning.

Imagine that you are with a student who comes across a word that he or she has never encountered.

There are three basic steps to follow:

1.   Decode the word.

2.   Decode and determine the meanings of unfamiliar words in the definition.

3.   Determine the meaning of the definition as a whole.

In the sample lesson, the word is *neuropterous*. Rather than skipping over the word, make use of this teachable moment. If you are enthusiastic about learning new words, your enthusiasm will spark students' interest in words. All students will reflect your confidence and enjoyment.

Neuropterous

A.   **Decode the word.**

1.   ***neu*** – Pronounced **nē-ū** or **nū.** *(Quickly said, the eu is has evolved to be pronounced like /ū/.)*   *(PSRS p. 54)*

2.   *rop* – Pronounced **rŏp.** *(A vowel by itself says its short sound.)*   *(p. 1)*

3.   ***ter*** – Pronounced **tur.** *(The er is one of the er, ir, ur combinations pronounced /ûr/.)*   *(p. 42)*

4.   ***ous***– Pronounced **ŭs.** *(The diphthong ou is pronounced /ŭ/ when followed by the letter s.)*   *(p. 56)*

B.   **Decode and determine the meanings of words in the definition.**

The definition used here is one as it might appear in an **unabridged** dictionary:

of or **resembling** the **neuroptera**.

[In this definition, **two words** might cause trouble.]

1. ***Resembling*** means *like or similar to*

2. *Neuroptera* –

> **n. pl. [neuro-, Gr. nerve; pteron, a wing.]**
>
> *An order of insects having four membranous, transparent,*
>
> *naked wings, reticulated with veins or nerves.*
>
> *Helligrammite and ant lions are members of this order.*

Note the abbreviations in the definition. Students should have been previously introduced to the significance of these abbreviations.

☞   **n. (n**oun)

☞   **pl. (** p**lural)

☞   **neuro-** (from the <u>Gr</u>eek neuro=nerve) and pteron (plural is *ptera*) meaning a *wing*.

Students should be required to look up the meaning of any unknown word in the definition.

☞   order   class, type, species variety

☞   of insects   of hexapod or six-footed bugs

☞	having four	having 4
☞	membranous	tissue, thin skin, film
☞	transparent	clear, see-through
☞	naked	bared, uncovered
☞	wings	front arms to allow flying.
☞	reticulated	constructed like the meshes of a net
☞	with veins	with blood vessels
☞	or nerves	or fibers or bundles of cords of fibers that connect body organs to the nervous system.

> **Hellgrammite and ant lions are members of this order.**

C. Determine the meaning of the definition as a whole.

Neuropterous means *of, or resembling, an insect with these characteristics.*

Glossary

The glossary is an alphabetized collection or list of specialized terms in a particular field of knowledge or used within a text, often appearing as an appendix to the text. It provides definitions for words used in the text. If the term, *neuropterous,* would be discussed in a science text, for example, it would probably also appear in the glossary, which is traditionally located in the back of the book. Words that are defined in the glossary are often printed in **bold** or *italicized* in the text.

Thesaurus

Exploring meanings of words in a thesaurus is akin to doing detective work. Students can find synonyms that provide hidden shades of meaning. Consider the word, *landmark.* Students have essential decoding skills necessary to pronounce the entry word as well as the words of the definition. Students will discover that a *landmark* is *a conspicuous object marking an event, boundary, or location.* Students may be able to comprehend that a landmark is something that is an object marking something. The student should be directed or assisted to look up any words whose meaning is unknown.

By doing so, students will discover that *conspicuous* means that something is *clearly visible, obvious, unmistakable, prominent, obtrusive, blatant*, and the like. Students then can do detective work, looking for other synonyms, other meanings of any of these unfamiliar words. Such activities can be reinforced in a variety of ways.

Numerous and diverse activities can be used to reinforce such word-sleuthing opportunities. Students may use newly found words in speaking and writing opportunities by sharing the meanings with the class and, then, by adding the word to a class list. Students may develop a personal word bank or journal. Competitions increase the challenge of learning new words. Having a thesaurus-word-of-the-day or dictionary-word-of-the-day is also beneficial. Other tools such as crossword puzzles, various books, and Internet sites are readily available. A tool for in and outside the classroom might be audio programs such as *Verbal Advantage* that can be found at this site: http://www.verbaladvantage.com/shop/product_details.cfm?prod_ID=8. Programs such as this can be extremely helpful for teachers, learners, and parents to enhance their vocabulary skills in only ten or fifteen minutes each day.

To reiterate, it is essential to develop the habit of researching the meanings of unfamiliar words as they are found in reading matter. Students should be advised to read a book with a dictionary, and, perhaps, a thesaurus nearby to be used when unfamiliar words are encountered. Also, students are to be encouraged to use a thesaurus when they are writing and to replace well-worn words with vibrant, new ones.

Once the fear of big and unknown words is dismissed, students' timidity to read challenging works may subside considerably. The original works of Edgar Allan Poe, for example, can be appreciated when the reader understands the subtleties of the words that Poe carefully selected to craft his classic tales. Ultimately, the confidence of knowing how to discover meanings of words as one reads will allow students to be unafraid to tackle more challenging pieces of literature, whether they be historical, classical, contemporary, fiction, non-fiction, or any other genre.

Discoveries of Meanings in Context

Context means the parts of a sentence or paragraph that occur before and after the word or words. In some cases, the reader simply can discern the meaning of a word by utilizing the information around it.

Consider the silly word in a sentence taken from *Phonics Steps to Reading Success*:

Last year we celebrated my grandfather's 100th vecklaipinkormaeple. We had a big party with ice cream and cake. He blew out 100 candles on the vecklaipinkormaeple cake.

What is a *vecklaipinkormaeple*? The reader can use clues to find the answer. The reader may search for some word clues in the surrounding parts of the paragraph that the reader might piece together to determine the meaning of this unusual word. The reader may understand the words, *celebrated, party, ice cream, cake,* and *candles.* All of these words are commonly connected to the idea of a birthday celebration. This might lead the reader to know that it possibly has something to do with a birthday. Therefore, the reader could substitute *birthday* for the word *vecklaipinkormaeple.*

*Last year we celebrated my grandfather's 100th **birthday**. We had a big party with ice cream and cake. He blew out 100 candles on the **birthday** cake.*

Vecklaipindormaeple then means *birthday*.

The student can be encouraged to (a) find what clues to the meaning might be in the passage, and (b) substitute the possible word to see if the word "makes sense." In this case, the word does make sense. It is to be noted that the phonics-skilled reader can *pronounce* the silly word as the author has written it. The reader then can use context clues to determine the meaning, not how to read the word. Although *vecklaipinkormaeple* in this example is an invented word, in most cases, the dictionary can be used to verify the meaning. Context clues, however, are often helpful when a dictionary is not readily available.

Vocabulary Context Clues

1. **Synonym/definition context clue***: The author restates a word or definition that means the same to clarify.

   EXAMPLE: *The man was afraid that he had not used a **tint** of pink paint. He was right. His wife had wanted barely detectable pink on the walls, but he had painted bright pink. In the next room, he made sure to use a tint of pink **by adding white to make a lighter gradation of the color.***

2. **Antonym context clue***: The author includes a contrasting word that is the opposite.

   EXAMPLE: *Elaine was **reluctant** to jump into the water. On the other hand, Yasmine was **eager** to dive right in.*

3. **Description context clue:** The author includes descriptions or explanations.

   EXAMPLE: *Young Jeffery was **famished** when he came in from playing all afternoon. He ate two bowls of cereal, a banana, two apples, and he was still looking for more food to fill him up. He eyed the dog food bowl, but Fido had eaten all of his food. Jeffery's **stomach was still empty**.*

4. **Inference context clue:** The author will include a definition through implication or inference.

   EXAMPLE: *Raymundo was a very **courteous** young man. He never talked when a teacher was explaining a lesson. He always showed respect for other students and adults. Even strangers made comments about how he would hold doors open for them. Raymundo always stood out in school in comparison to other students. They would walk through doors without considering the persons following them. They would walk by someone who may have dropped papers or books and never bother to help. Yes, Raymundo was not like them; he was always very **courteous**.*

There are challenging opportunities for vocabulary acquisition such as looking for context clues to define meanings. Students can be encouraged to see them as mystery challenges to be overcome rather than barriers to fear or avoid. Have students understand that gaining vocabulary knowledge is like putting money in the bank. The wise person seeks to accumulate vocabulary wealth. As students read at or just above their competency level, they will continue to discover new words to discern and learn.

Conclusion

Vocabulary building is a key component of a complete reading program. It now goes without saying that a solid foundation in phonics-based decoding is a prerequisite for reading and acquiring new vocabulary words. In addition, tools that build vocabulary, such as dictionaries, thesauri, and glossaries, are essential. Instructors play an indispensable role in modeling and widening learners' linguistic repertoire and use of vocabulary-building aids.

For Further Consideration

- What vocabulary-building tools do you use regularly for yourself?

- Has there been any word used in this book that was unfamiliar to you?

- Do you skip over unfamiliar words or try to define them? Do you use context clues, dictionaries, and the like to enhance your vocabulary?

- Do you attempt to actively increase your vocabulary knowledge and usage?

- Do you think that vocabulary can be built up exclusively from words in context?

- If so, how? If not, why not?

- How do you react or respond when you hear someone, particularly a young person, speaking with many four-letter expletives?

- What is your opinion of educators who use expletives or street slang in the classroom?

- What problems do you or your students face in reading comprehension?

References

[1] Lutz, W. (1996) *The New Doublespeak: Why No One Knows What Anyone's Saying Anymore*: New York: HarperCollins.

[2] *Fifty Years of Educational Endeavor.* (1930). The McClure Company, Inc.: Stanton, Va.

[3] Weaver, C. (1994). *Reading Process and Practice: From Socio-psycholinguistics to Whole Language.* Portsmouth, NH: Heinemann, 41.

CHAPTER EIGHT

MAIN IDEAS AND RELATIONSHIPS

"Remember that you are giving students proven tricks of the trade. Good readers use their tricks to improve comprehension." Anonymous

---

FOCUS POINT: Reading comprehension depends on skills beyond decoding and owning a good vocabulary. Additional skills that factor into reading comprehension are (a) picking out the main ideas and (b) spotting transitional words and phrases that signal supportive ideas, associations in time, comparisons, contrasts, and cause and effect relationships. **These essential tools must be utilized if one is to become a competent reader. In another fashion, utilizing these same tools as one writes is critical to good writing.**

The Main Idea

An important initial step in reading comprehension is that of ferreting out the *main idea*, also called the theme, or the point of a passage or paragraph. To do so, one must identify key phrases that represent the crux of meaning around which are found secondary and supportive materials. Imagine that the author is a builder, and the paragraph is a house. This literary house will have a roof. In other words, the paragraph will have a *main idea* that covers all that is under it.

The main idea is usually written in a general statement called a *topic sentence.* Read the following paragraph to determine its main idea.

> Yelling at a child is an ineffective way to encourage a child to change his
> or her behavior. First, yelling results in animosity and aggravation. The
> child will not hear the adult's intended message, but only the loud, rude
> voice. Additionally, having learned that yelling is acceptable, the child

might yell back at the adult in defiance. Ultimately, yelling teaches youngsters that authority can express its power in shouts, screams, and bellowing.

Analyze this paragraph by comparing it to a house. The topic is at the apex of the roof, while the main idea is the entire roof, under which all supporting material fits.

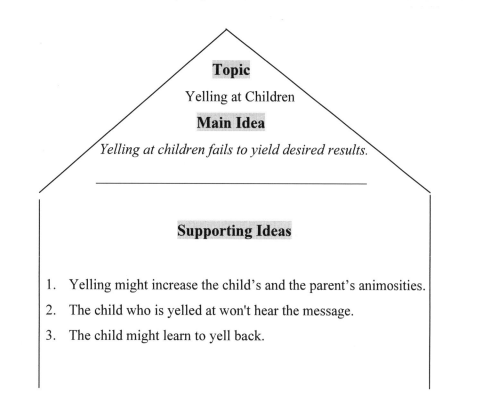

Topic

Yelling at Children

Main Idea

Yelling at children fails to yield desired results.

Supporting Ideas

1. Yelling might increase the child's and the parent's animosities.
2. The child who is yelled at won't hear the message.
3. The child might learn to yell back.

The Topic, the Main Idea, and Supporting Ideas Work Together

Using the house analogy for the paragraph, enables students to analyze a paragraph for its meaning. Although slow and deliberate at first, the process of analysis becomes second nature after a while. Much practice is necessary to increase the speed of processing information in order to scrutinize it. If the reader understands the structure of a paragraph, it will give the reader tools to discover the meaning.

Characteristics of the topic, main idea, and supporting ideas are summarized below.

The Topic

1. Can be expressed with minimal wording.

2. Is often found in boldface in textbooks or magazines.

3. Answers the question: *Who or what is this passage about?*

4. Should be neither too broad nor too narrow.

    a. Too broad a topic for the sample paragraph: *Disciplining Children*

    b. Too narrow a topic for the sample paragraph: *Children Yelling*

    c. Perfect topic for the sample paragraph: *Yelling at Children*

The Main Idea

1. Is most frequently stated in the topic sentence.

2. Is often the first sentence.

3. May be in inter-paragraph sentences.

4. Can sometimes be found as the last sentence of the paragraph.

5. May be written as the first sentence and then rewritten as the last sentence.

6. Can cover more than one paragraph.

Supporting Ideas

1. Develop the main idea.

2. Can be major details, that is, primary points that support the main idea.

3. Can be minor details, that is, points that expand major ideas.

4. May occur in outline form:

    Major detail

      Minor detail
      Minor detail

Major detail

Minor detail
Minor detail

The topic is the subject of the passage. The main idea is the author's primary point about the topic. Authors often put the main idea in a single sentence called the *topic sentence*. Although not common, the topic sentence can appear in a paragraph other than the first one. Normally, the topic sentence is the first sentence. If it comes after the first sentence, the topic sentence is usually preceded by one or more introductory sentences. Other sentences in the paragraph provide *supportive details*. Consider another sample paragraph:

Developing one's vocabulary is easy. Reading books can develop one's vocabulary. Using a dictionary can develop one's vocabulary. Whatever you do, remember that it is important to use a variety of approaches to develop vocabulary. In fact, asking a friend for help can also enable you to learn more words.

The sentences in this example are numbered to demonstrate the pattern.

1. *Developing one's vocabulary is easy.* [Supporting idea.]
2. *Reading books can develop one's vocabulary.* [Supporting idea.]
3. *Using a dictionary can develop one's vocabulary.* [Supporting idea.]
4. *Whatever you do, remember that it is important to use a variety of approaches to develop vocabulary.* [Topic sentence.]
5. In fact, asking a friend for help can also enable you to learn more words. [Supporting idea.]

An author might include two topic sentences, one at or near the beginning of the passage and one later on, usually at the end. Here is a variation on the paragraph shown with two highlighted topic sentences, one in the middle and the other at the end of the paragraph.

> Developing one's vocabulary is easy. Reading books can develop one's vocabulary. Using a dictionary can develop one's vocabulary. Whatever you do, remember that it is important to use a variety of approaches to develop vocabulary. In fact, asking a friend for help can also enable you to learn more words. Remember, the opportunities to develop vocabulary are limitless.

Hints for Efficient Reading

Newspaper and magazine articles often have topic sentences in the first and last paragraphs. The first paragraph exposes the main idea, called *the lead*. The importance of putting the most significant information in the first paragraph, most likely, was reinforced during the era of the Civil War when the telegraph lines could have been cut at any moment. The reporter, therefore, needed to make sure that the most essential elements of *who*, *what*, *when*, and *where* were written in the first paragraph in case that is all that was transmitted before wires were cut. The report could be expanded in subsequent paragraphs but with less-essential information. Also, in the newspaper business, space is sometimes limited, and the editor is required to cut out internal portions of an article. Often, the final paragraph reviews the main idea and provides concluding remarks.

In today's busy world, finding the main idea in newspaper and magazine articles can be helpful. The headline or subject line indicates the topic, such as "President Visits China." If the reader is interested in finding out more, then the first paragraph usually gives the main idea, citing the essentials of *who*, *what*, *when*, and *where* of the President's visit. Although the article may cover several columns, the last paragraph usually rephrases the main idea with a summarizing comment. For instance, the final paragraph may inform the reader by stating, "The President's visit to China was uneventful, although his meetings with representatives are expected to lay the groundwork for further meetings." If the reader is interested, he or she can then read the entire article to discover supporting ideas and details about the visit.

On the other hand, if the first and last paragraphs do not peak the reader's interest, at least the reader has gained some background knowledge about this current event.

Teach Words That Indicate Relationships Between Ideas

When a writer uses words or phrases that indicate a transition or relationship between ideas, the writer facilitates the reader's comprehension of the material. Words that point to relationships of ideas help readers to connect ideas. For example, the phrase *on the other hand* is a relationship indicator that alerts the reader to an upcoming concept that may be opposite to a previous statement. Other examples of words and phrases that show relationships in ideas are *for example, as stated, in support, therefore, consequently, then,* and *so.*

The next sections list words that provide specific types of relationships or transitions that occur between and among ideas. The lists are by no means comprehensive.

Lists are available in various print sources. (Examples are noted at the end of this chapter.) Students can be encouraged to find other phrases and synonyms that signal transitions or relationships. For example, by using such *search words* on the Internet as *grammar, transitions, relationships,* and *writing,* one can find helpful sites. Students can also write their own examples to reinforce the concept of transition words and take note of transitions when they are encountered. Teachers can find many places that provide handouts and worksheets for review and practice.

Teach Words That Indicate Additional Ideas

Phrases and words that indicate additional supportive ideas are *also, additionally, another, other, moreover,* and *furthermore.* Words that enumerate supportive points are *firstly, secondly, thirdly, next, finally, lastly,* and *for one thing.* Other additional words are *and, in addition, than, too, also,* and *both.*

Teach Words That Indicate Emphasis

Phrases and words that emphasize information are *even, indeed, in fact, of course, truly, certainly, surely, really, in truth, again,* and *besides.*

Teach Words That Indicate Time of Occurrence

Some words that signal time of occurrence are *once, previously, during, now, then, when, while, later, first, initially, meanwhile, earlier, immediately, simultaneously, subsequently, eventually, in the future, in the past, in the meantime, currently, eventually, at that time, thereafter, finally, at last, presently,* and *at length.*

Some relationship words have similar meanings, but good writing avoids the monotony of repeating words *over and over and over* again. Here's an example of dull writing.

> *First,* we went to the library. *Then,* we selected some items. *Then* we went home and, *then,* we read our books.

The same sentences can be rewritten to show a variation in phrasing.

> *First,* we went to the library *during* which time we selected some items. *Eventually,* we went home. *Then,* we read our books and, *finally,* went to sleep.

The brain seeks patterns. Therefore, when the reader utilizes the pattern of time relationships, comprehension of what is read is more extensive. Readers should be able to comprehend the passage of time and ordered sequence of events by noting the transitional words *first, during, eventually, then, finally*. Of necessity, recipes, rules, and assembly directions usually contain words that provide order. Time is clearly identified in texts, such as history books, that tell about sequences of events. In other words, understanding time sequence provides a pattern with which the brain can identify.

Teach Words That Indicate Examples

Some words and phrases indicate examples. They introduce situations or lists that support ideas that were previously introduced. Such words are *for instance, including, for example, such as, to demonstrate, specifically, to illustrate,* and *in particular*.

Teach Words That Indicate Comparison

Words that signal comparisons are *in the same way, similarly, as, just as, just like, in like manner, similarly, in a similar manner, in like fashion,* and *analogous to*.

Teach Words That Indicate Contrast

Some words that signal contrast are *yet, nevertheless, although, however, on the contrary, on the other hand, still, even though, unlike,* yet, *notwithstanding, nevertheless, nonetheless, instead of, as opposed to,* and *conversely*. The following paragraph illustrates the use of words that signal contrast.

> Readers with good skills need little encouragement to read a long novel or a challenging text. *On the other hand,* readers without honed comprehension skills, even if they can decode well, prefer to read materials written at a low level or will scan pages of picture-filled magazines.

Teach Words That Indicate Cause and Effect

Words that show cause and effect are *accordingly, if, then, due to, consequently, therefore, thus, result in, as a result, because, causes, effects, affects,* and *leads to.*

Teach Words That Indicate Conclusion or Summary

Words that show conclusion or summary are *finally, in the final analysis, on the whole, thus, to conclude, in sum, in summary, in brief,* and *in a word.*

Teach Words That Indicate Suggestion

Words that can be used to indicate a suggestion are *for this purpose, to this end, with this in mind, with this purpose in mind, therefore, specifically, especially, in particular, to explain, to list, to enumerate, in detail, namely,* and *including.*

Conclusion

Important components of reading comprehension are identifying main ideas and relationships between ideas in passages. The main idea is the author's primary point, frequently circumscribed within a single topic sentence. Other sentences in the paragraph provide supportive details, sometimes signified by transition words and phrases.

Authors often use words and phrases that indicate relationships and transitions. Although not all writing, good or bad, uses such clear signals, it is necessary for students to recognize signal words and their meanings. Understanding the use of these transition indicators is essential when students are reading materials in which the writer has used such indicators, and when students are writing so that they are able to include such words on their own. Teachers may have students create their own lists of transition words, perhaps, with sample sentences. Due to limited class time, teachers may prefer to assign this task as homework.

For more information, please see books such as:

- *The Gregg Reference Manual* by William Sabin.
- *The Brief English Handbook* by Edward A. Dornan, Charles W. Dawe.
- *The Least You Should Know About English* by Paige Wilson, Theresa Glazer.

For Further Consideration

- Why is being able to identify the main idea and supporting ideas essential to reading comprehension?
- How does the ability to decode efficiently influence one's ability to identify the main idea?
- Why is background knowledge important in reading comprehension?
- How would awareness of relationship indicators while reading help one improve his or her writing?

CHAPTER NINE

PURPOSE AND TONE

"I will prepare so I will be ready when opportunity presents itself." Abraham Lincoln

---

> **FOCUS POINT:** The guiding principle for an author's writing is called *purpose*. The attitude the author has toward his or her subject is called *tone*. Being able to determine the purpose that an author has for writing a passage or text and to detect the author's tone are crucial for reading comprehension. These skills also empower the reader to be discriminating and evaluative.

Purpose

Purpose is the guiding principle, the motive, the rationale, or the basis for an author's writing. It answers the question "why?" The author might want to portray a mood, create an emotional impact, persuade, or convey critical information. The author may be writing to a specific group, often called a *target audience*. He or she may choose specific words for that reason. Three common purposes of writing are detailed in the following sections.

Informing the reader: An author might want to convey facts and relate or disclose information about a situation, topic, or procedure. For example, an author might want to document which specific states require riders to wear helmets when riding bicycles and motorcycles. The piece might include facts such as the dates the laws were passed, how many times the laws are enforced, and the approximate number of riders in each state.

Persuading the reader: A writer might try to influence the reader's thinking, and sway the reader toward the writer's opinion. Persuasive writing might include only those facts that support the writer's point of view. Sometimes, but not always, the presence of words such as *should, ought,* or *must,* alert the reader to the writer's strong convictions regarding the topic. An example of such a sentence might be as follows:

Motorcycle riders should always wear safety helmets to protect their heads in case of an accident. (Note the use of the persuasive word, *should.*)

In another illustration, the author might write about the important role that the eating of fresh fruits and vegetables plays in maintaining a healthy diet. The topic sentence might be as follows:

No healthy diet is complete without generous amounts of fruits and vegetables. The author might continue to illustrate other benefits of eating fruits and vegetables to maintain longevity.

On the other hand, the author might carefully omit examples of individuals or groups that eat almost no fresh fruits and vegetables. Nonetheless, they live to a ripe old age. Thus, the author is being persuasive by presenting only one opinion and by omitting information that may have an undesirable effect on the reader.

Entertaining the reader: A writer's primary purpose might be to amuse, delight, charm, cheer, gladden, gratify, or provide humor for the reader. This can be done through fictional or non-fictional works. The writer might also have a secondary purpose of informing or persuading the reader.

For example, consider this sentence: *I didn't know what it meant to have ambivalent feelings until I saw my cantankerous neighbor, whom I hate, drive over a cliff in my new Mercedes Benz that I love.* While the reader might learn the meaning of *ambivalent* as having mutually conflicting feelings or thoughts at the same time such as love and hate together, the writer's main purpose is to amuse and provide humorous entertainment for the reader.

Tone

Tone in writing represents the writer's feeling, spirit, character, mood, frame or state of mind. The tone of the writing makes known the attitude that the writer has toward the subject or topic just as a speaker's verbal tone can cue us. A writer's tone can also give clues about his or her purpose for writing a piece and for whom the piece is written. Specific phrases, adjectives, adverbs, certain verbs, forms of statements, and details that the author has selected specifically may signal the reader as to whether the author's attitude is one of joy, sadness, despair, anger, frustration, and the like.

For the reader with an extensive vocabulary, determining tone is a relatively uncomplicated matter. Consider the following statement: *"Can't forest fires be controlled? Look at the catastrophic toll on wildlife."* Is the tone primarily that of frustration, hopefulness, or sadness? Of course, it is one of frustration based on serious concern at the extensive damage to wildlife. The following sentence has a different tone. *"Her promotion was merited."* Is the tone one of dislike, approval, or disappointment regarding the promotion? Most assuredly, it is one of approval because the author is saying that the person should have been given the promotion because she deserved it or earned it. Here, again, however, vocabulary knowledge is important because the reader must know the meaning of *merited.* If not, comprehension is limited, making it impossible for the reader to begin to determine tone.

Another aspect of tone is that of formality or informality. For example, if the author writes, "He flipped his lid," instead of, "He was greatly agitated," the reader can identify this as informal writing. When the author writes, "Your behavior exacerbates me intensely," instead of "You really bug me," it serves notice to the reader regarding the formality of the tone. Knowledge of word meanings, such as *exacerbates*, is critical.

Selected Descriptive Words That May Indicate Tone

admiringly	doubtfully	melancholy
affectionately	enjoyable	morose
amazingly	frightened	peculiarly
ambivalent	frisky	pessimistic
angrily	gentle	playful
appreciate	gleeful	positive
arrogant	greedily	praising
bitterly	graciously	remorseful
bewildered	haughty	resentful
calmly	hopeful	revengeful
careful	horrific	sinister-like
cantankerous	horrendous	sorrowful
catastrophic	hostile	stingily
conniving	jokingly	sympathetically
delightful	jovial	tragic
disgustedly	joyous	treacherous
disingenuous	laughable	vengeful
disturbing	loving	viciously

Irony

Irony is stating one thing, but meaning the opposite. Irony usually employs humor to make a point. Irony can occur in comedy parlance, as for instance, when a visitor says, *"How do you clean your floors? I can eat off the floor in your kitchen. That's because so much food is on it."* The tone is insulting and mocking with a touch of humor.

A frank, straightforward way to communicate the same idea might read: "You are a terrible housekeeper; food has spilled everywhere and you haven't cleaned it up." On the other hand, saying or writing it this way probably wouldn't have the same walloping effect.

Another example might come from a shopper looking at a pair of bargain shoes. When the sales clerk brings out a pair of shoes costing $500, the customer might ironically say, *"That's a bargain at only $250 per shoe."* What the shopper really means is, "That is considerably too much to pay for a pair of shoes."

Another illustration of irony may be noted when the CEO of a company wins $5 in an office betting pool, and the young mail clerk complains, *"He definitely needs that $5 more than I do!"* His tone is self-pitying and scornful. A clear-cut way of expressing the same idea with no humor might be, "He doesn't need the money as much as I do."

Circumstances can also reflect irony, as in this example:

He went through the rooms filled with books, looking for money or jewelry, anything of value, but he found nothing. Frustrated and disappointed, he left without realizing that the old books were actually rare and worth millions of dollars.

Active Reading

The more aware, alert and the better prepared the reader is to uncover purpose, tone, and meaning, the more successful the reader will be at comprehending and analyzing what is read. Being an *active reader* is the opposite of being a passive reader who just reads or "calls" words. Passivity turns the reader into a mere sponge, unthinkingly taking in what is read, or, worse, unable to comprehend what is read. Active reading is critical.

In the classroom, students will encounter mostly textbooks and non-fictional materials that are meant to be strictly informative, although some reflect the authors' biases or agendas. Readers must be alert to authors' biases. Readers must learn to read magazines, newspaper articles, editorial columns and even textbooks with critical, comparative, and evaluative attention. If not, the subtleties of the written word might be lost to the passive reader. By contrast, the active reader comprehends more clearly and is able to detect underlying messages. If the reader is unable to determine whether something is written ironically or straightforwardly, as information or persuasion, the reader can be easily duped, possibly confused or misinformed. Detecting clues in purpose and tone is essential in an active reading process.

Conclusion

Being able to determine what an author intends to convey (purpose) and how the author expresses his or her attitude and feeling (tone) is key to successful reading comprehension. A writer presents ideas with specific purpose and tone. The most common purposes are to inform, to persuade and to entertain. The tone is affected by the writer's attitude toward the subject as well as toward the audience for whom the piece is written.

For Further Consideration

- Why is it important to be aware of a writer's tone? What misinformation can occur when the tone of the writing is misinterpreted?

- Think about a time when you may have changed your mind about an issue as a result of the writer's persuasiveness.

- If you were to write a piece on a subject about which you were trying to inform the reader, how would you approach it? What tone would you use?

CHAPTER TEN

OPINION, FACT AND ARGUMENT

"Chew up the meat and spit out the bones." Unknown

FOCUS POINT: Being a successful reader is not determined solely by the reader's ability to decode or comprehend the literal meanings of words. Despite the fact that the reader may decode words effectively and has an adequate vocabulary, the reader may be unskilled in judging the merits of evidence. The reader must be able to distinguish between opinion and fact and to judge the adequacy of a writer's argument.

Opinion

When an author writes *an opinion*, it might be a myriad of things. It might be a belief, a judgment, an idea, a thought, an impression, a notion, an assumption, a conviction, a persuasion, a way of thinking, a point of view, or even a sentiment or a feeling. Another person may have a totally different point of view and neither person can be objectively proven right or wrong. Therefore, opinion is said to be *subjective*.

Consider the following statement, *"My first grade teacher was the best teacher in the world."* Someone else might believe that his or her teacher was the best. Even if both people have different, legitimate views, their statements are merely opinions. Here's another example: *"The most important invention of the modern era was a wireless phone."* Perhaps someone else thinks that computers, airplanes, or automobiles were the most important modern inventions. If so, the statement is merely an opinion; that is, a belief or conclusion that is held with confidence by the individual, but cannot be substantiated by absolute knowledge or proof by anyone else.

A movie, book, or restaurant review by a knowledgeable and well-known expert is still a matter of opinion, based on that reviewer's personal preferences, perspectives, likes, and dislikes. Have you ever gone to see a movie that had rave reviews in the newspaper, but you thought it was awful? Obviously, your opinion differed from the opinion of the paid reviewer.

Often, that which is opinion is erroneously elevated to the status of fact. Opinions about politics, health issues, social concerns, media advertising, and even science and history sometimes masquerade as facts. When it comes to reading, it is imperative that students be able to identify when something is an opinion. Let the reader beware. Let the reader be *aware*. A critical and evaluative reader can distinguish an opinion from fact.

Fact

A fact is a statement or idea that can be proven by means of *objective evidence*. Objective means it is unbiased, unprejudiced, impartial, exact, and provable. An instrument of measurement or first-hand knowledge may prove a statement to be fact.

For example, the statement "The boy is 5 feet 5 inches tall," can be proved or disproved using a tape measure or yardstick. Therefore, it is a fact. On the other hand, an *opinion* might be that the boy is tall when compared to his twin brother who is five feet one inch, or short when compared to a professional basketball player who is six feet eight inches tall. In another instance, eyewitnesses at the scene of an accident can also attest to the *fact* that two cars crashed. These eyewitnesses also may have different *opinions* as to which driver was responsible for the crash.

On a cautionary note, not all writing can be classified strictly as fact, fiction, or opinion. For example, the historical fiction novel combines fact, opinion, and fiction in a large body of work. A discerning reader with sufficient and accurate background knowledge can confidently detect that which is fact, fictional license, and the author's opinion. On the other hand, readers, who may not have sufficient background of the subject, may readily believe everything that is written because it is done so in a historical, seemingly factual, format.

Argument

I always like a good *argument*. A first-rate argument is the best form of debate. I am not talking about yelling, screaming, inappropriate language, and name-calling. This foolishness can never be considered a good argument, no matter who wins.

A good argument, however, is a less coercive, less emotional presentation of factual evidence that supports a point of view about some matter. Facts or evidence can be used to advance a specific point of view about a subject.

We often hear of an attorney *presenting an argument*. In general, an attorney attempts to use logic, reason, and presentation of facts to prove or disprove a case. However, the attorney might attempt to cloud the issue or sway the jury by introducing irrelevant statements. Such argumentation is not limited to the courtroom. The written word is a powerful tool of persuasion and persuasive writers present their arguments in ways similar to those of attorneys. The readers act as judge and jury. The readers must carefully analyze the writer's points and decide whether the points are factual and relevant.

With this in mind, mature readers realize that they are required to be decision-makers in their daily private, work, and civic activities. Arguments occur on editorial pages, in politics, and in commercial advertising. Students today must be trained to question the validity of an argument and be adequately prepared to critically evaluate attempts to sway their opinions.

In some cases, the writer may attempt to support the main point authoritatively with extraneous information that may be factual but does not address the main point. This may be intended to leave the impression that the argument is filled with facts. These irrelevant points deviate from the main point, and purposely or unintentionally, serve to distract the reader. An author might attempt to add credibility to her position supporting a law forbidding cigarette smoking in public buildings by saying that her father was a doctor who treated many people with lung disease. While this may be interesting and factual, it is unrelated to the facts pertinent to the specific argument.

There is a famous line from an old television series, *Dragnet*. When Detective Sergeant Joe Friday interviewed witnesses to a crime, they frequently added in unrelated bits of information. Sergeant Friday's oft-repeated directive was, "Just the facts, Ma'am." His request was for the witness to give facts pertaining only to the crime scene. In like manner, the reader should be focused on just the facts that are pertinent to the argument.

Reading Critically

Critical reading, therefore, is essential when sorting through the written arguments encountered in daily life. To read critically, the analytical reader must do the following:

1. Identify the main point.
2. Determine whether the supporting points are relevant or irrelevant.
3. Discard irrelevant points.
4. Determine whether the author's supporting points are adequate.

Consider the main point and relevancy of supporting points in this example:

Sample of a Main Point

This political candidate is honest.

Sample of a Relevant, Supporting Point

This political candidate has a clean record. She has kept every campaign promise she ever made. She has disclosed all her private and personal files for public scrutiny.

Sample of an Irrelevant Point

The political candidate is always nicely dressed.

A critical reader should be able to identify irrelevant points. Sometimes they may be noticeable like flashing neon lights such as in the following paragraph:

Matt is determined to be successful. He gets up before dawn to do his homework. He practices four hours a day to improve his football skills. He is good looking, enjoys jazz music and likes to have fun. He has a weekend job to pay for his school and sports expenses. Nothing gets in the way of Matt's journey to success.

In this paragraph, the author includes some engaging facts about Matt. Matt is good looking, enjoys jazz music. He likes to have fun. However, these statements are not relevant to the main point that Matt is determined to be successful.

Readers must identify such irrelevant points in an argument. These points can inhibit accurate comprehension.

Supporting points must be adequate to convince the reader. Did the author include enough persuasive points to defend the main point with reason? Can you identify the supporting points? Look back at the paragraph about Matt. How many supporting points are there?

Topic sentence:

Matt is determined to be successful.

Relevant supporting sentence 1:

He gets up before dawn to do his homework.

Relevant supporting sentence 2:

He practices four hours a day to improve his football skills.

Relevant supporting sentence 3:

He has a weekend job to pay for his school and sports expenses.

Rephrased topic sentence:

Nothing gets in the way of Matt's journey to success.

The three sentences in the middle of the paragraph are relevant supporting points. Now examine the samples and determine the adequacy of supporting statements in each.

Example A: Inadequate supporting details

It is hot in the summer in Phoenix, Arizona. Nevertheless, Phoenix is a good summer vacation destination because hotel rates are low. You should plan to come to Phoenix on your next summer vacation.

Example B: Adequate supporting details

Although it is hot in the summer in Phoenix, Arizona, it is a good summer vacation destination. As the temperature goes up, hotel rates go down. All resort hotels have luxurious pools with poolside service to take your mind off the heat. Many restaurants offer delicious, inexpensive summer specials with discounts to lure people out of their air-conditioned hotels and into well-appointed, air-conditioned restaurants. Because the winter visitors have departed, traffic congestion is reduced. Therefore, if you are looking for a good summer deal, want to enjoy fine food, and avoid the crowds, come to Phoenix for your summer vacation.

Being a Critical Reader Means Being an Active Reader

An active reader either draws on his or her background knowledge or researches the issues before jumping to conclusions about what he or she reads. These techniques are vital when combing through the gnarls and snarls of an argument. Assuming that (a) the reader can decode all the words; (b) the reader knows the meaning of the words used; (c) the reader identifies the writer's tone and purpose; and (d) the reader distinguishes fact from fiction, the active reader can then take a critical view of what he or she reads. Many readers are amazed to discover how easily they can recall the smallest detail of an argument, if they employ the techniques of active reading.

Inferences

Inference is an indirect understanding of what we read.

When we read, we bring with us certain assumptions. Sometimes the author will rely on those assumptions by writing something, hoping that we will infer something different.

Consider the following statement: *The store's owner admitted that his store sold the same poison that killed his girlfriend.*

Now, consider the parts of the statement.

1. There is an owner of the store.

2. He admits that his store sold poison.

3. He has a girlfriend.

4. His girlfriend is no longer alive.

5. Poison killed his girlfriend.

6. The poison that killed his girlfriend is the same kind that he sells in his store.

The reader may infer (or come to a conclusion or assumptions based on experience, information, or knowledge) that the store's owner poisoned his girlfriend. In this case, the author presented some information and the reader may have read "ideas" into what was written, beyond what the words said. When we make inferences, we find meaning that is hidden in the words and phrases. We become sleuths.

Sometimes, however, we "sleuth" incorrectly. Now, consider what else the author has added. *The police, however, found out that the girlfriend was actually married to a poison manufacturer who admitted to poisoning his wife because she was cheating on him.*

An active reader must be critical, focusing on the facts and open to many interpretations of ideas.

Standardized Testing Strategies

Although teachers should never *teach to the test*, teaching students skills in critical reading and analyzing arguments can significantly improve a student's test scores. One strategy is that of being able to identify irrelevant or distracting information. Remind students to be alert for irrelevant information or distracters that are usually included in items that test the students' comprehension. Students, who know how to identify main ideas, topic sentences, and supportive sentences and can discern the adequacy of supportive sentences, have the skills to confidently, analytically, and successfully take tests.

Conclusion

In any first-rate argument, the writer states his or her opinion at the outset. The writer then presents evidence to support the opinion. The reader must engage in active reading, that is, be attentive to the ideas and ways the ideas are presented. The reader must analyze the evidence and determine whether it adequately supports the author's opinion. Additionally, an active reader continually makes inferences, evaluates, and analyzes what he or she reads to distinguish fact from opinion.

For Further Consideration

- How is knowledge of the essential elements of argumentation related to comprehension?

- When have you read an argument that had irrelevant or inadequate supporting points?

- Read the letters to the editor on the pages of your local newspaper. Identify the arguments and determine whether the supporting points are relevant and adequate.

CHAPTER ELEVEN

DYSLEXIA: LEARNING DISABILITIES OR LEARNED DISABILITIES

"A child miseducated is a child lost." John F. Kennedy

FOCUS POINT: The term *dyslexia* has commonly been used to mean having difficulty using words or language. Such a broad definition allows the diagnosis to broadly apply to hundreds of thousands of students, who, far from being learning disabled, simply have been taught to read using inadequate and inefficient methods. The popular rise of the diagnosis of dyslexia seems to have occurred simultaneously with the abandonment of phonics instruction in favor of whole word, sight-reading, and whole language approaches to reading instruction. Dyslexia is not always a learning disability, but often can be *instructionally induced* and a *learned* disability, correctable and reversible with systematic, direct, and explicit phonics and reading instruction.

A Broad Definition

Dyslexia is a term that pops up frequently in contemporary television shows, on the radio, in print media, and even in daily conversations. Almost everyone, it seems, has heard about it. Most people know someone who is "dyslexic." Some people think it has something to do just with reversing the order of letters in words.

In most scientific research studies, the term *dyslexia* is defined as having difficulty using words or language. In her book *Dyslexia*, Wendy Moragne writes:

> Dyslexia is derived from the Greek *dys* that refers to difficulty,
> and *lexia* which refers to the use of words. The condition called
> *dyslexia* refers to a difficulty using words or language and people
> with this condition are called *dyslexics.*[1]

Marion Sanders in her *Understanding Dyslexia and the Reading Process* defines dyslexia as "faulty reading."[2]

A nineteenth-century ophthalmologist originally coined the term, *dyslexia*, to describe a condition of his patients who had experienced trauma to the head and brain. The patients had been able to read *before* the trauma. Afterward, they were unable to correctly process the written word. Thus, he reported that they had *dyslexia*, that is, *difficulty while reading or wrong reading*.

In 1925, a neuropathologist, Samuel Orton, popularized the term. His observations led him to conclude, "severe reading problems were due either to cerebral dominance or to abnormalities of the language system of the brain."[3] Since Orton's patients had some type of neurological problem, "unfortunately, these ideas led to the belief that poor readers have brain damage."[4]

The meaning of the term dyslexia has evolved and broadened. Today, dyslexia has come to mean any significant trouble with reading and spelling. A plethora of symptoms are associated with dyslexia and the term gives no indication of its varied causes and possible remedies. Far too often and too hastily, teachers, psychologists, counselors, educational professionals, parents, and those in various medical fields, tend to label students as *dyslexic*. It is easy to make a casual diagnosis, but if it is the wrong diagnosis, the consequences can be very harmful to the individual.

A few years ago, I met a young man who had been diagnosed by his school's professionals as being dyslexic when he was in first grade. He had never been taught to use phonics. By the time that I met him, he was eighteen years of age and had spent thirteen years in school being instructed in special education classes. He was graduated from school, illiterate, and able to read less than ten words. As an adult, he learned explicit phonics strategies, is now literate, and reads books that he buys for himself. He has a long way to go because he has many wasted years behind him, but over time and with practice, he will continue to improve. He complains, "When a kid can't read, why do the teachers always think that it's the kid's problem?" It is a wise observation, arising out of painful, personal experience.

The Popular Press and Dyslexia

In July 2003, *Time Magazine* offered a cover story titled "Overcoming Dyslexia: What New Brain Science Reveals and What Parents Can Do." It is typical of other articles, well written and geared toward the public. The article compiles a common list of symptoms of dyslexia, transcribed below. Based on my experience, I have adapted the symptoms and offered my thoughts. My observations and comments about the "symptoms" follow each item and are enclosed in brackets. It is hoped that the reader may come to understand the necessity of considering whether it is possible that caring but inadequately prepared teachers unknowingly have given ineffective instruction. The result may be reading disabilities and/or reading deficiencies often thought to be *dyslexia*.

AGES 5 TO 6: DOES YOUR KINDERGARTNER [OR OLDER STUDENT]...

1. **Use invented spelling for words, cannot write name, or has illegible writing?**

   [*Comment*: Some whole language reading programs specifically direct students to use invented spelling. Therefore, the child might simply be doing what he or she was instructed to do.

   Regarding handwriting, in some schools, good penmanship is neither taught nor expected. Parents should ask which types of handwriting procedures have been taught. Could it be that the instruction is lacking? Remember, many older students never have been taught correct manuscript or cursive handwriting, or had high standards placed on their penmanship.]

---

2. **Cannot discern spoken syllables or compound words like *bookmark*?**

[*Comment*: Kindergartners do not necessarily have the concept of syllables (book·mark) or the combining of words like *book* and *mark* to make compound words like *bookmark*. Children should not be expected to figure this out themselves. This is something that explicitly must be taught. For example, what is a *bookmark?* Students may think it to be a *mark on a book*?]

3. **Has difficulty with rhyming words such as *sit* and *mitt*?**

[*Comment*: It is imperative to check the student's hearing and vision by qualified medical professionals. If no hearing or visual problems exist, again, it is necessary to look into the manner of instruction. Was rhyming and the explicit teaching of phonemes and phonemic awareness part of the curriculum? On the other hand, the student might have picked up the habit of inattentive listening. For example, one adult student did not know what a *window* was when he came across it in his reading, although he was able to correctly pronounce it using his decoding skills. He had always thought he heard people talk about "closing a *wendell*." It wasn't until he decoded and read "window" that he learned its correct pronunciation.]

4. **Does not understand the letter symbol/sounds relevance? (Does your child know only letter names but not the sounds that they make?)**

[*Comment*: Some non-phonics approaches put the child in charge of his or her own learning and language acquisition.[5] On the other hand, Wendy Arnold says, however, that "...you must be...taught the rules...and not be expected to work them out yourself."[6]

Look into the mode of instruction and parental involvement before assuming the reader is dyslexic. Some parents and teachers believe that the learning of the letter names necessarily precedes the knowing of the sounds. Again, ask the question if the child has been adequately taught to connect the two.]

5. **Does not recognize phonemes? (Can your child tell you what word in the following list start with the same sound as *dab*: *map, mad, card, dip*?)**

[*Comment*: See *Comment* #3.]

AGES 6 TO 7: DOES YOUR FIRST-GRADER [OR OLDER STUDENT]...

1. **Continue to struggle when trying to recognize and manipulate phonemes?**

[*Comment*: Has the child been instructed in a systematic, explicit phonics program? Perhaps the child has been instructed using combination methods or embedded phonics, and the like.]

---

2. Is confused or unable to read small, common words, such as *mat, map, mop, top,* or *pot*?

[*Comment:* The child might be in a whole language, a whole-word or a sight-word class where these words have not yet been introduced. Therefore, the child has limited word recognition and background knowledge. Additionally, if the child has *not* been taught explicit phonics, he or she might not have the decoding skills to read even small words. The use of flash card drilling can actually cause problems rather than correct them. As one of my adult students told me about his reading word lists and flash cards in elementary school with his classmates, "I just said what the kids were saying. The words all looked alike to me. I guessed." He still sometimes confuses small, common words when he subconsciously relies on his sight-reading training, but readily corrects himself when he uses phonics strategies.]

3. Make frequent word substitutions such as *car* for *auto* or *pond* for *pool*.

[*Comment:* Making substitutions is generally an acceptable strategy taught by most whole-word/whole language instructors. Therefore, the substitutions may not indicate dyslexia on the part of the student. This may suggest that the teacher has failed to correctly teach the connection between sounds and letters.]

4. Fail to recognize common, irregularly spelled words, such as *said, where,* and *two*?

[*Comment:* When "inventive spelling" is taught as an acceptable strategy, then the child may not be able to detect common, irregularly spelled words. His or her teachers may even have given lavish praise for written creative expression replete with spelling errors.]

5. Complain about how hard reading is and refuse to do it?

[*Comment:* Human nature often causes all of us to avoid activities that are difficult for us to do. I have to admit that I have neither the knowledge nor adequate skills to change a flat tire efficiently. I have seen others change tires; I lack training and practice. For me, it is hard and, therefore, I avoid changing tires. Similarly, when a student has been given neither the knowledge nor adequate skills to read efficiently, he or she will complain about its difficulty and refuse to do it. Monroe and Backus wrote in 1937, "Refusals may also indicate that the child simply has no method of attacking words, and is intelligent enough to recognize when he does not know."[7] As Shirley L., an adult in her early 40s, writes, "Before I met you, I had never read a book in my life! I thought I was learning disabled. Now I buy books for myself and my family gives me books for gifts."

Do not *assume* that the student has been taught properly, even if the child has gone to a "good" school.   As noted earlier, teachers, even good teachers at good schools, don't know what they don't know, and they don't know that they don't know it.]

AGE 7 AND OLDER: DOES YOUR CHILD...

1.   **Mispronounce long or complicated words, saying *amulium* instead of *aluminum*?**

[C*omment:* The reader may have been taught to use substitution or guessing strategies that do not require exact reading. The reader may not know how to use essential left-to-right strategies.]

2.   **Confuse words that sound alike, such as *tornado* for *volcano*, or *lotion* for *ocean*?**

[C*omment:* The child simply may be using the *guessing* or *substitution* strategies that he or she learned in school.]

3.   **Speak haltingly and over use vague words such as *stuff* or *things*?**

[*Comment:* Individuals cannot grow beyond what they know. The child may be lacking in the essential vocabulary development, relying only on "prior knowledge" and not knowing various shades of meanings that would allow him or her to adequately express ideas. Again, extensive vocabulary must be modeled, taught, and its use reinforced. My seven-year-old granddaughter told me she was in the middle of a *conundrum,* making a decision. *Conundrum* is part of her vocabulary because it is a word that she has heard used in our family. Moreover, she is encouraged to ask questions about the meanings of new words that she hears. In addition, at age seven, she has strong phonetic skills and enjoys reading which is an activity that enhances her vocabulary development.]

4. **Have trouble memorizing dates, names, and telephone numbers?**

[*Comment:* Individuals who have not been explicitly taught phonemic awareness and left-to-right reading strategies may be more prone to rely on *memorization* of the names and numbers *as a whole* in the same manner as they have been taught to memorize whole words. Therefore, they may have a similar difficulty duplicating dates, names and telephone numbers as they have in spelling correctly.

The reading of both words and numbers rely on left-to-right strategies. The student who has developed whole-word strategies may consciously or subconsciously apply those same strategies to the reading of numbers. Therefore, the same confusion that may appear in letter reversal may also appear in number reversal. Although this may not always be the case, it is important that one discovers if there is or is not a background in whole word reading that may be correlated to "whole number" confusions. Just as stroke victims have to be retaught and new brain pathways established, it may be that those individuals who have not developed the left-to-right strategies may have to be taught to do so.]

5. Have trouble reading small function words, such as *that, an,* and *in*?

[*Comment:* This can be explained by information noted in the earlier commentary of the confusion that can be caused by the memorization of words on sight-word lists or other words learned by sight and not phonics strategies.]

6. Guess wildly when reading multi-syllabic words instead of sound them out?

[*Comment:* Although whole language proponents do not advocate "wild" guessing, some advocate "smart" *guessing*. The following quote may shed additional light on why students may guess:

> *Keep in mind that if the miscue [mistake] is grammatically and semantically appropriate for the reader's dialect or simply reflects imperfect mastery of the grammar of English, it should be coded as entirely acceptable...* [8]

Nonetheless, a mistake or guess is not accurate reading. The guessing strategy can be discarded and mistakes avoided with application of phonics strategies.]

7. Skip parts of words, reading *conible* instead of *convertible*, for example?

[*Comment:* This may be attributed to sight-reading instruction and use of guessing strategies, as well as lack of left-to-right phonics strategies. If students have never heard "convertible," and do not have left-to-right decoding strategies, then they cannot possibly make an intelligent guess as to what it is. Therefore, they may attempt unsystematically to "read" the letters in the word that they see, but miss some of them. This can be corrected with systematic phonics training, reading each phoneme (sound) left to right.]

8. Substitute easy words for hard ones, such as *car* for *automobile*?

[*Comment:* As we have seen, unlike phonics instruction, whole language instruction does not require that good reading must be word-perfect reading. Therefore, students may not have had teachers who considered any departure from the text such as substituting, without changing essential meaning as being problematic. Therefore, *car* and *automobile* are essentially the same. The child simply may be constructing the meaning as directed. Furthermore, the child may also be using visual clues as taught and using the term most commonly used for a family passenger vehicle, a car.]

9. **Spell terribly and have messy handwriting?**

[*Comment:* Accuracy in spelling is not an outcome promoted in whole language instruction. Weaver explains, "Children's constructed spellings are often called invented spellings, functional spellings, or even temporary spellings. I prefer to call them *constructive* spellings…to emphasize the fact that the child is operating upon **self-constructed** rules and strategies for spelling."[9]

It is imprudent to consider this a symptom of dyslexia if the child is only doing what a teacher has told him or her to do. It may be because the child has never been taught or encouraged to spell with accuracy or to write correctly and neatly.]

10. **Have trouble completing homework or finishing tests on time?**

[*Comment:* Should we not ask other questions first, before we see these problems as possible symptoms of dyslexia?

a. Has the student been taught to read using essential reading skills, thus enabling the student to read the homework or tests without difficulty?

b. Has the student been taught how to use effective and time-efficient strategies?

c. Has the teacher provided clear and adequate instruction for the student to be able to do the homework and finish the test in a timely fashion?

d. Could the student's experience be similar to that of Jano at the beginning of Chapter One of this book?]

11. **Have a deep fear of reading aloud?**

[Comment: A singer once commented that she did not do live concerts because she had a deep fear of forgetting words of the songs. After the introduction of the invisible teleprompter, she felt comfortable again to sing publicly. If you were keenly aware that you could not read words correctly, that you only knew to make substitutions, guesses, or to skip words, would *you* have a deep fear of reading aloud? That is why so many students prefer to "read silently." They know that they don't know; they also don't want others to find out.][10]

This *Time Magazine* article offers broad insights of many professionals into the variety of symptoms associated with reading difficulties that lead to the diagnosis of dyslexia. These insights are to be respected because they are coming from a unique perspective. However, one might say that all or most of these symptoms are also traits of students who have been taught to read using non-phonics programs.

For example, a picture on the first page of the article is of a girl posed in front of lists of words similar to what some educators call "word walls." Often, this is a reading-instruction technique used to assist students in memorizing words by *sight*. In the article, one child is reported as being able to figure out words like *electricity* but has trouble with shorter words like *four* or *year* with similar visual configurations. Because of information in previous chapters, you understand how confusion could be possible. Few words look similar to the word *electricity*. It is long, and has a unique configuration.

By way of comparison, let me tell you about a young man who learned to read and speak Russian in college. He learned to read the language phonetically. He explained, however, that there were some long words with unique configurations that he did not have to use phonics to sound out. He recognized them by their uniqueness. Likewise, the young boy might be able to identify *electricity* in the same manner as a young non-reader may identify but not read the familiar word, *McDonald's*. However, the words *four* and *year* are words that many students are taught to memorize by sight as well but these words' configurations have much in common. Notice the similarities between them. For some children, these similarities visually are confusing. However, a phonics-trained student could not possibly confuse them because the first sound that is pronounced in four is /f/ and the first sound that is pronounced in year is /y/. When read from left to right, there can be no confusion because, to the phonics-trained reader, the *ea* vowel team is not the same as *ou*. To others, it is confusing.

The well-researched *Time Magazine* article concludes that the child, who can read *electricity*, but confuses other words, may have *dyslexia*. The authors use the broad, popular definition of dyslexia. The author also writes that the child has had "good schooling" and exhibits "above-average intelligence." As pointed out frequently in other chapters of this text, good teachers in good schools may unknowingly use faulty instructional methods, even for students with above-average intelligence. The child's inability to read well might not have anything to do with the child's intelligence or capabilities. It may be a problem that is "instructionally induced," however. It is imperative, therefore, that the teacher and parent understand how the child has been taught to read and what learned strategies the child is using, before the child is labeled as having a physical learning disability of dyslexia or an instructionally induced disability of dyslexia. Strategies to reverse or correct dyslexia should not include drilling on sight words. Instead, left-to-right phonemic decoding is essential, no matter the age of the *dyslexic*.

A Personal Tale

When I was in my early teens, I took a sewing class at a fabric store that offered free sewing lessons. Someone who was very knowledgeable and skilled in sewing taught the class.

Never having sewn anything in my life, I came to class filled with eagerness. On the first day, the instructor told us that our final sewing project was to make a dress. Only a few students were in the class, but the teacher seemed to be overwhelmed with time constraints, and she had an overabundance of impatience. She presented instructions once and then spent most of her time with students who already had high levels of sewing skills. When I had a problem, the instructor would say, "Rip out the stitches and do it over."

I ripped and did over and ripped and did over. I began to refer to myself as "Pat, the Ripper." I was frustrated. As hard as I tried, I fell further and further behind. At every class, my frustration level increased. By this time, my teacher was of little help, although I remember still asking questions because I wanted to do well. When it was time to begin work on my final project, I went shopping with my mother to buy a dress pattern and material. As I looked at the material and the picture of the dress on the package, I still held out hope that I would be able to accomplish this goal.

However, the class sessions were coming to a close and all my ripping and re-sewing was slowing me down. One night, a few days before my dress was due, I asked my mother to help me. She had sewn many dresses for me. She was caring and in her own way she thought she was helping me when she said, "This will take you too long. Let me do it for you."

The dress was finished although *I* didn't sew it. Nevertheless, I received a certificate that I had completed the sewing class although I hadn't really learned how to sew. To this day, I have *dys·sew·ia*. I can sew, but not well. As a result, I don't like to do it. I avoid sewing.

Is something physically or mentally wrong with me, or could it be that the instruction or help that I received was less than adequate?

Scientific Studies of Dyslexia

It seems obvious, therefore, that educators and parents do not have scientifically specific guidelines to accurately identify what constitutes dyslexia in the same way that a medical professional or a parent can accurately determine that a child has a temperature of 102.5 degrees by using a thermometer. Without such specific guidelines and with a little knowledge, educational professionals and the public are led to believe that checking off a few symptoms can identify if someone is dyslexic.

In 1994, over thirty million adults were considered dyslexic.[11] With such ambiguities in the definition of dyslexia, as well as the checklists of symptoms of dyslexia, or without an understanding of ineffective reading instruction that can create such symptoms, it is no wonder that the number of those labeled as dyslexic continues to increase. Practitioners in a variety of fields tend to use broad definitions of dyslexia and are not held to any limiting standards. On the other hand, scientific researchers are attempting to use a narrower, less ambiguous definition of dyslexia.

Consider the two following definitions of dyslexia:

1. A narrow definition of *dyslexia*, considered "pure dyslexia," restricts the term to specific difficulties in word identification, that is, the ability to correctly read words in isolation.

2. A broad (popular) definition of *dyslexia* includes difficulties with word identification, reading comprehension, associated difficulties in spelling and writing, and a wide range of difficulties with spoken language.[12]

The next critical step, however, is to ask whether the problem is dyslexia that is an actual neurological learning disability characterized by reading difficulties, or whether it is dyslexia that is a difficulty caused by inadequate and ineffective instruction.

Based on what we now know about failed reading instruction, the concerned parent, teacher, or dyslexic adult might be wise to find the answer to that question first.

If the "dyslexic" individual has not been instructed in what we now know to be scientifically proven essentials of phonemic awareness and phonics, the source of the *dyslexia* symptoms may begin there and should be aggressively treated with corrective reading instruction before going further. Not all teachers, although they may be caring and committed educators, have adequate training or knowledge in the teaching of true phonics.

Without a doubt some individuals have true, neurological dyslexia. **Nevertheless, classroom teachers and even trained school psychologists, or "certified dyslexia experts," who are not neurologists, are not qualified to determine if there is a neurological cause of the dyslexia symptoms.**

You may discover, however, if you do an Internet search, for example, that there are innumerable programs offering solutions for dyslexics. Not all of these programs have been developed by or are serviced by scientific experts; sometimes they are created by well-intentioned, highly dedicated, skilled individuals. Nevertheless, it is essential to evaluate their research reports cautiously as was addressed in *Chapter Four*. For example, one site boasts that its program is so effective and unique that it is not possible to collect quantifiable data. Just as in the days of the Old West, there are many types of the "snake-oil Sam" vendor offering scientifically unproven solutions to eager clients.

In searching the Internet to find sites offering discussions about or programs dealing with dyslexia, you will find multiple lists of symptoms. Remember that the symptoms listed on dyslexia sites are usually only *indicators* of the possibility of physical or neurological causes for dyslexia. Overall, some of the symptoms found on one site will be found on others, but there may also be unique symptoms noted. In some cases, the unique symptoms are directly related to the solutions identified by the site's providers. For example, there are various solutions offered that deal with cerebral stimulation, visual or auditory accommodations, neurological solutions, multi-sensory approaches, and the like. They may or may not be valid approaches.

Although a few providers seem to be aware of the importance of phonological awareness, not one of the sites reviewed for this publication addresses the question, "How was the individual *taught* to read?" In my opinion, that is a critical *first* question.

Furthermore, information that you read might simply be culled from resources, such as books or articles that are not scientific, but are considered topical research. Such research on the topic of dyslexia, for example, may be written by experts, so deemed because of their wide knowledge accumulated through years of study in the field. Obviously, much of the topical research can sometimes be a trustworthy, necessary source of reliable information. Nevertheless, as has been mentioned previously, the reader must be an *informed cynic* when considering the validity of topical research or any research claims. The information in this book can assist the reader in asking and answering questions.

Is Dyslexia Instructionally Induced?

An abundance of valid, as well as soft-science data exists regarding dyslexics, dyslexia, and potential solutions to correct this reading disability. Nevertheless, one treatment has been shown to yield consistent results for intervention in reversing or alleviating dyslexic symptoms. "The most successful programs emphasize the same core elements: practice manipulating phonemes, building vocabulary, increasing comprehension, and improving the fluency of reading."[13]

In addition to teaching phonemic awareness and explicit phonics as a corrective measure for dyslexia, other interventions exist. These include highly structured instruction that is systematic, sequential, and provides simple-to-complex learning objectives.

In some cases, multi-sensory structured language instruction is also required that helps develop cognitive processes by which the student can know, and confidently use, rules and structures of reading, spelling, and writing as opposed to guessing or discovering them on his or her own. In some cases, it may be that the student had never been given the appropriate opportunity to develop these cognitive processes either at home or in the classroom.

For generations past, before the natural-acquisition-of-knowledge philosophies were in vogue, the basic education in the United States included highly structured instruction that was systematic and sequential, providing simple-to-complex learning objectives. Students developed cognitive processes by which they could know and confidently use language rules and structures. Phonics instruction fit well into this format. Reading skills were honed as core knowledge was taught. Guessing or discovering the rules on one's own was unacceptable.

Also in the past, students were taught the grammatical structure of sentences through diagramming. Diagramming sentences allowed students to use highly regulated rules to create a visual schematic illustration of how words and phrases were used grammatically and how they were related to one another. The ability to analyze sentence structure through the visual scheme in diagramming also contributed to one's being able to comprehend complex sentences, thus, bringing clarity out of grammatical confusion.

Again, a structured learning activity that developed the cognitive process, such as diagramming, was also discontinued decades ago. Instead, students were encouraged to use other means of literature exploration and less-structured instruction to gain knowledge of the English language.

The friction between those who supported structured learning as opposed to natural learning has been detailed in previous chapters. For purposes of this discussion on dyslexia, it might be good to have a brief review.

In 1779, Frederick Gedike, a German schoolteacher, developed a whole word reading acquisition approach. After introducing the whole word, he helped the students analyze the word according to the individual sounds the letters made. Then, students were to synthesize the parts that they now knew into the whole word again. Gedike believed the process of analyzing and synthesizing words was to be followed with more systematic phonics instruction.[14]

Horace Mann (1796-1859), the renowned educator, admired Gedike's approach as well as the method that Gallaudet used to teach the deaf to read. Mann adapted the skeletal form of Gedike's whole word reading instruction to teach English in the United States. Although Gedike's approach used explicit phonics instruction, Mann omitted explicit phonics in his alteration of Gedike's method. Mann's renowned position and the considerable weight of influence that his prestige carried in the education dialogue allowed his own unique theory to take root and expand in American schools.[15]

The rise of dyslexia parallels the abandonment of phonics instruction. Phonics was replaced by whole word, sight-reading and whole language approaches to reading instruction. Therefore, students lacked the structured, direct instruction of explicit phonics knowledge that had been the primary tool their predecessors used to decode English words. Hopeful educators believed that, as students read independently, they would automatically come up with this knowledge somehow without structure or instruction.

Nevertheless, the correlation between whole language strategies and symptoms of dyslexia is troubling. Whole language methodologies do not support explicit phonics. Explicit phonics instruction, however, is now proven highly effective in reversing dyslexic symptoms. Given this information, is there a possibility that perhaps whole language instruction contributes to *instructionally induced dyslexia*? Moreover, it is sad and troubling that millions of individuals live with the constant, albeit erroneous, belief that they have a learning disability. As Jim J. told me, "Thanks for showing me how easy it was to learn how to read. Thank you for showing me that I am okay, that there is nothing wrong with me. Thanks for taking away the feeling I have lived with for most of my life that I was no good."

As an added note, I did not create this change in Jim; it was his learning of the essential skills required for successful reading that made it possible for him to read. I was merely the individual who taught him how to use those skills.

Conclusion

Before a student, who exhibits difficulty with reading, is labeled dyslexic, trained, medical professionals should eliminate any actual and *identifiable* physical causes, such as problems with hearing or vision.

Before any other treatments are considered to aid so-called dyslexics, these individuals should be taught to read using systematic, direct instruction of explicit phonics. If an individual has instructionally-induced dyslexia, most likely, systematic, explicit phonics instruction will eradicate the symptoms. A word of caution, as noted in previous chapters, should remind teachers and parents that old habits take time, practice, and patience to reverse. Students frequently may slip into comfortable old habits of guessing, substitution, and the like. The instructor is to be aware of this and to give the reader help by identifying when he or she is using old habits. For example, the instructor might remind the reader by saying, "You don't have to guess at words; use your phonics rules. Instead of guessing, what rule could you use here?" Thus, the reader can replace ineffective strategies with effective phonetic strategies. In the future, perhaps much time, money, and personal distress could be eliminated if all emergent readers were explicitly taught phonics in the first place.

For Further Consideration

- Think back on your own schooling experiences. Have you encountered individuals who were labeled as being dyslexic? How were their lives affected?

- How would you set up a scientific experiment to study the relationship of dyslexia to reading methodologies? How would you define dyslexia?

- Can you cite any rigorous scientific studies on dyslexia? What were the findings?

References

[1] Moragne, W. (1997). *Dyslexia.* Brookfield, Connecticut: The Millbrook Press, Inc., 17.
[2] Sanders, M. (2001). *Understanding Dyslexia and the Reading Process.* Needham Heights, Maine: Allyn and Bacon, 2.
[3] McGuinness, D. (1997). *Why Our Children Can't Read and What We Can Do About It.* New York: Touchtone Simon and Schuster, 117.
[4] Ibid, 117.
[5] Weaver, C. (1994). *Reading Process and Practice: From Socio-psycholinguistics to Whole Language.* Portsmouth, NH: Heinemann, 65.

[6] Arnold, W. (2004). *Phonemic Awareness* [Msg 1942]. Message posted to ExtensiveReading@Yahoogroups.com.

[7] Monroe, M. and Backus, B. (1937). *Remedial Reading: A Monograph in Character Education.* Cambridge, Massachusetts, 85.

[8] Weaver, 254.

[9] Weaver, 76.

[10] Song, S. (2003). Is your child dyslexic? *Time Magazine,* 55. (Questions adapted from *Overcoming Dyslexia* by Shaywitz, Sally, M.D. and *Straight Talk About Reading* by Susan Hall and Louisa Moats as cited in this source.)

[11] Cronin, E. (1994). *Helping Your Dyslexic Child.* Prima Publishing: Rocklin, CA., 13.

[12] Sanders, 2.

[13] Cuadros, P., Land, G., Scully, S. and Song, S. (2003, July 28). The new science of dyslexia. *Time Magazine,* 58.

[14] Sanders, 129.

[15] Sanders, 129-130.

CHAPTER TWELVE

FREQUENTLY ASKED QUESTIONS ABOUT PHONICS INSTRUCTION

"Always do more than is expected of you." General George Patton (1885-1945)

FOCUS POINT: Teachers of post-primary students might find certain hints helpful for effectively teaching phonics strategies. These eleven questions address the most frequent concerns teachers might have. This chapter provides simple, practical hints and information, in the form of questions and answers, to assist the teacher who teaches post-primary students to read or to read better.

Question 1

If my post-primary students don't know their consonants, what do I do?
How do I teach the consonants?

♦ If a student needs to learn all the consonants, use **commercially made** consonant cards or **make your own**, one card for each consonant sound. You can make your own cards by using clip art from a computer program or by cutting and pasting pictures from magazines. Use pictures of objects whose names begin with each of the consonant sounds. For example, use a car for *c*, a dog for *d*, and a pig for *p*.

Note: When you teach a sound for a letter symbol, teach the sound at the beginning of a word (*/d/* **as in *dog*),** but, at some point, also teach the sound at the end of a word (**as in *red*).** This instills phonemic awareness. It also emphasizes that sounds at the end of words are just as important as sounds at the beginning of words.

Consonant Chart Sample Words and Suggestions

B   ca**b**

C   pi**c**ni**c**   • Use the hard /k/ sound. The soft /s/ sound is taught later in the *Phonics Steps for Reading Success* program.

D   ha**d**

F   sti**ff**

G   do**g**

H   **h**at   • An *h* at the end of a word is usually silent, so using one at the beginning of a word is the best way to teach the /h/ sound.

J   **j**ump   • The letter *j* is not commonly found at the end of words.

K   in**k**

L   fue**l**

M   swi**m**

N   pa**n**

P   ta**p**

Q   **qu**it   • Teach *qu* as the /kw/ sound. In English, *q* is always followed by *u*. Also, in English the /kw/ sound is always spelled *qu*.

R   **r**ip   • Teach this as the tearing sound of *r* in *rrrrrrrrrip*. Do not teach the sound as /er/ or /ruh/.

S   ga**s**

T   ho**t**

V   gi**v**e   • In English, words that end with a /v/ sound, usually have a silent *e* at the end.

X   bo**x**   • Teach the *x* as the /ks/ sound, as in fox and six. An *x* at the beginning of a word usually has a /z/ sound as in **x**ylophone, although these words are rare.

Z   bu**zz**

How do I teach the vowels?

- *Suggestion:* Consider teaching the <u>short vowel *sounds* first.</u>

These are the "short" vowels' **sounds:**

/ă/   **A**nn's **a**pple

/ĕ/   **E**d's **e**gg

/ĭ/   **i**n the **i**gloo

/ŏ/   The **O**x says, "Aahh."

/ŭ/   The **U**mbrella is **U**p.

___

- *Note*: A long vowel (as it is called when it is pronounced by saying its letter *name*) is different from its *sound* as noted above.

These are the "long" vowels' **names:**

/ā/ as in **a**p**e**   /ē/ as in **e**at   / ī / as in **i**c**e**

/ō/ as in **o**at   /ū/ as in **u**s**e**

- *Suggestion:* Teach the long vowels <u>after</u> teaching the short vowels. Teach long vowels as "vowel teams" (such as *ai, ay, oe, oa* in *paint, tray, toe, boat*) and as "long vowel teams with a consonant blocker" (such as *o-e, a-e* in *rope, tape*).

Words with **short** vowels' *sounds*	Words with **long** vowel *names*
cap	cape
hop	hope
pad	paid

- Exceptions such as *old, -ight, er, ir,* and *ur* can be taught later.

Is it true that all students learn differently and therefore phonics is not the best decoding method for everyone? Isn't the learning of words by sight easier for some than having to apply many phonics rules?

♦   Memorizing sight words by their shapes is limiting and confusing. Given the hundreds of thousands of words in the English language, it would be a daunting task to memorize the look of each word.

♦   Put yourself in a student's place. Try to memorize these words by their shapes:

cat	=	♏︎♋︎♦		you	=	⬭◻♦
cap	=	♏︎♋︎◻		did	=	♎⧓♎
can	=	♏︎♋︎■		dad	=	♎♋︎♎
if	=	⧓↗		Dan	=	♎♋︎■
can't	=	♏︎♋︎■♦♦		run	=	◻♦■
fish	=	↗⧓♦♒		read	=	◻♏︎♋︎♎
the	=	♦♒♏︎		this	=	❋♒⧓♦
a	=	♋︎				

Consider the problems of a learner with significant learning problems trying to memorize words by shape and patterns. Note the words: ♏︎♋︎♦   ♏︎♋︎◻   ♏︎♋︎■. The shapes and patterns can be confusing.

Do the following assignment after you have memorized the words on previous page.

Write the English translation of these sight word sentences.

♍♋■ ⍓□◆ ❑♏♋♎ ❄♒♓⬧?

1] ⧫♒♏ ♐♓⬧♒ ♍♋■🕯⧫ ❑◆■.

2] ♎♋♎ ♍♋■ ♐♓⬧♒.

3] ♎♓♎ ⍓□◆ ❑♏♋♎ ❄♒♓⬧?

4] ♍♋■ ⧫♒♏ ♍♋⧫ ⬧♏♋❑ ♋ ♍♋□?

Now Ask Yourself These Questions

- Which word was **not** on the sight word list? How did you *read* it?
- Did you have to guess to fill in the word?
- Did you *read it* or did you *match shapes*? Is this an effective way to learn to *read*?
- If you had to memorize the words and read other texts, could you do it fluently?
- Study for a spelling test. Then, have someone give you the test or test yourself by covering up the words.

- The fifteen words on the previous page use an alphabet of an unfamiliar language.

- If you were a student who had difficulty learning or had a real learning disability, would it make sense to have you memorize all of these **words** by sight?

- How many words could you memorize? Would you get confused?

- How would you learn hundreds of thousands of words?

- If you could learn these words by sight or figure them out on your own, how many words could you learn in a day, a year, twelve years?

- How long would it take you to memorize most or all of the words in a dictionary?

- How long would it take you to read the definitions of those words?

- If each of the twenty-six symbols below could be combined to make 44 sound patterns for all of the words in a dictionary, would it be possible to learn to read most or all of those words ? Could you read the definitions?

♋ ♌ ♍ ♎ ♏ ♐ ♑ ♒ ♓ ♉ & ● ○
■ □ ▫ ❑ ❒ ◆ ◆ ◆ ❖ ◆ ⌧ ⬚ ⌘

Question 4

Can I combine or blend phonics strategies with sight-word, whole word, or whole language strategies?

Answer: Combining various strategies causes confusion.

NON-PHONICS STRATEGIES	PHONICS STRATEGIES
◆ Students might be taught to memorize whole words by the way the words look.	◆ Phonics strategies teach students to translate letter symbols to their assigned sounds.
◆ Students can spend an entire school year memorizing only 200-350 words, although English has hundreds of thousands of words and students entering 1st grade have between 20,000 and 30,000 words in their spoken repertoire.	◆ Phonics uses a systematic approach to teach the 43-46 separate sounds and sound-spelling relationships.
◆ Students become dependent on the teacher and can only read materials with controlled vocabulary.	◆ Students are empowered to read and understand all the words in their speaking vocabulary and to read and pronounce many others.
◆ Decoding unfamiliar words is often done by chunking or whole-to-part strategies.	◆ Phonics allows students to read and pronounce any word and its definition in a dictionary. Phonics helps students increase their ability to independently expand their vocabularies.
◆ Students are allowed to guess at words, instead of sounding them out.	◆ Instruction expects decoding to be precise and rejects guessing.
◆ Sight-word methods are designed to have students learn through immersion in reading and writing activities, because proponents equate learning to speak with learning to read.	◆ It takes about one year to complete instruction of an entire phonics program. Students then require only practice and occasional guidance.
◆ Inventive spelling is acceptable.	◆ Phonics instruction can be taught by anyone equipped with phonics rules, books, and phonics games.
◆ Students' reading errors are uncorrected, if guesses fit the context.	◆ Students become good readers and spellers, who like to read.
Some concepts in this column have been adapted from Constance Weaver's *Reading Process and Practice From Socio-Psycholinguistics To Whole Language*, Heinemann, New Hampshire, 1994.	◆ Students will have to memorize only a very few highly irregular words.

Question 5

Should I have my students use context clues to figure out how to read unfamiliar or unknown words?

◆ Context clues are extremely helpful in determining the **meaning** of an unfamiliar or unknown word. Use of context clues aids in comprehension. **Systematic phonics** supports the use of context clues to assist the reader in comprehending sentences and individual words.

◆ **Phonics readers** are fairly accurate in reading unfamiliar words, particularly those with regular pronunciations. Context clues can often help the English speaker adjust the pronunciation of a word.

- For example, in the sentence, "I *worry* about my sick puppy," the reader may initially attempt to apply the "*or* rule" [See *Chapter Six, Phonics Steps*, Rule 22]. Context helps the reader recognize the word and pronounce it according to the local, regional dialect. "Worry" is commonly pronounced "w**ur**ry."

- If context clues or prior knowledge are insufficient to determine the meaning of a word, the reader can read the dictionary definition. Phonics students can easily read dictionary and glossary definitions.

◆ On the other hand, using context clues to try to figure out how to read or decode a word slows fluency and inhibits accuracy. Consider this passage:

The man handed the old suitcase to the young woman. It was a real *conundrum* for her. At first, she didn't know what to do with this problem. She took the suitcase, stepped back, and left without saying a word.

(An older student with sight-word training might be able to use context clues to derive the meaning of the word *conundrum*, but figuring out its pronunciation is cumbersome at best, without the use of phonics strategies.)

> **Why do my older students frequently misread words?**
> **For example, they might read *blend* instead of *bend.***

♦ Many words begin with the consonant blends of two- and three-consonant patterns, like: bl / br / cl / cr / dr / gl / gr /pl / pr/ sl / fr / tr / sk / sm / sn / sp / st / sw / tw / spl / scr / str.

♦ Having students memorize these blends is similar to and as confusing as sight-word memorization.

♦ Each letter in a blend preserves its own sound. For example, *b* and *l*, or *d* and *r* are not the same as **digraphs** (ch, wh, th, sh, ph) that form **one unique sound with two letters.** Digraphs <u>must</u> be memorized.

♦ Teaching children to memorize consonant blends adds **unnecessary instruction** and **memorization time**. Frequently, much more time is spent drilling consonant blends like *st, str, sr,* and *sp* than is spent on the sound of each letter *s, t,* and so on.

♦ Post-primary students, who were taught to memorize consonant blends frequently read only the first letter of the blend, then guess. They might use the wrong blend and read *blend* instead of *bend,* or *bland* instead of *brand.*

♦ While reading, some students insert an unwritten consonant, rendering the word **meaningless** and **interfering with comprehension.** A student might read *dristrict* instead of *district,* not because the student is dyslexic or learning-disabled, but because the student guesses at blends as his or her first response. Such **one-letter errors** lead to poor comprehension.

♦ To correct these problems, **remind students to read each letter from *left to right.***

♦ **Patience is the key. Old habits are not overcome overnight. Put yourself in your students' shoes. Respect and understanding are essential keys to good teaching.**

How is phonics to be taught by a teacher with an accent or a dialect of English pronunciation?

♦   If a teacher has accepted the challenge and responsibility to teach Standard English to student learners, the teacher should make *every effort* to model excellent English pronunciation and grammar.

♦   Generally, one's accent or dialect is not a problem in daily conversation. However, problems arise when teaching. For example, one teacher was dictating spelling words *hat*, *tap*, *map*, and *cat*. However, with the pronunciation of her primary language reflected in her English, she dictated *hot*, *top*, *mop*, and *cot*. This can cause great confusion, not only for English language learners, but for native English speakers as well.

♦   A teacher responsible for teaching students to read and speak in Standard English and write using Standard English grammar needs to master his or her own Standard English skills. An example of a problem that may result follows in this true anecdote: One new English speaker, a teacher, asked a colleague about the best time to have her students write in their *journals*. However, because of the influence of the teacher's native language, the colleague thought the teacher asked, "When is the best time to have my students write in their *urinals*?" If necessary, the teacher should use audio aids to improve his or her own Standard English pronunciation.

♦   Students should also be encouraged to use audio and other reinforcing aids in Standard English pronunciation. The *Phonics Steps to Reading Success* program and other reading or language programs have word-for-word audio assistance to reinforce Standard English pronunciation.

What quick "tricks" can I use to help me teach my students?

Cardinal Rule: Always encourage the student to sound out independently. Conversely, never contribute to a student becoming a *handicapped* reader, always needing reading aids or *crutches*.

Here is what <u>not</u> to do:

a.   Do not allow guessing a word from the picture.

b.   Do not allow guessing a word from its context.

c.   Do not allow guessing a word from memorized or previously read text.

d.   **Do not give non-phonics hints.** Never take an easy way out to help a student by saying, "Look at the picture," or "It rhymes with …," or "It sounds like…," or "It is a word that means the same as…."

e.   Do not make your students memorize more sight or stock words than is necessary. Truly phonetic words, such as *can, ran, it*, and *eat* do not need to be memorized by sight. These are frequently used words, but they are easily read phonetically.

Here is what to do:

a.   Remind the student to read from **left to right.**

b.   If a student is misreading words, have the student place a pencil or a finger at the *beginning of each word* and **glide the pencil or the finger from left to right**, to keep the eye focused. *Do not* place the pencil or finger over or under the middle of the word, as this might cause the student to revert to trying to read the *whole word,* but not left to right phonemically.

c. If the word can be sounded out using the rules of phonics, assist the student to think of **phonics rules** that apply. For example, ask, "Is that a vowel team? What is the vowel team rule?"

d. If the word has an irregular pronunciation or local regional dialects influence it:

(1) Assist the student to think of **phonics rules** that do apply. For example, *word* does not have to be memorized as a sight word. A student can read it by following the "or rule" and say *w<u>or</u>d*. (In my experience, if the English-speaking students read, "*w<u>or</u>d*," they will self-monitor and say, "*w<u>ur</u>d*." English learners initially must rely more on dual-language dictionaries.) Words spoken with a "schwa e" similar to /uh/ as noted in dictionaries may have evolved because of lax enunciation. For example, *salary* is often pronounced *sal/uh/ry or /sal/ree.* Yet the new reader can apply rules to read *sal/ar/y* fluently and continue without hesitating. Applying **phonics rules** to new words accurately aids fluency, confidence, and comprehension.

(2) If the word has an irregular spelling or pronunciation pattern as in the word ***might,*** you can say, "This word has a troublemaking team *i-g-h-t.* What does the team say? Which letters are silent?"

(3) If you haven't yet taught a rule that applies to a troublesome word, or if it is a word that has a major exception, such as ***Chicago*** or *thorough*, read the word to the student.

(4) If the student comes across one of the very few irregular, but frequently occurring words that must be learned by sight, such as *was* or *they*, the word may be memorized as a sight word.

Should I teach phonics apart from other subjects?

In one word -- NO!

Although phonics must be taught systematically and explicitly, the mastering of phonics concepts is but one part of reading skills acquisition. Reading, writing, and spelling are the academic triune essentials of all learning, not three separate and distinctly isolated subjects. These skills form the foundation of literacy and acquisition of knowledge. If your students have not developed these foundational skills in their early years, you must help them do it.

When teaching the principles of phonics, use decodable text so the student can read and apply what he or she has learned. Decodable text is text that is matched to the corresponding knowledge of the learner. Older learners, however, often do not have the luxury of mastering reading skills while working with only decodable text and nothing else. Usually, they are required be in other classes and to read vocabulary-rich textbooks such as history and science. Older individuals, who are new phonics readers, can readily apply phonics strategies after the first sessions. Moreover, for any skilled readers, virtually any text in English is decodable; however, there may be some words whose regional variation may be unknown or unfamiliar to the student. Therefore, all teachers must include help in decoding words as needed.

Phonics instruction is but one of the essential elements of scientifically-based reading instruction. To stress *again*, the elements are:

- **Phonemic awareness:**   The ability to hear, identify, and manipulate phonemes in spoken words.

- **Phonics:** An understanding that a relationship exists between the written letters of language and the sounds of spoken language.

- **Fluency:** The capacity to read text accurately and fluidly.

- **Vocabulary:** The knowledge of words and their meanings that students must have to communicate effectively.

- **Comprehension:** The ability to understand and gain meaning from what has been read.

Phonics skills are essential to reading and spelling. Accuracy in reading skills diminished when phonics instruction was abandoned. The teaching of phonemic English as a hieroglyphic language, to be memorized word-by-word, negatively affects both writing and spelling.

With intensive, systematic, direct and explicit phonics instruction, the student learns to read and spell correctly at the same time. The student writes the phonemic sounds as they are heard in left-to-right order. With such training, the student can easily use the written word to convey his or her thoughts.

Helping The New Phonics Student Overcome Bad Habits

Students taught by a sight-word approach are at several disadvantages and may carry these ineffective habits into all other classes. Although students may have been taught to use phonics decoding strategies, their teachers may have to work with them to overcome the following limiting habits:

1. They are limited to expressing themselves only in the words that they have memorized.

2. They revert to their foggy concepts of why and how new words should be spelled, so they avoid using new words or incorrectly spell them.

3. Because of past experiences, they might experience embarrassment or intimidation at having to read or spell polysyllabic words.

4. They might find excuses to avoid writing or resort to copying the work of others.

Reading, writing, and spelling are interrelated. The student who cannot read with comprehension cannot hope to find written expression easy. Moreover, the student, who can read well, has skills to be able to write, speak, and think well. Such students become independent thinkers, not dependent on others to read, write, or think for them.

In summary, when teaching **reading** through phonics, it is imperative to reinforce each concept with spelling practice. In addition, students are encouraged to pay attention to the **spelling** of words as they read, particularly noticing any parts that may cause trouble, as in the case of words like *night* and *beautiful*. Armed with that added awareness as well as a dictionary and thesaurus at hand, students should also be encouraged to expand their **writing** horizons. Over time, successes will overcome their fears.

Question 10

If I have never had phonics training, how can I teach what I don't know?

As an educator, you must be a lifelong learner. If you have not had training in phonics skills, be assured that programs exist for older learners. For example, Rio Salado College in Tempe, Arizona, offers an online endorsement course, *EDU 270 AB*, that teaches secondary decoding and reading strategies. It also uses *Phonics Steps to Reading Success* that has been designed to teach decoding skills to older learners. If you are a teacher, you could learn as you tutor a student. *Phonics Steps to Reading Success,* the program with which, obviously, I am most familiar, needs little or no preparation. It has an unabridged audio for personal and classroom use. Various formats are available such as overheads, print, and PowerPoint.

It is important that you, as an educator, also become a scholar, searching out the most knowledge and best tools, not only for you but for your students as well. Seek knowledge and be inquisitive. Find answers that are valid and sensible. If you don't get the answers you need, keep searching.

Why have most teachers not been trained to teach phonics?

Here is a simple answer. Most teachers and teachers of teachers were not taught to use phonics as children. They learned to read using various forms of *sight-word* or *natural* methods. The *natural methods* have been around for over 150 years.

A more complex answer can be found in Sykes' *Dumbing Down Our Kids*, published in 1995:

> In the late nineteenth century, a proto-educationist named James Cattell journeyed to Leipzig to study the psychology of learning. Cattell was later to found Columbia University's department of psychology and to train some of the most influential American educationists of the century. Most importantly, he provided a scientific gloss to the abandonment of traditional methods of teaching reading. Through a series of experiments, Cattell found that adults who knew how to read can recognize words without sounding out letters. From that, he drew the conclusion that words aren't sounded out, but are seen as "total word pictures." If competent readers did not need to sound out words, he declared, then there was little point in teaching such skills to children. 'The result,' wrote Lance J. Klass in the Leipzig Connection, 'was the dropping of the phonic or alphabetic method of teaching reading, and its replacement by the sight-reading method in use throughout America.'

As many of his successors would do, Cattell confused the 'attributes' of readers (or in later edspeak, 'the expected behaviors' or 'outcomes') with the appropriate way of acquiring those attributes. Of course, skilled readers did not stop to sound out words; long practice had made that unnecessary. It was thus an 'outcome' of learning to read: the mechanics of reading, including the ability to sound out words, enabled the reader to achieve that outcome. But since the actual process of sounding out words is not the desired 'outcome,' educationists decided that they could dispense with it.[i]

Reginald Damerell is also critical of those in the colleges of education who opposed teaching phonics. He writes the following in his 1985 book *Education's Smoking Gun: How Teachers' Colleges Have Destroyed Education in America*:

Most affected are the teachers in the nation's 100,000 public elementary schools. They were the education majors. Not all of their education professors shared the views of the attackers of [phonics] literacy.... But those professors [who supported phonics] kept silent. By keeping silent, they contributed to the diminished importance of the 3Rs.[ii]

On a final note, educators must be knowledgeable scholars who participate in dialogue about this issue, remaining neither ignorant nor silent. If you are a teacher, parent, or a concerned citizen, you must know how to answer, or where to look for answers, when anyone poses questions. *The Secret Club* should be just the beginning.

TEACH OTHERS HOW TO READ AND THEIR FUTURES WILL HAVE NO LIMITS!

References

[i] Sykes, C. J. (1995). *Dumbing down our kids: Why American children feel good about themselves but can't read, write or add.* New York: St. Martin's Griffin, 107-108.

[ii] Damerell, R. (1985). Education's smoking gun: How teachers' colleges have destroyed education in America. *New York: Freundlich Books,* 77.

CHAPTER THIRTEEN

REAL LIFE STORIES

"Some people struggle and work hard to climb their mountains. When they reach the top, they are wise from experience and are able to pull others up." Pat Doran, *My Steps Journal*

FOCUS POINT: Most of the stories you are about to read are those of real life people who learned how to get into the "club." There are also stories of people who shared with students the "keys to the club," namely, phonics strategies and other essential reading skills. The stories focus on how individuals benefited when there seemed to be no hope. This chapter is included to demonstrate how widespread reading deficiencies are and to illustrate that reading issues not only affect so-called "at-risk" youth, they also affect individuals of all ages. Some of the names and identifying circumstances have been changed to protect the identity of individuals.

STORY 1: CHARLES

It was my first day of teaching in the classroom after being taught by phenomenally skilled professors in college. I assumed that I was well prepared. That is, until Charles, a fifth grader, taught me a very important lesson about erroneous assumptions.

As I faced my students for the first time, I was nervous, even though I had been practice-teaching in classrooms under the guidance of talented master teachers. Moreover, students in my teacher preparation program were required to take a solid core curriculum that included various rigorous courses such as mathematics, history, and science. The work was exacting and challenging.

We were required to take a solid block of courses dealing with pedagogy, such as methods to teach science, social studies, and reading. They wanted us to be ready for *anything*. In addition to the subject-area teaching-methods classes, the students in the teacher preparation program were required to learn how to write lesson plans, to create tests, to encourage excellence in student achievement, and to follow, but also go beyond, the limitations of the curriculum guides. We felt fortunate that our instructors were knowledgeable, demanding, and dedicated.

COMMENT: As part of the course requirements for the teaching of intermediate reading-level literature, we were required to read from an assigned list of books. We were to create "file card" book reports written for one hundred books of children's literature. The file cards could then be made available to our students as suggested or recommended books.

Since my course curricula focused on instruction in the intermediate grades, the assigned books were the genre of text-rich books mostly written in the 1950s and 1960s. One of the books is the wonderful *Young Fu of the Upper Yangtze*, an award-winning story of a young boy who lived in China during the perilous 1920s. It is a marvelous introduction to Chinese culture.

Our instructors encouraged us to gain more background knowledge about what we read, to become scholars. For example, finding out more about China and its history would allow us to provide our students with other interesting information in order to motivate them in their own quest for knowledge.

With the strong background that my college of education experience provided, the students and I were going to make a great learning team. I didn't want *to waste a learning minute*.

COMMENT: Through the years, this phrase, "Don't waste a learning minute" became a valuable slogan. It was particularly helpful when a student might be tempted to misbehave or lose focus. When that occurred, I would say, "Could you do that some other time; we don't want to waste a learning minute." Surprisingly, it usually worked, particularly because the students in the class knew that there was much learning going on. This could never have worked if I had been filling their days with busy work. Students know when they are being taught and when they are learning.

As often happens, and as every teacher knows all too well, problems are inevitable. I was finally at the chalkboard, enthusiastically following the teacher directives of the math curriculum textbook and my expanded lesson preparations.

The first chapter served as a review of fourth-grade work. I began to take students through each step, using practical, effective, and creative teaching materials. The pre-computer era visuals and chalkboard demonstrations caught the attention of the students. Any of my college instructors would have given an A+ for the lesson plan design and execution. However, what was going on in my classroom wasn't college theory or practice. I was ready, but apparently the class wasn't. Charles made that perfectly clear when he raised his hand.

"Yes," I asked, calling on him.

"I don't know what the heck you are talking about!"

The students giggled at Charles, thinking that he was trying to be disruptive, a smart aleck.

"What do you mean?" I asked calmly, although I was a bit taken aback.

"What's all that stuff you're talking about?"

After the giggles ended, I asked if anyone else was confused. To my dismay, *every hand* went up. Neither Charles nor the class could understand *anything* about the lesson.

Although my teacher preparation program was excellent, I had never been taught what to do when students, without necessary foundational knowledge, were assigned to my classroom. Therefore, I had erroneously assumed that teachers could start on page one of the textbook on day one and finish the book before the end of the school year. Obviously, I learned the hard way. What I was trying to do was not unlike a builder trying to put a roof on a building before the walls were up. It was a serious dilemma. My students and I had to work hard and fast, but I made sure that they were caught up with their fourth-grade work before they attempted to do the fifth grade work.

Clearly, it is quite possible that the fourth grade teacher faced a similar dilemma when she discovered that she was expected to teach students functioning one or more years behind their assigned grade level. There is a negative cumulative effect caused when inadequately prepared students are passed on from one grade to the next. Not only does it affect the ability of students to learn what is expected of them at any grade level, but it also affects the productiveness of subsequent teachers.

Moreover, I learned early on that educators should not assume that students have background knowledge to move forward. Teachers must make sure that the walls are in place before they attempt to put on the roof. My gratitude goes to Charles. His gifts of youthful naiveté and courageous honesty were able to teach me a valuable lesson. Although I know that I failed many times over the years, the lesson that I learned from Charles caused me to establish important goals. Because of that experience, I realized that in addition to presenting well-prepared subject matter, I needed to determine what was lacking in my students' knowledge and respond to their needs.

◆ ◆ ◆

STORY 2: GOVERNMENT EMPLOYEE

My husband and I were sitting in the airport, waiting to board a plane to visit our son, Peter, who lived in Washington D.C. I am a chatty person and strike up conversations easily. A middle-aged woman sat down next to me. We began visiting, exchanging small talk. As we spoke, she told me that she was a government employee. Her job was to travel across the country making presentations to various organizations regarding compliance with federal regulations.

She asked me what I did for a living. Of course, I spoke about my phonics program and about the numbers of adult illiterates or functional illiterates in our country. I also shared a few stories with her. She listened intently and asked some questions. At one point during our conversation, Chris, my husband, excused himself to get coffee for us. As soon as he left, she leaned toward me, put her hand on my arm and almost secretly asked, "Can you help adults?"

"Yes, of course."

She said, "Could you help me? I can't read well. It takes me three or four hours, sometimes more, each night to just get through material that I have to read for my work. I am so afraid of being found out. I think I have a learning disability. No one knows that I can't read well."

We talked and, of course, I asked her if she had been taught to use phonics. She told me that she didn't know how she was taught to read, but that she had to guess a lot to figure out what was written. She was terrified of making mistakes if she guessed wrong. I told her that phonics instruction might help her considerably if that was missing in her education.

I gave her my business card, and she said that she would call me. I never heard from her.

Because of what I do and my obvious concerns about adult illiteracy, adults like this hard-working woman find it easy to talk with me and tell me their stories. However, the embarrassment they experience often keeps them from actually getting help. Hopefully, after our conversation, she had an understanding that phonics may help her and, perhaps, she found help somewhere. It is my sincere desire for her that she was able to find someone who could help her.

Often when I travel, I find myself in conversations similar to the one I had with this woman. Individuals quietly share with me their frustration at not being able to read or tell me stories about their sons and daughters, parents, or friends. Over the years and across the many miles of my travels, I have met or heard about many individuals with reading difficulties. All had gone through many years of schooling. Most of the adults had high school diplomas; some were college graduates. Moreover, I have not met a single person who told me that he or she had significant problems with reading, spelling, and comprehension after being taught to read using explicit phonics strategies. Phonics-trained individuals are proud of their reading and spelling skills. Moreover, phonics-trained individuals commonly have a love of reading; non-phonics individuals commonly do not.

Common sense should tell us that if people who have had phonics instruction are generally successful readers and good spellers, then phonics might be the missing piece in the education of those individuals who are *not* successful readers and good spellers.

Furthermore, it makes even more sense to make sure that every teacher, every administrator, every parent, every business leader, and every concerned citizen demand that students be taught explicit phonics strategies. Age is not an excluder. If individuals have not been taught to read using explicit phonics strategies in primary or early grades, then they must be taught at some point, whether it is in upper grades or even college. It is not too poetic to say that you, as teacher, parent, or business leader may be their only hope. It *is* possible to prevent the fear and embarrassment that was present in the life of the woman in this story. At the forefront of the search for knowledge, educators must take responsibility for making sure that all students know how to read using explicit phonics. There isn't any other scientifically proven viable option.

◆ ◆ ◆

One day in late spring, my husband, Chris, and I combined a holiday and a visit to a town where I had been invited to meet with two junior high students, Jack and Carla. These twins were soon to enter high school. Their parents were concerned about the twins' low reading abilities as well as their increasingly negative attitude about school. The mother had purchased the *Phonics Steps to Reading Success* program on the advice of a school counselor who had heard me speak at a conference. Both parents wanted me to meet with their children.

The teenagers were far below in their reading levels. I had previously sent a set of uncomplicated and straightforward reading tests, namely, the AGS *Reading-Level Indicator: A Quick Group Reading Placement Test*, for them to take. Their father administered the tests and returned them to me so that we could get a general idea of the independent and instructional reading levels of both teenagers before our first meeting.

The levels at which students read, as well as the discrepancy between their independent and instructional reading levels, are significant bits of information for both parents and teachers to know. The **independent reading level** is that level at which a learner can read with little or no frustration and with a high level of accuracy and comprehension. It is the level at which the reader comfortably and accurately can read the material required for taking tests, doing homework, and enjoying independent recreational reading at appropriate grade levels. The **instructional reading level** is the level at which the material is more challenging, but is below the reader's frustration level if it is accompanied with normal classroom instruction and support.

The test results showed that eighth-grade Carla's instructional reading level was 9.5 and her independent reading level was 5.0. Therefore, although Carla has the ability to do ninth-grade-level work in the classroom during instruction time, she can only test and read independently if the work is on a fifth grade level. In other words, Carla's educational experience is the same as it would be if a fifth grader, reading on fifth-grade level, were required to do eighth grade work. Carla's father told me that her teachers say that Carla has trouble with *comprehension*. However, once he saw the test results, he was able to understand the problems caused by the discrepancy between her independent reading ability and the level of the materials she was assigned to read in school. In contrast, Jack's results indicated that he was reading at a much lower level. His scores showed that his instructional level was a 3.9 and his independent R.L was 2.9. It was obvious why he was placed in special education classes. However, Jack is not alone in the school. According to the parents, approximately one-fourth of the high school students in the school are in special education classes and one-half of all junior high students would be in special education classes in the following school year. Unless there are some significant environmental problems, there should be no reason why so many students in one area have actual learning disabilities.

Everything I have learned from adult individuals whom I have tutored has taught me that the stigma and humiliation of being in special education classes, especially in high school, is sometimes overwhelming. It was not surprising that Jack's attitude was not always respectful at school because, apparently, he doesn't respect educators or like being in school. Carla was also displaying a negative attitude and lack of commitment to education. The school administrators were considering suspension for Jack and, possibly, his sister, Carla.

When I arrived, I met with the teenagers and their father, as their mother had been called away. I went into their living room where we talked for a while. I explained to these teenagers what I did and why.

Upon entering the living room, I took my place on the sofa while the teens sat across the large living room on the ledge in front of the fireplace. Both were leaning over, hands clasped, elbows on their knees, respectful, but disengaged. The physical distance between us reflected the emotional disconnect they experienced with their teachers at school.

As I spoke with them and their father, they were very polite, but not talkative. "Can you read?" I asked them both.

"Yes." Their answers were the same.

"Do you like to read?"

"No."

"Are you good spellers?"

"No."

"Do you remember how you were taught to read?"

"No."

"Did you have phonics?"

"No, I don't think so… I don't know… Maybe… I don't know."

Finally, picking up the *Phonics Steps* program, I stood up, walked across the room to them and sat in the space between them on the fireplace bench. I opened to one of the introductory lessons in the *Phonics Steps* program and pointed to a silly, long word, *mapontazet.* I asked them each to read the word. I wanted to find out how they handled reading unfamiliar, multi-syllable words.

It was sad. I felt badly for both of these young people. Carla, the better reader, read halfway across the word, saying, "map•on•t...." Then she garbled something that sounded like *zanzet.* Jack, struggling, only pronounced some of the sounds randomly, *ma... t...on...z...*, but gave up, frustrated and embarrassed.

I told them not to worry. I could show them something that would explain why both of them were having difficulties.

First, I showed them the vowel chart with the short vowels and picture clues, *apple* /a/, *eggs* /e/, *umbrella* /u/, and so on. I explained that generally, when a vowel is alone between two consonants the vowel says its short sound, /a/, /e/, etc. Then, they were asked to read across the word, left to right and to change the shape of their mouths to pronounce the sounds that each letter *makes.*

Carla pronounced another word, *binrumsod,* with no problem. She was impressed with herself. Her smile spoke loudly of her pride and of a re-awakening of her self-esteem.

At that point, my husband returned to pick me up. Without interrupting us, he sat down on the couch and observed silently.

Jack read another silly word, *wanitudimsan.* He read it correctly as well, with the exception of a pause at the *u.* As I looked at him, I could see that he was thinking, then, he pronounced the *u* as in *umbrella* and continued to read the word correctly. After he read this word, I asked him, "What were you thinking when you paused?"

He told me that he was remembering the picture of the umbrella to remember what sound the letter *u* made.

I asked him, "Has anyone ever taught you how to do that?"

He said, "No."

I asked the two if any of their teachers had told them to guess, to skip words, or to read the first few letters and try to finish with a word that "made sense."

Both answered, "Yes."

Then, I proceeded to tell them that method is *not* the way to read, and their teachers, although probably very sincere, were wrong because guessing, skipping, and other similar strategies usually result in mistakes, frustration, and failure. I briefly explained to them some of the things you've learned in this book.

I further explained that most likely their teachers were taught to teach these strategies. I told them that some college textbooks used for teacher training give these same directions. I had one of these college books with me and showed the teens and their father where the book's author points out that "reading is just a guessing game."

Carla looked at her dad, started smiling, and said something under her breath. Carla wouldn't repeat what she said, but her dad had tears in his eyes. He later said, "Carla smiled because she and Jack have been telling me all along that the teachers weren't teaching them to read right."

Then, I asked Jack to read other things to me. He had no problems, even with multi-syllable words with short vowels. His confidence seemed to be increasing.

After that, I gave the two a spelling quiz using two, made-up words, *datponilzet* and *lamifudimsan*, from another page in the program. I told them to re-pronounce the words slowly as they wrote and to write the *sounds* that they heard *as* they heard them. Both spelled the words 100% correctly! These decodable words also were easily encodable because they contained only consonant sounds plus the short vowels that they had just learned. Nevertheless, they were long, multi-syllabic words and the twins had never seen the words, much less studied how to spell them. Both teens remarked that they were never taught that way to spell. They explained they had been taught to try to memorize words or to "get close" to correct spelling. When they did have spelling tests, they never got good grades.

I told Jack, "There's nothing wrong with your mind. If you had an actual disability that kept you from learning and reading well, you couldn't have taken in this information so quickly. My suggestion is that you remove that label of 'learning disabled' off of you and stick it on something else."

What happened next was incredible to behold. Jack looked at me, and his face flushed. He smiled and sat up straight as though someone had lifted a hundred-pound weight off his shoulders. Both my husband and their father had tears in their eyes as they watched in silence.

We all talked a bit more and developed an action plan for these two for the summer. Chris and I said our good-byes and left. The father was grateful, thanking us.

When we were driving away from the house, I asked Chris to comment on what he observed. He said, "When you told Jack to take the learning-disabled label off and put it on something else, the transformation was amazing. The change was undeniably visible."

I have seen this phenomenon occur numerous times. Watching Jack was like watching a boy being healed from a crippling, debilitating affliction. I believe that is what happened. Jack's spirit was healed from the debilitating sense of believing that he was "learning disabled." He discarded the stigma of inferiority that zapped his sense of confidence.

The twins continued using the program. Later, I learned that the special education teacher agreed to work with Jack. There is one final note to be made about placing students into special education classes. The serious, long-term damage that is done when students are put into special education classes *erroneously* is beyond our imagination, particularly if the cause of the student's problems is due to ineffective instruction and is not effectively corrected. I asked one of my adult students, a former illiterate, to tell me his opinion of his experiences in special education classes.

He said, "Being in special education classes was humiliating. It hurt. But, if those teachers had actually taught me something, I could have put up with it."

He complained that he watched Sesame Street shows during his special education classes for third, fourth, and fifth grades while the teacher did paperwork. Throughout his years in school, he watched videos, did *word searches,* and was given other handouts that he couldn't read. Teachers even gave him oral tests so he could pass the classes. Yet, he never learned to read until he was almost forty years of age when he learned to use phonics strategies.

After they learn to read, some of the adults I've tutored felt comfortable telling me they had thoughts of committing suicide or prayed to die when they were younger. For them, the thought of returning to school each day was too painful. When I asked these adults if they ever told anyone of their feelings, they responded in various ways but with the same message, "Would you?"

One young man said he would arrive at school early and wait until the door to his special education class was open. He would go into the room as soon as he could. He said, "I'd hide out all day in my classroom so that no one would know I was in special education classes. I only dated girls at other schools because they couldn't find out I was in special education classes. It really messed up my social life."

◆ ◆ ◆

STORY 4: THE TEACHER WHO COULDN'T READ

John Corcoran (his real name) is a friend of mine. He has inspired me more than he will ever know.

John graduated from high school and college, eventually becoming a high school teacher. However, he never learned how to read until he was close to fifty years of age. His incredible story is written in his book, *The Teacher Who Couldn't Read*. It is about how he, a bright and talented young boy, "slipped through the system and was welcomed into it as a teacher."

John wrote, "You receive your high school diploma, but you can't read a word of it. To survive in a world of literates, you become an expert at deception, relying on clever schemes to make up for your disability. You go to college. And when you graduate, you move from the dummy row in the back of the class to the head of the class...you become a teacher" (Corcoran, 1994).

When I first met John and he shared his story, his humility and honesty struck me. By the time I met him, his story was well known. Despite his fame and success, he was not proud of his "dark side" when he had to lie to compensate for his illiteracy. Eventually, John learned to read using phonics. His story challenges and inspires anyone who reads it.

◆ ◆ ◆

STORY 5: FREEDOM TO READ

I don't have a frivolous passion for phonics as a pet teaching theory or reading methodology. Instead, I have a passion for what works, and for helping learners become successful, independent, lifelong readers. My colleague and I began *The Freedom Reading Foundation*, a non-profit organization to help combat illiteracy, particularly by providing services to teach older individuals scientifically proven, essential reading skills. The name of this program reflects our philosophy--when one can read, one has the freedom to pursue one's destiny of success.

Recently, a *National Geographic* issue focused on contemporary worldwide slavery. There was one poignant story about a former female slave. In this story, the woman said that on a daily basis the adult son of her owner would take her into a small building behind the house. His family believed that he was having his way with her (sexually), an acceptable practice among slave owners. In truth, however, he was teaching her to read. If either of them had been caught, the punishment would have been severe beatings or possibly death. Eventually, this woman escaped captivity, but it was her ability to read that gave her real freedom.

Similarly, one of my students, who once had been functionally illiterate, told me that he used to feel as though his mind was behind bars, with no hope of ever getting out. He told me, "Nobody ever understood. It was always like being in jail."

The ability to read brings freedom in other ways. I received a phone call from a young woman, Judy, who was using the *Phonics Steps to Reading Success* decoding skills program in a small, inner city charter school. One boy had transferred to the school. He had been kept back three times in the seventh grade because his behavior and academic skills were so inferior. Judy was working as a consultant to the school but was not a certified teacher. Nevertheless, she had some knowledge of the *Phonics Steps* program and an abundant, innate desire to help young people. With Judy's help, the boy learned to read and his behavior improved. Moreover, on his own, he was able to use the *Phonics Steps* program to help other students develop their word attack skills.

This student was asked to make a presentation to the school board about his reading progress. At the school board meeting, the man who introduced the boy explained that he learned to read using *The Phonics Game*. The boy proudly corrected the presenter, "I used *Phonics Steps to Reading Success*."

Although the boy felt he needed to make the correction, the error of the presenter is an insignificant mistake. All programs that teach systematic, explicit, phonics skills such as *The Phonics Game, Action Reading, Hooked on Phonics, Phonics Steps to Reading Success,* and the like are effective. It may be that various programs have different targeted audiences. For example, some programs may be developed for emerging readers as a complete reading program for young children or for English learners. Others, such as *Phonics Steps*, are remedial, word-attack skills programs for older students to be used alone or as supplements to other complete phonics reading programs. Nevertheless, it doesn't matter how it is done or who gets the credit, as long as individuals learn the essential skills, systematically and explicitly, enabling them to be successful, independent readers. Ultimately, it is the freedom that effective reading skills give to the individual that is the goal of reading.

♦ ♦ ♦

STORY 6: ROBERT AND EDWIN

An inner-city principal hired our company, Edu-Steps, Inc., to teach decoding skills to selected English learners and at-risk students during the time that most of the school's students were on a mid-year school break. The students that we were to teach scored far below grade level in their academic work. The sessions were held Monday through Thursday mornings from 8-11:30 with 180 minutes of instruction time each day. I was to teach the sixth through eighth graders. My colleague taught the third through fifth graders.

When I walked into the junior high classroom, the teacher picked up some books and papers and began to walk out of the room. He noticed two boys that were sitting next to each other. He stopped and sternly said to them, "Don't you try to pull that on this nice lady! You know you two are not allowed to sit next to each other. Now, move."

One boy got up to move to the other side of the room. The teacher then turned to me and said somewhat under his breath, but loudly enough for the nearby students to hear, "Be careful of those two. They are nothing but trouble. The one who changed seats is a 'SPED.' Good luck with *him*!"

> **COMMENT:** This teacher meant to tell me that the one who changed seats is a *special education* (SPED) student. It is my opinion that terms like these are particularly demeaning to individuals who are already struggling with interior humiliation and sense of failure.

When the teacher left the classroom, I told the students, "I honor your teacher's requests. So should you. But, now, your teacher has handed the classroom over to me, and I have a different approach. When I teach, I allow my students to sit anywhere they choose. If, however, they do not follow my rules or if they become distracting to others, they lose the freedom to choose where they sit, and *I* will make the choice. There are no second chances."

I continued, "Now, you may move to sit where you choose. Just make sure you can see the screen in the front of the room clearly." In an instant, these two young men were sitting next to each other.

After taking attendance and making a few preliminary comments, I administered one form of the AGS test (referenced in Story 3 about Jack and Carla) as a pretest. This test takes approximately fifteen minutes to administer and, although not extensive and detailed, gives two valuable bits of information. By testing sentence comprehension and vocabulary, the test results report a student's instructional reading level and independent reading level. The reading level score is reported in terms of school years and months. As already mentioned, the *instructional* reading level is that level at which the students can read in a classroom with teacher's instruction and guidance. The *independent* reading level is that level at which students can read to do homework, take tests or read when no one is around to help.

The results of this quick quiz indicated that these two, tall, seventh-grade teenagers with problematic behaviors also had significant reading deficiencies. Robert, who appeared to be the more emotionally mature and more socially confident of the two, had a 6.8 instructional reading level but only a 4.5 independent reading level. Edwin had a 2.0 instructional reading level, but struggled even more because of his 1.0 independent reading level. Both boys were frustrated and neither liked being in school.

Robert was able to understand seventh-grade material. Nevertheless, when he took tests that were written for seventh graders, he was already behind because he was limited by his 4.5 *independent* reading level. Although he may have known many or all of the answers if asked orally, the grades he received on independent tests or homework labeled him a failure. (Refer to the story of Jano in Chapter One.) To distract his peers from his failure as a student, Robert used his outgoing personality and innate leadership qualities to try to compete with his teachers for his classmates' attention. In other words, he misbehaved.

Edwin, on the other hand, lived with the constant reminder that he was not smart and would never be smart. He was a special education student. He knew that everyone in the class knew that he was a "SPED." He, too, caused problems. For one thing, he could not do the work in class so he found other things to do, like joking with Robert who was a willing accomplice.

Understanding the problems caused by these reading deficiencies, I introduced the students to the *Phonics Steps to Reading Success* program and told them that their reading would improve by the end of the session if they paid attention. I told them that they would be challenged, held to high standards and asked them if they were ready to work hard. Reflecting my confidence and enthusiasm, they responded enthusiastically.

The instruction moved along quickly. Robert was very confident and cooperative. Edwin initially wanted to avoid his turns at reading, as was his habit, but he was required to take turns and was pleased when he realized that he could pronounce the words on the lists.

At first, when he answered, he was uncharacteristically soft spoken. I assured him and the rest of the class that we were all there to support each other. This classroom was a place to learn. I told them, "No one has to be 100% perfect 100% of the time." Consequently, no one was allowed to laugh at anyone's mistakes. If, out of habit or rudeness, any student did laugh, that student would be expected to respectively say, "Excuse me." In this positive environment, no negative discipline issues arose during the entire session. We were all able to move forward.

During these lessons, students read in unison or took turns by reading "round robin." They took 3-, 5-, or 8-word spelling quizzes at the end of each page introducing a new decoding strategy. Most students voluntarily shared their spelling errors so that the entire class could benefit by learning from each other's mistakes. They learned about affirming each other's attempts or successes with a one-clap compliment.

At the time, a district representative stopped by to observe the class. She was keenly aware of the problems in many inner-city junior high classes and commented on how impressed she was watching students volunteering their mistakes and witnessed them affirm and support each other. Such an environment of cooperation and learning made for an enjoyable and successful experience for all concerned.

> **COMMENT:** The one-clap compliment is a strategy that can be used by either teacher or students to spontaneously congratulate anyone in the class for being successful or for displaying a positive behavior. For example, students are complimented when they spell all words correctly or perhaps have only one error. As another illustration of the strategy, I use the "one clap compliment" to congratulate students who show courage to share their errors so that the class can learn to avoid the same mistakes.
>
> The one-clap compliment is a practical, effective and minimally disruptive way to reinforce positive behaviors, to correct answers, and so forth. The traditional applause approach can be distracting in the day-to-day activities in the classroom when a few students may attempt to gain negative attention by prolonged applause, thus, drawing attention from the deserving student.

Edwin participated in the lessons. Some of the words were very easy for him to read; others took a bit more effort. He applied phonics rules as he read from left to right. He sometimes struggled, but eventually succeeded. I gave him one-clap compliments. Soon, the other students spontaneously recognized his successes in the same way. He beamed with pride.

By the end of Tuesday morning, we had completed about twelve pages of the *Phonics Steps to Reading Success* program. Before the beginning of class on

Wednesday, Edwin handed me a pencil and paper. He said, "Will you write a note to tell my grandma that I am being good for you?"

"Why don't you tell her yourself?" I asked.

"I tried, but she doesn't believe me. I'm never good."

"You're good in my class. Why are you good in here?"

"Because you're teaching me stuff, and I am learning it."

It was true. Moreover, Edwin was not alone. The entire class worked hard and learned a lot. It was amazing to see these junior high students so excited about learning the basic decoding skills that had so recently been unfamiliar to them.

Since they had only eighteen hours to complete a program that most classes complete in thirty hours, the students agreed to work intensely and they did. On the final day, each was given a certificate, and we took a class picture. The students posed proudly with their certificates, knowing that not only had they completed the program, but that they had learned much.

Although we wanted completed pre-and posttests for all students, we were not able to test everyone because of stringent staff and time restrictions. For various reasons, only eleven students were present for both tests. Because of the severe time limitations, the pre- and posttests were used only to give a general idea of the students' improvements. However, the students who took both of these tests demonstrated an *average* improvement of one whole grade-level after only eighteen hours of instruction. This noted increase was based on comparison of their pre- and post-session scores.

Keep in mind that during the sessions, only decoding skills were taught. The attention to vocabulary development was limited to that of providing definitions of some of the words on the lists. For example, when we would complete reading a page in the program, I would ask the students, "Are there any words for which you would like the definition?" I would then provide the definition, and either the students or I would use the word in a sentence to reinforce the meaning. Then, we would move on.

The scores showed an increase on the posttest because of the students' new ability to apply word attack skills to enable them to read words they already knew as part of their aural and oral vocabularies. It allowed them both to decode the test items and to comprehend at a higher reading level.

The following results will at least shine a bit of light as to Robert and Edwin's general improvement after only **eighteen hours of instruction**:

- **Robert's Reading Levels**:
    - Instructional **pre**test score: R.L. 6.8
    - Instructional **post**test score: R.L. 9.5

    - Independent **pre**test score: R.L. 4.5
    - Independent **post**test score: R.L. 5.0
- **Edwin's Reading Levels**:
    - Instructional **pre**test score: R.L. 2.0
    - Instructional **post**test score: R.L. 3.1

    - Independent **pre**test score: R.L. 1.0
    - Independent **post**test score: R.L. 2.4

Phonemic awareness and phonics decoding skills are but two of the five essential elements necessary for successful reading. During the short period, the students did not have time to work on fluency, vocabulary and comprehension. However, one can only imagine how much more these students and their classmates would gain in consecutive years of work that included all of the essential elements. Nevertheless, it is better to provide one part of essential skills in a short amount of time rather than avoid teaching it because there is not enough time to do a complete program.

Ultimately, Edwin was right. I was teaching him "stuff" and he *was* learning it.

◆ ◆ ◆

STORY 7: BILLY

Billy, age 12, was assigned to my classroom when he entered our school mid-year. His mother told me that there were family problems and that she knew her son was "unsettled." She also explained that the teacher at his former school told her that her son had an attention deficit problem and could not be in class if he was not taking Ritalin.

Admittedly, this boy's behavior was a challenge. Nevertheless, he did extremely well in our classroom. We provided for him a structured environment and systematic instruction of information that he could use to replace the ineffective reading strategies that were causing him so much frustration. To be sure, I had to adjust some of my preferred ways of teaching. Instead of moving about the classroom, I had to keep in physical touch with him at all times. In fact, for the first several weeks, I kept at least one finger on him, on his head, shoulders, hand or arm at every moment. As a result, my movement was limited dramatically.

Personally, I did not enjoy this restriction on my teaching style. It was extremely difficult for me to do, but as educators well know, we frequently step outside of our well-established comfort zones in our efforts to help students.

Equally important to my change was the response of the class. The students adapted with no difficulty to my more limited movement. We were a learning team. Instead of my going to them, they came to me. Learning went on without disruption. Subsequently, Billy's behavior and academic achievement improved. He blossomed in our classroom. Gradually, the invisible teacher-student umbilical cord lengthened.

Moreover, Billy's mother was encouraged by his progress. She explained that his behavior at home improved. However, she was sad when several months later family circumstances required that they move back to their home state. To be honest, although I was glad that we helped her son, humanly speaking, I was looking forward to returning to my freedom to move about the classroom. It had not been an easy time. In reality, it had been a challenge for all of us to have him in the class, but we all grew from the experience.

The day Billy's mother withdrew him from school they stopped by our classroom. Billy's mother brought her son to see me one more time because he had told her, "I have to say good-bye to my teacher. She will miss me. I am her *favorite* student."

◆ ◆ ◆

STORY 8: JAMES AND DAVID

As an adjunct instructor, I was assigned to teach a remedial reading class at a local junior college. The class included Latinos, Caucasians, African-Americans, and a Japanese student. James was the oldest student, a personable, tall, thin, 47-year-old,

African-American man with an angular physique. Another student, David, was a disinterested male in his late teens. Also of African-American descent, he wore garb traditionally associated with gang members in the inner city where I had taught for many years.

For the first session, David was disengaged. He slouched in his chair or rested his head on his arms that were folded on his desk. He responded minimally, only when called upon. At first, I couldn't understand why he had signed up for the college class because it was obvious that he didn't like being in school. Later, I learned that he wanted to be a fire fighter, and had been told that he needed to take remedial reading. On the first day, however, David's demeanor was one of an angry young man that had no love of learning. Nevertheless, he was a bright young man, as was obvious by his responses in class, but his reading skills were minimal. After the first class was over, and before we met the following week, I pondered about how to motivate him. At first, nothing came to mind, but then I developed a plan.

Halfway through the second session for the class, it was obvious that David was present, but in body only. He seemed to be internally unsettled. I went over to him. I held out my hand with my palm up and said firmly, calmly, with no anger or threat in my voice said, "Give it to me! Give it to me now!" He looked at me. The class was stunned, silent.

I continued, "Give me that million dollars that I gave you when you walked into the classroom this morning!"

Confused, he simply stared at me. He asked, with his expression but not words, "What million dollars? What are you talking about? You're crazy!"

I proceeded with my questioning asking, "What's the matter? Are you *stupid*? Don't you know what I am talking about? Maybe you are just too *lazy* to get up and get it. Maybe you are just *dumb*; you don't know where you put it! Could it be that you are all three? Maybe you are stupid, lazy, AND dumb."

The tension in the room was thick. Before I had an opportunity to explain what I was doing, James stood up in the back of the room. Out of the corner of my eye, I saw the 6'7" frame of James' thin body rise out of his chair. He pointed at me.

"I know what you are doing," he said.

I responded, "And what *am* I doing?"

He said, "You're trying to tell us that we have been called *stupid, lazy,* and *dumb* all of our lives because we haven't been able to give back what was never given to us in the first place! Ma'am, you just replayed most of my years in school. My teachers called me those names, but they passed me on 'cause they didn't want to hurt my self-esteem. Well, I can't read and it cost me two marriages. What woman is going to stay with a man who can't earn a good living 'cause he can't read? Where is my esteem now?"

"Bingo!" I responded with enthusiasm. "You win! You, James, have been able to figure out what the highly educated teachers and educators of teachers have not been able to figure out! There are millions of individuals walking around this country, thinking that they are learning disabled, *retarded*, not *wired right*, or just not as smart as others are because they can't read well or read at all. Moreover, for most, it is because these people have never been taught what you are learning here."

James added that he had learned more in a few hours in this class than he had in all of his years in school.

I wish there had been one of those hidden cameras in the room recording the students' expressions, hearing the silence, watching that tall, lean body standing up in the back of the room, but most of all, recording the change in David. It was as though a string was attached to the crown of his head, pulling him straight up into an upright position. From that point on, his normally expressionless face often had a smile. He learned quickly, responded more in class. His work was excellent.

David probably would have earned an A for the class. However, for some reason, although he had perfect attendance until the last day, David did not show up to take the final exam. I called his home phone, but there was no answer. I sent several letters to his home address, but never heard from him again. He was a special man who carried a heavy burden. Hopefully, the skills that he learned and the knowledge that he gained about himself will help him in the future.

It is troubling to realize that it wasn't until they went to college that James and David gained the skills and ability to read. They were fortunate and wise in that they continued to pursue knowledge. What about the discouraged or fearful individuals who never made it to college, believing they would fail?

David is an example of a well-known, but sometimes forgotten truth. It may be that educators have only a small window of opportunity available to them to help a student. Therefore, striving for excellence in instruction is the only option available for teachers. Students who sit in any class cannot be dismissed as being *lazy, stupid,* or *dumb*. It is the job of teachers to teach. It is every teacher's responsibility to fill in foundational information gaps with skills and knowledge.

◆ ◆ ◆

STORY 9: CLARA'S STORY

Clara had brought her nine-year-old granddaughter to the college where I was an adjunct instructor. She had contacted various people there to find someone to help the child improve her reading skills. Seventy-two-year-old Clara recognized that her granddaughter had the same problems with reading that had caused her pain most of her long life. She was going to get the child help.

Clara was the youngest in a family of five children. All of her older siblings had been taught to read using phonics. However, when she was a little girl, entering first grade in the mid-1930s, the family moved. Consequently, Clara didn't have the same first-grade instruction that her siblings had. Clara's new first-grade teacher had recently graduated from teachers' college with *new* ways of teaching reading that did not include phonics.

Because Clara was the only one in her family who could not read well, everyone in her family thought that she was a *slow learner*. As a young woman, she married a man who became a minister and, subsequently, a pastor of a church. Then, as the pastor's wife, Clara's life became more complicated. Throughout the years, Clara found herself making excuses to avoid attending many church functions where she may have been asked to read. She lived daily with a sense of inferiority and a fear of her *secret* being found out.

Her granddaughter's tutor at the junior college told her about the importance of phonics instruction and suggested that Clara contact me. She did, but when we first spoke, she cautioned me that she probably couldn't be helped because she had a "problem in her brain that kept her from understanding" what she read. This attractive, sophisticated, and gracious woman believed that she had some kind of learning disability. Early on, she told me that she could "call words," but in reality, she read only familiar words that she had learned or figured out on her own. When she got to words that were unfamiliar, she inserted words or phrases that she thought might make sense.

Soon, she began her tutoring sessions by going through *Phonics Steps to Reading Success.* She completed it in only ten hours over several days. I teased her and told her that she was easy to teach, and that it didn't take long for her to go through the program because I didn't have to work around behavior problems and bathroom breaks! But in reality, Clara completed the program quickly because she was very intelligent.

She worked to overcome her guessing, substitution, misreading, and fear of big words. These old strategies were causing her to misread several words in passages, thus interfering with her knowing what the author had written. In effect, she had attempted to *paraphrase* what the author had written and often she did so incorrectly. As a result, she could not understand what she was reading.

At the end of the ten hours of instruction, I told Clara that she didn't need me any longer. She could practice her newly learned skills on her own. At that point, she understood what was holding her back and had the decoding tools to move forward. Then she said, "But what will I do without you?"

I asked, "What would you have done fifty years ago if you had these decoding skills?"

Clara responded, "Oh, my! I would have gone to college."

"And, is there a problem now?"

We talked further. I said, "You are *never* too old."

The following semester, with trepidation, Clara did enroll in college. This energetic, determined senior citizen took a few classes that didn't interfere with her daily exercise regimen at the gym. She surprised herself when she earned A's in all of her classes. She also earned more respect in her family, and, more importantly, she said that she felt "grateful, elated, and thankful." She added, "I'm not the same person I was when I first met you."

Is it possible to teach older individuals how to read? Ask Clara.

♦ ♦ ♦

STORY 10: JIM JANSSEN, *HONOR ROLL ILLITERATE* (IN HIS OWN WORDS)

Jim Janssen was illiterate until he was thirty-eight years old. When Jim was in the beginning of second grade, a school psychologist told his parents that Jim was "dyslexic." His parents were told that he would not be able to learn to read.

Accommodations were made for him throughout his school years, but he was not taught to read. Despite being illiterate, Jim was on the honor roll four years in a row in high school. He says, "I couldn't even read the words on the certificate. I couldn't even read *honor* or *roll*." He is currently writing his autobiography, *Honor Roll Illiterate*. The following story offers a glimpse into his experiences.

Tammy became my wife after high school but we had known each other since seventh grade. I never told her about my inability to read, my *dyslexia*, until we were in twelfth grade. Until then, I did what I did best. I would get out of the situations when she would ask me something. For example, one day she asked me to write in her yearbook. I told her that I didn't think that it was right because of the fact that her mother spent a lot of money for the yearbook, and people shouldn't be writing all over it.

Tammy would send me letters in school. I never wrote her back. Later in the day, she would ask me, "Did you read my letter?" I would tell her that I did, but had to use my powers as an *illiterate psychic* to read her mind. I would notice words or clues that she dropped in our conversations, and I figured that she was writing about those things.

Also, Tammy never knew what classes I was in. I would hang around with her, and she would say, "Oh, I'm late for my class." Then, she would run off.

I always waited until Tammy and everyone else was in class before I would go to my class. The other kids at school never knew that I was in special ed classes. I was good at hiding my secret from Tammy and everyone; however, I was always getting into trouble with my teachers for being late. When I finally was in class, I would sit in a place in the classroom so that no one would be able to see me from the doorway.

After a certain amount of *tardy reports,* students were given a detention that meant that they would have to stay an extra hour after school was out. To me, it seemed worth it — an hour after school — to keep my friends from finding out. I was staying after school almost every day because I was late for all of my classes. If I didn't run fast enough then I would get a couple of tardy slips in one day. Some of the classes were closer to where I was with Tammy, but sometimes the classes were across the campus. But, my strategy worked. I fooled everyone all through my high school years.

When Tammy finally found out that I couldn't read and when I told her it was because I was dyslexic, she went to the library and did some research. Afterwards, she told me that there was no way I was dyslexic. Tammy knew, but I didn't find out until I was thirty-eight and learned to use phonics.

I also did things to survive with other situations in my life. Sometimes at work, people would have something printed off the Internet and hand it to me. I would have to try to read their facial expressions. If someone handed me something and he had a smile on his face, I would pretend to read the paper and laugh. Sometimes it was hard. Sometimes, because of people's lack of expressions, I couldn't read their body language just like I couldn't read what was on the paper that they were handing me. Then, if I couldn't read the person, I would try to interpret the cartoon. If there were no cartoons or picture clues, I didn't know how long to take to pretend to read something, so, I guess, maybe some people thought I was a speed reader; others might have thought that I was a really, really slow reader.

I look back on my life now and I know that I was lying to everybody when I couldn't read. I feel badly about that. No one should have to lie about this. Kids should be able to learn how to read when they are kids. If the teachers can't teach someone how to read, they need to find someone who can teach them to read. If they can't find someone else to teach the kids how to read, then they should do what it takes to learn how themselves. **It's a tough life being illiterate.**

♦ ♦ ♦

STORY 11: DANNY

Danny's sister raised him from the time he was two-years-old. She heroically took over raising her eight younger siblings when their mother died. Danny never talked about where his father was. He grew up in an inner-city area in the South, and he was identified as a special education student in first grade.

Throughout his school years, he explained that he developed the strategy to match shapes of words on the work he was given. He couldn't read anything, yet he was given written work to do every day. He was also given written tests to take. Teachers always told him he was doing a *good job.*

He was quiet, obedient, and respectful. Although his older sister was overburdened with many responsibilities, she did an excellent job raising him. However, she trusted the school system and each year, Danny fell farther *through the cracks.*

At least, Danny could run and carry a football. As a result, his high school coach helped Danny's sister get him a football scholarship to a school in a state on the other side of the country, far from his home. It was a brave move for Danny. Being illiterate and alone, moving to a far-away state to attend college and play football was a major challenge, but he wanted to succeed. When he got to the college, however, Danny found that he could only practice with the team. He could not play in their games because he could not read well enough to take classes.

Someone at the college contacted me and hired me to teach Danny how to read. When I first met him, at age eighteen, he could only read the words, *an, in, on, the,* and *I like football*. It was at that junior college that he learned to read for the first time in his life. He learned to read well enough to take some basic classes in college.

His literacy skills continued to improve daily. He also continued to exercise, doing demanding physical workouts each day, hoping to be ready for that *big break.*

When his break came, he was in great physical shape. As he was trying out to be a member of a professional football team, he pulled a muscle in the tryouts. It was a time of intense discouragement for this dedicated and fine young man.

As I write this, Danny's leg is on the mend. His training will resume shortly. He is still young and his chances for having a sports career are not over. Moreover, he continues to work at learning academic skills. My husband has become his tutor to help fill in grammar, writing and reading gaps. Danny buys books for himself and has an entry-level job with benefits and a future. He has not given up his dreams or effort to succeed in professional sports and is still pursuing college.

Danny is one of the most special young men I have ever met. He has experienced great personal tragedy. He has overcome poverty and has been able to withstand the attraction of drugs, gangs, and violence that drew in many of his childhood friends and classmates. He is a man of integrity, determination, and gentleness. He is an inspiration to anyone who knows him. My family has a great affection for him and is honored to have him in our lives.

♦ ♦ ♦

STORY 12: BRENDAN

When Brendan was born, he had multiple birth defects, one of which was a hearing impairment. Consequently, Brendan's pronunciation is somewhat affected because he speaks based on how he hears words, just as we all do, but the hearing impairment does not allow him to hear all sounds clearly. For example, he has minor difficulty hearing and clearly pronouncing a few sounds such as /s/ and /x/.

During his early primary schooling, Brendan had been placed in special education classes. Later, a school psychologist gave Brendan a battery of tests. The result? A line on the summary page on the front of this extensive, detailed report stated that Brendan had an extremely low Intelligent Quotient (I.Q.) of 40. This indicated that Brendan was severely mentally challenged and limited. Therefore, based on this report, his curriculum was likewise limited. When Brendan was almost sixteen-years-old, his mother contacted my colleague and me to see if we could help her son.

We began to use the *Phonics Steps to Reading Success* program with him. We were surprised and pleased that he learned quickly. At first, we found that he was trying to "read" us, his teachers, in order to give us the answer that he thought *we* wanted. He was like Jim Janssen, using his *illiterate psychic* survival strategies. Nevertheless, we continued to encourage him to trust himself.

Within less than one year of our working with him for only one hour a week, he was successfully doing fifth-grade reading workbooks independently.

He was frustrated and bored at school. On the other hand, his mother said that she also experienced frustration and a sense of intimidation at staffing meetings with teachers and psychologists because they wouldn't listen to her. She said that they dismissed her opinions and she always walked out of the meetings feeling humiliated and beaten down. His mother complained, "His teachers tell me that he isn't capable of doing what I see with my own eyes that he can do."

With his academic achievement so low, Brendan's teachers explained that they had to prepare him to be able to get a job. As a result, he was placed in a vocational education program. For example, for one of these classes, Brendan's daily assignment during his 40-minute vocational education class was to sharpen pencils to be used throughout the school. He complained, "How many pencils do I have to sharpen before I can learn something else?" Brendan told his teachers that he hated it, but the teachers told him that they were training him to get a job for the future.

Because of Brendan's ability to learn quickly to read, it was difficult to comprehend why he was not being challenged in school and why his mother's pleadings were being ignored. It wasn't until Brendan was reading at a fifth-grade level that his mother showed me an evaluation of Brendan's ability. On the first page of the report, the school psychologist who had tested and evaluated Brendan had written an executive summary of the entire report summarizing that Brendan had an I.Q. of 40. However, on the *last* page following many pages of detailed analysis, the school psychologist wrote that Brendan's hearing aids were not functioning properly during the test and, therefore, **the test results were invalid.** No indication of this was on the first page and it was the first time that his mother had paid attention to that all-important last page. To the best of his mother's knowledge, the teachers had been basing their decisions about Brendan's ability by that erroneous and meaningless I.Q. number written on the first page.

Because of receiving tutoring in phonics strategies, by the time he was eighteen years old, Brendan was able accurately to decode almost anything he read and was able to comprehend at a fifth- or sixth-grade level. He lacked a developed vocabulary and analytical skills, but his teachers insisted that he was "not ready" for such work. They still insisted that Brian would never be able to read above a primary level.

His mother then hired an independent consultant to evaluate Brendan. The consultant noted that Brendan's decoding skills had advanced several years in one year. With that information confirming what she had known, Brendan's mother withdrew him from his high school and enrolled him in another. She initially met with his new teacher, explained about his private tutoring, and showed her the work at the sixth-grade level that Brendan was able to do independently. The teacher agreed to begin working with Brendan at that level and would evaluate as he progressed.

As a result, this special education teacher raised the bar for Brendan, challenging him and motivating him to advance further. Because Brendan's records from the other school were slow in arriving at his new school, the new teacher had not developed any preconceived opinions about Brendan based on faulty, misleading information. Therefore, she never considered treating Brendan as though he had an I.Q. of 40. By the time the records arrived, Brendan had proven to her that he was capable of much more than his previous teachers had thought. Sadly for Brendan, this talented and caring teacher was at that school only a short while before she moved to another state. Nevertheless, in the few months that she worked with Brendan, she had a significant and positive influence on his learning and self-esteem.

Today, Brendan decodes extremely well and reads very fluently. In an interesting irony, it seems that because no significant effort had been made by his earlier teachers to teach him to read, Brendan had not learned bad habits such as guessing and word substitution. It was for that reason, as well as his higher level of intelligence, that Brendan learned to decode rapidly. Nonetheless, Brendan has much ground to cover. He could have remained in special education classes until he was age twenty-two, but he and his mother decided that he would have the opportunity to learn more on his own.

Currently, he no longer attends school. Instead, Brendan continues with his tutoring every two weeks and works on daily assignments to expand his spoken and written vocabulary, both of which were lacking in his formal education. As part of his on-going learning, he uses various reading materials, his dictionary and workbooks by Townsend Press as his primary learning aides. He is continuing to learn, wanting to gain knowledge that was never presented to him when he was in school. He has many years' worth of work to make up.

Brendan's future life story would have been significantly different had he remained on his path of illiteracy and had not encountered the special ed teacher who successfully raised the bar for him. Instead, he has a job at a local grocery store and is given rave reviews from customers, co-workers, and supervisors. Although he still lives at home, Brendan has his own checking and savings accounts, is driving and has real dreams for his future. He is working to be able to go to college, get married and to live an independent life. It is a dream that his ability to read will help him to fulfill.

♦ ♦ ♦

STORY 13: HUNTER

Hunter has severe Cerebral Palsy that confines him to a wheel chair and allows him minimal use of only one hand. His parents are involved, loving and committed to their son's welfare. Hunter speaks haltingly, but is articulate although his verbal processing is slow at times. His parents contacted us when Hunter was sixteen-years-old. By that time, Hunter knew only the names of a few letters of the alphabet and could not read anything. He was being disciplined at school by losing free time and the like because he was balking at doing assigned work. When we spoke to him, he said, "Every day they ask me to write my name, address and phone number." He added angrily, "They ought to know it by now!"

His mother said that she had boxes and boxes of papers of the same thing printed repeatedly, including *hundreds* of pages where Hunter had traced his name, address, and so forth, as follows:

Sample of the tracing pattern:	His mother had pages of the following traced information.
	1. Hunter,
	2. Their street address,
	3. Their city,
	4. Their phone number,
	5. The word, *pizza*.

Every day, when Hunter entered the classroom, he was given pages with words that he was to trace. Throughout his school days, there was little or no intellectual stimulation for this young man.

After meeting with the parents, we began to work with him once a week. First, we taught him his alphabet sounds. Then, we proceeded to use primary, multi-sensory activities. There was no doubt that Hunter needed much practice and reinforcement, but, as my colleague had commented, " During the eleven years he had been in school, if his teachers had taught him just two consonants' sounds every year and one vowel sound every two years, he could be reading."

We met with his teacher and expressed concern over his comments that he hated writing the same word, *pizza,* every day. His teacher told us that they had asked him what his favorite food was, and he told them that he liked pizza. She said, "We want our students to work, ultimately, to become independent. Now, when he goes into a restaurant, he can look at a menu and order his favorite food."

His mother told us that it seems to make sense that if he can only read one word, *pizza*, he wouldn't need to look at a menu. Instead, he would just ask, "Do you have pizza?" The time and materials were wasted having this young man tracing the letters, *p-i-z-z-a,* when he could have been gaining phonemic awareness and learning phonics concepts. Moreover, he was being disciplined for not cooperating with his teachers by refusing to do the same as he had done for hundreds of days and thousands of pages before.

His mother wrote, "Your…methods to teach reading have given [Hunter] a new lease on life. For ten years, his teachers had him tracing letters. We have boxes of papers of his work. You taught him how to read. We have a lot of work ahead of us, but now we have hope."

◆ ◆ ◆

STORY 14: SUBMITTED BY THERESA MANRIQUEZ, M.ED.

My reading philosophy has evolved greatly since the time I first stepped into the classroom. After I graduated from Arizona State University, I was hired to teach reading to seventh and eighth graders.   I wasn't particularly overjoyed with the offer. I would have rather taught math, science, or social studies, anything but reading. I knew I was not particularly strong in this area. In fact, I always struggled with reading as a child, and, although my reading abilities improved, I was always one of the slowest readers. For whatever reason, fate, destiny or perhaps divine intervention, I became the reading teacher for the seventh and eighth graders at a south Phoenix K-8 elementary school.

I truly believe that I received my gray hair in my first few years at this school. Only a handful of students were on or above grade level in reading – or in any other subject for that matter. In fact, the majority of the students were reading at about the third or fourth-grade level and it troubled me to know that they would be in high school in a year or two.

I did not have a conviction that what I was doing was actually helping my students. Nevertheless, I was doing everything that I was taught in my undergraduate studies, and I even let the instruction be more student-directed. I used cooperative learning often, found low-level and high-interest materials. I tried to maintain individual *running records* (recommended by whole language proponents for miscue analysis) for 180 students! I even pulled out my old college whole language textbook to try to figure out what more I could do.

My students were making little gains. At this rate, their futures did not look promising. I continued with what I was doing because the university instructors and textbooks all conveyed the message that students learn at different rates and at some point, they will "catch on." I never really believed this statement because here I was a teacher, who graduated from the university with honors, and *I* never really "caught on."

Nevertheless, my junior high students were getting ready to go on to high school. They should have already "caught on." Yet they were lacking basic fundamental knowledge. I knew what they were lacking. They could not pronounce words. Their vocabularies were limited. Their comprehension was limited or completely lacking. However, I had no clue as to what was the most efficient and effective way to teach the information they needed since I lacked the knowledge myself.

My personal reading philosophy began to develop about two years after I began teaching. Until this point, I was trying to get by with the philosophy that was given to me by others. I started to work on my master's degree the semester after I began teaching. Classes were offered at my school district.

One of the required courses was curriculum development that introduced me to the concept of *brain-based learning*. I was definitely intrigued because I wanted to know how to teach my older students to read. The instructor told us that the brain was a pattern-seeking organ. I later came to understand that explicit, systematic phonics is orderly, follows rules and has patterns. In retrospect, I think the reason the instructor did not openly mention "explicit systematic phonics" was because the district strongly promoted the whole language philosophical approach to the teaching of reading. Even after the *No Child Left Behind Act*, based on solid, longitudinal, and rigorous research results reported by the National Reading Panel, was in place, whole language was still identified to be the approved approach of reading instruction used in the district according to its official web site.

The district did not promote the proven systematic, direct instruction of the essential elements of reading. That is, students were not taught **phonemic awareness** (so that readers know the sound/symbol relationships), **phonics** (so that readers know the rules of English pronunciation and spelling), **fluency** (so that readers do not have to stumble, struggle and guess as they read), **vocabulary** (so that readers can understand the meanings of the words that they read), and **comprehension** (so that the readers can understand the intent and meaning of the author). Instead, they were given excuses. We were all told, "We're doing the best we can do." Then we needed to improve; however, I didn't know what to do to be better. I didn't know then what I know now.

Subsequently, I found the answer to be the systematic instruction of reading skills, but this created a new conundrum for me. All the published information then about explicit, systematic phonics material was for the primary level and my students would have "killed me" if I even fancied the thought of giving primary work sheets. More importantly, I had no idea where to begin. *I* didn't even know the basic rule of when a vowel will say its *short* sound and when it would say its *long* sound. I could not teach what I did not know.

My continued searching led me to a greater belief that phonics was the answer. Nonetheless, all of my undergraduate professors spoke strongly against phonics and drilled into our mind that, if we were to ever teach it, it would do far more damage to our students than we could imagine. If phonics instruction was damaging and, if what they taught me didn't help, how and what was I to teach?

Soon after I took the curriculum development class, a teacher at my school, Pat Doran, gave an in-service on explicit systematic phonics. She brought some of her research materials--a stack about a foot high. She had used this research to create the materials to teach her sixth graders phonics. I was surprised that I had not been exposed to any of this information in my undergraduate studies. The research upon which the information was based wasn't new, yet it was exactly what I was looking for to teach my students.

The in-service was not long enough to teach me what I needed to know, and the idea of teaching phonics to my students actually frightened me. It was not until I observed Pat teaching her entire program that I felt comfortable in presenting it to my class. She worked with me, and we taught the students that had been assigned to my classroom for summer school. As she worked with the class, I took detailed notes. Not only did I take notes on the material, but also on her teaching methods, what she said and how she said it. Pat is a skilled, veteran teacher.

She came to my class the following year to observe my teaching. She made a few suggestions that I put into practice immediately. These suggestions worked and I had more success that year than all my years of teaching combined. I also had a sense of control of the curriculum.

Earlier in my career, I taught what and how I had been told to teach. My college professors had told me what would be effective, and I taught as they had instructed me with the belief that they were right. However, my students experienced little academic growth. With this new weapon, I taught phonics to my junior high students during the first four weeks of the school year. The results were amazing! That year was also the first year I could call on any student to read in any of my classes with the knowledge that the student would not put us to sleep. For the first time, students did not skip over words or say, "whatever" when they encountered unfamiliar words. Moreover, the capable readers did not feel the need to blurt out the word(s) on which the slower readers were *stuck*.

Yet, there was more. I was amazed at how much I learned that year. My spelling improved, my reading speed improved, and my self-confidence improved. I no longer found myself having to reread as often. My own comprehension improved. It made things much easier for me. That year, I learned along with my students.

I was troubled, however. I wondered how many other teachers needed phonics and weren't aware of it? From that point on, I became dedicated to teaching phonics, and to teaching others how to teach phonics. Moreover, I know that I continue to struggle with my grammar and writing skills. Despite my advanced education, I realized that little stress was placed by my instructors on the importance of striving for personal excellence: for example, in speaking and writing, using correct grammar, becoming a widely read scholar, and of expecting excellence from my students. Accordingly, I am living proof of what I always tell my students, "You are never too old to learn, to change, and to improve."

◆ ◆ ◆

STORY 15: CHRISTA R., IN HER OWN WORDS

As a self-contained classroom teacher of upper intermediate students, I was required to teach all subjects to students who were reading several, if not many years, below level. A few had only basic primary reading strategies. Only a couple of students were on level and above.

I had been aware and deeply concerned that my students were sorely ignorant of history. First, their reading abilities did not allow them successfully to read the textbooks or any post-primary reading-level books on historical subjects. Since I was a teacher new to that grade level, teachers and administration suggested that to cover the assigned curriculum I should use the unit approach, complete with learning centers, activity units, educational films, group projects, and so forth.

Coincidentally, around the same time, I began to notice late night talk show hosts using "man-on-the-street" interviews to humorously reveal individuals' appalling lack of historical and geographical knowledge. Most likely, the people interviewed, who demonstrated such profound ignorance, have at least a high school diploma and have been taught by certified teachers. I didn't want to be one of those teachers. I couldn't accept the *status quo*.

Having read about the effectiveness of phonics and knowing my students were missing those skills, I gleaned information from multiple sources. As all caring teachers do, I found out what my students needed to learn, and what I needed to do to teach them. In this case, my students lacked knowledge of effective phonics strategies. Once they learned to use these strategies, all of my students, including those who were already at or above average reading levels, increased several levels in their reading skills.

The writings and suggestions of E.D. Hirsch were very influential in redirecting my teaching techniques. For example, I began to consider the social studies textbook as a reading text. Like most teachers, I wanted my students to actually read their text to gain solid information, not cursory concepts. With basic decoding skills under their belts, my students were ready.

The history textbook we used was excellent with a typical, effective instructional format including chapter headings, main ideas, supporting information, photographs or illustrations, chapter reviews and tests covering general and specific information. The well-devised format utilized various means to elicit reader response and foster vocabulary development. It had graphs, maps, recommended fiction and non-fiction materials. Poetry and music selections provided on audio recordings added a richness of information-based learning experiences. As a result, many students were inspired and on their own initiative developed charts, graphs and wrote creative reports. Moreover, because the text provided some knowledge, many of the students were also voluntarily selecting library books on historical subjects.

It was important that we followed guidelines of the state standards. Subsequently, and specifically, because these students were reading successfully by using essential reading skills, their scholastic achievement expanded into other subject areas of math, language arts and science curriculum. Their ability to read efficiently made this possible for all of the students, even those who had been struggling and had previously given up. It was exciting to see the bright students, now even brighter, having confidence to tackle more difficult academic challenges with tools they could use for far greater independent success.

As for me, because of the success of these students and others as well, I have been motivated to learn more and each day to be a better teacher than I was the day before.

♦ ♦ ♦

STORY 16: MAUREEN R., PRINCIPAL (IN HER OWN WORDS)

I am the principal of an alternative charter high school. [After using the Phonics Steps decoding-skills program]…one of our most noticeable changes has been with one of our ninth-grade students. The student's IEP (Individual Education Plan) states that there should be no oral reading done in any classroom because the student has difficulty reading in a public forum. The mother of this student quickly brought this to our attention because the student's English teacher requires each student to give an oral presentation for a grade. Two weeks after we started the *Phonics Steps* program this student went to her English teacher after class and asked if she could read to the class the next day the short story that she had written. Her teacher reminded her that she did not have to give oral presentations, but [the girl] said she thought the class would enjoy her story, and she wanted to read it aloud. Her classmates loved her story and actually applauded her when she was done. Since that time, this special education student has actively participated, not only in her English class, but in all of her classes. Her mother also noted the dramatic change for the better in her daughter's self-esteem and attitude at home.

Conclusion

This book isn't about a specific program or me. Rather, it is meant to offer hope for those many individuals who can be taught what it takes to get into *The Secret Club*. No matter what their age, whether they are 9- or 109-years-old, with the exception of those who have significant natural or chemically induced mental impairment, everyone can be taught the essential elements to successful reading. **It is imperative that individuals who have not been taught to use phonics strategies should not be allowed to believe that there is something wrong with them because they cannot read or read well.** They must not be expected to "figure it out for themselves." Everyone who can read successfully can help those who cannot.

You are invited to contact me and to share your stories at http://www.edu-steps.com or at www.freedomreading.org.

FOCUS ON TECHNIQUES THAT DEVELOP

STUDY AND TEST-TAKING SKILLS

BY PAT DORAN AND JANET MARTIN
FREEDOM READING FOUNDATION, INC.

"Sometimes we look at others who are successful and attribute their success to random luck. What we don't see, however, is that 'luck' usually has been brought about by many long hours of very hard work."

Anonymous

Message to instructor: This appendix is in a worksheet format. It been added for teachers, parents, and students to use after a phonics foundation is laid. Often, students have had academic accommodations made for them. As a result, these skills and strategies have not been taught. Many are at a loss as to how to develop specific study skills or test-taking strategies.

We hear of students who experience "test anxiety." Frequently, the underlying cause of their test anxiety initially is their lack of research-based, explicit phonics and essential reading skills. In addition, students may be lacking the techniques needed to develop good study habits and test-taking skills due to their low reading levels and high frustration levels. (See Jano's story.)

Once students have good phonemic skills, read with fluency, have tools to continually develop their vocabulary, and have effective comprehension skills, they have the foundation for success. The next step is to focus on techniques that develop good study habits and test-taking skills. Once this knowledge is acquired and utilized, test anxiety is reduced; success is increased.

Do not assume that students have acquired good study habits and test-taking skills. The following information provides you with suggestions to help students develop study skills. These elements are critical for students if they are to do well. You may duplicate the following pages for use in your classroom. Students may use them as personal check sheets. Upper-level students should frequently review these study and test-taking skills. Moreover, these check sheets can be particularly helpful as an *individual improvement plan* to use when a student is struggling or is finding the work difficult. Remember, however, that these strategies are beneficial **only** if students are able to decode well and know how to use the necessary tools when they encounter unfamiliar words. Likewise, students must have adequate fluency, vocabulary and comprehension skills.

Name _____

I. Student Study Plan

❑ I will plan a **regular time to study**.

❑ I will find a **quiet place** where I can use a table, desk, or stable writing surface and not be distracted.
   [TV and radio should be off. However, Baroque music (Yes, Baroque music!)if playing softly in the background can help my brain to concentrate.]

❑ I will find a place with **good lighting**.

❑ **I will have all of my materials** to complete my assignments.

   [ ] Books, dictionary, thesaurus, _____, _____.

   [ ] Pencils, pens, markers, highlighters, compass, ruler, _____, _____.

❑ I will set important mini-goals:

   [ ] I will finish _____ by _____ [ ] I finished by _____.
                    Assignment and/or pages   *Time*

   [ ] I will finish _____ by _____ [ ] I finished by _____.
                    Assignment and/or pages   *Time*

   [ ] I will take a break from _____ to _____ [ ] I began working by _____.
                                 Time   *Time*

   [ ] I will finish _____ by _____ [ ] I finished by _____.
                    Assignment and/or pages   *Time*

   [ ] I will finish _____ by _____ [ ] I finished by _____.
                    Assignment and/or pages   *Time*

   Note: A break and some fresh air can often help to refresh you while studying. Get up,

   walk around, and stretch. Avoid turning on the TV or calling a friend, as these activities

   tend to be distracting and time-consuming. Set a goal to complete your homework first;

   then reward yourself with watching TV or calling a friend.

II. What I Do In Class

❑ I listen intently to what the instructor is saying. [*Your being an active listener is essential for your academic success.*]

❑ If I am not taking notes, I keep my eyes on the instructor or the information that has been presented on the board/screen.

❑ I **don't** rest my head in my hands, thus, signaling to my brain that it is "rest time." [*The only thing holding up your head should be your neck! Be in work position at all times.*]

❑ I take notes in class, especially trying to get my instructor's **exact** wording for definitions, rules, etc. [*When you are unsure, or if the instructor has spoken too rapidly, ask for clarification or repetition. If the instructor does not respond in class, ask him or her after class. Write down unexplained, unfamiliar words to be looked up in the glossary or dictionary at another time.*]

❑ I write down the main idea and supporting details either in **outline format** or **information-web format** with the main idea in the center box and supporting details on lines radiating from main idea.

❑ I **do not** write everything that the teacher says.

❑ I review my notes when the information is fresh, either right after class or that evening.

❑ I rewrite my notes, either by hand or on computer, and fill in all of the important details. [*Some students may want to inquire about learning how to write **shorthand**, a symbol-based speed-writing skill once taught in business classes. It can be a very helpful skill to have for times when you have to take extensive notes quickly but have no electronic devices available.*]

❑ I write down questions to ask the instructor.

❑ I take notes when I read assigned materials.

❑ I **don't** doodle or play with my pencil, etc. [*This can become a "toy," providing a distraction from the lesson. As a result, you may begin to daydream; you will be in class in body only, but your mind will be far off. You will miss much information.*]

❑ If I become restless, I move my shoulders or ankles unobtrusively in circles to increase circulation. [*Always be respectful of other students and the instructor.*]

III. Before I Begin Each Chapter or Lesson

- ❏ I read the title.

- ❏ I read major headings.

- ❏ I study photographs and captions. [*These will add to your understanding of the written word.*]

- ❏ I read opening paragraphs.

- ❏ I look at the questions at the end of the chapter. [*They will help you to focus on the most important information as you read.*]

- ❏ I look over the lesson briefly for bold words, graphs, charts, and illustrations.

IV. As I Read the Lesson

> **To the student:** Become an *active* reader. Authors, editors, and book publishers include various elements in text materials. All of these elements are included after extensive and intensive planning. Part of comprehension is not to simply decode words and get basic ideas, but to gain a full understanding of all of the material being presented. Therefore, as you read the text material, actively study these other elements of information.

I will:

- ❑ Read the main headings.

- ❑ Read the subheadings and each paragraph.

- ❑ Take note of main ideas, main points, and supporting points.

- ❑ Look for words that indicate transition or relationships.

- ❑ Study the graphs and charts.

- ❑ Pay close attention to the words that are written in **bold type**.

    - ▪ The first time that they appear, they are usually defined.

    - ▪ The words in bold are also usually defined in the glossary in the back of the book.

    - ▪ These words are words whose meanings you must learn. [*Often they appear on tests and could be used in the writing of your answers.*]

- ❑ Create a vocabulary file with index cards. [*You may want to punch one hole in the corner of each card and put the cards on a large "O" ring that can be purchased at most hardware and some office supply or specialty stores. This makes them easy to carry and to use when you have spare minutes.*]

    - ▪ Write one word (or fact) on the front of each card.

    - ▪ Write the chapter number, page, and definition (if required) on the back.

    - ▪ Use these cards to study by yourself or with a study partner.

V. As I Review the Lesson

To the student: Although your academic responsibilities are demanding, it is wise for you to review material frequently and not to wait for test time to cram the information into your memory bank.   You should "not waste a learning minute." Using the minutes before class begins to review information is helpful. While waiting for a ride or a bus, you could find that it is a good time to review vocabulary words or main points. If possible, find a friend who is willing to work with you. Reviews are essential to allow you to "own" the information rather than to "borrow" it for a test and then forget it.

If I want to do well on tests I should:

- ❑ Review chapter questions.

- ❑ Review my notes.

- ❑ Drill my facts and any new words or words that were written in **bold**.
  [Make a pile of cards. Take the cards off the "O" ring if you have used one. Have a friend quiz you or study by yourself. Any facts or words that you know immediately are put in pile A; any facts or words that are not known quickly are put in pile B. Then, re- study information on cards in pile B. After studying, take cards in pile B and re-quiz yourself. Any facts or words that you know immediately, put those in pile A, known information. Repeat this procedure until all of your cards go into pile A on the first round.]

- ❑ Review key ideas.

- ❑ Review any lists, rules, timelines, etc. that my instructor has stressed.

VI. When I Prepare for Tests

To the student: If you have been utilizing the previous tips that you have been given, you should take the next steps to prepare for the test.

I must:

- ❑ Make sure that I have completed all lesson reviews and chapter reviews that may be in the text.

- ❑ Study my notes.

- ❑ Study key ideas.

- ❑ Study my vocabulary cards.

- ❑ Reread any chapters and unit summaries.

261

VII. As I Take Tests

I should:

- **Be confident** because I have the skills to read and the strategies to comprehend.

- **Have confidence in myself** because I have studied well.

- **Not panic**. [*Your body will go into "survival" mode and you may not think clearly.*]

- **Take a deep breath**. [*Rotate your shoulders to relieve stress.*]

- **Note how many items** are in the test for each testing period before I begin.

  - I decide how many minutes that I am allotted for that test or section of the test.

  - I divide the number of items by the number of minutes. [*That will give an idea of how much time you must spend on each item. For example, for 60 items to be completed in 30 minutes, take no more than an average of 30 seconds on each item.*]

  - I will remind myself to watch the clock to keep my pace. [*You do not want to have 15 questions remaining and only 5 minutes of time left.*]

- **Listen carefully** to or read **all** directions, even if I think I know what they say.

- Make sure that I **provide all information that is asked** and **in the form that is required**. [*For example, if you are asked to put an X to indicate the correct answer, do **not** put a √ or other mark. You may lose points.*]

- **Thoroughly and carefully,** read **each of the multiple choice answer possibilities, every word** in a statement requiring a true or false answer, or when choosing the correct word.

I will make sure that I:

- Do not skip any words as I read!

- Make sure that I am reading each word **exactly** as it is written, left to right.

262

Important points to remember:

- ❏ There will usually be one or two "distracters" that could be the correct answer. Try to logically eliminate the incorrect one based on the information that you have studied.

- ❏ Do not spend a lot of time on a test item about which you are not sure of the answer.

  - ▪ Mark the answer of your best guess.

  - ▪ If possible, put a small dot in the margin next to the test item to indicate which items you should return to. [*If you cannot make any marks on the test, make a mental note.*]

  - ▪ Come back to it when and if you have time.

  - ▪ Remember to erase the small dot when you are finished.

When I respond to questions requiring an essay answer, I will:

Read the directions for each essay question **thoroughly**. When you are writing your answer, follow this pattern:

- ▪ *Rewrite the essay question as part of your topic sentence or main idea.*

- ▪ *Write the supporting points clearly and logically making sure that each point falls under the umbrella of your topic sentence.*

- ▪ *Write concluding points or re-phrase the main idea in one final sentence or paragraph.*

  For example, if the item asks you to **name** *and* **discuss** *three branches of the U.S. government, do not just name them.*

  1. *Rephrase the question as the main idea.*

  2. *Identify 1st branch in a main idea and include supporting points*

  3. *Identify 2nd branch in the main idea and include supporting points.*

  4. *Identify 3rd branch in the main idea and include supporting points.*

  5. *Use transitional or relationship words and phrases.*

  6. *Include pertinent vocabulary in your answer. (Remember to include essential words that were stressed by your instructor or were bold in the text.)*

  7. *Conclude with a rephrasing of the main idea.*

- ❏ Slowly read the response to myself, making sure that I did not omit words.

- ❏ Check my grammar, punctuation, and spelling.

The Test Results

If you got 100%, congratulate yourself. You can be proud of your efforts.

If you didn't get 100%, don't grumble or be discouraged, crumple up the test and toss it away.

Find out how you might have done better.

Look at the mistakes you made.

Compare them with your notes. [*Sometimes the instructor makes an error in scoring a test.*]

Find the correct answer and learn it. [*Tests are just as important in highlighting what you don't know as they are in telling you what you do know.*]

If you ran out of time and had to rush, improve your time-awareness strategies for the next test.

If you did not follow directions, improve that strategy for the next time.

If you did not have adequate class or study notes, improve that for the next time.

Remember: ***If you always do what you always did, you'll always get what you always got!***

Get help! It is not a sign of weakness. All **great** thinkers and leaders seek out support and advice from others. Always keep looking for someone who will support you as you strive for excellence.

REMEMBER

A friend is someone who helps you to be your best. Avoid friends who do not value your success in school. These are not real friends; they are only people that you know.

No matter what happens, always strive towards excellence! You may not always achieve your goal, but at least you will be going in the right direction.

Don't be discouraged in school from working hard. Some unsuccessful students may ridicule classmates who are interested in doing well in school. In school, a hardworking student may be called "nerd," but don't forget that after graduation, that "nerd" will most likely be called "boss." Successful people who seem "lucky" have achieved their success through hard work, determination, overcoming obstacles and being prepared when the door of opportunity opened for them. Good "luck" to you!

Bibliography

Adamson, John William. Ed. (1922). *The Educational Writings of John Locke*, Cambridge University Press. Retrieved October 27, 2004 from http://www.cpm.ehime-u.ac.jp/AkamacHomePage/Akamac_E-text_Links/Locke.html.

Arizona Republic Newspaper. (1997, February 19). *Sound It Out: Phonics Works Better*, 1.

Arnold, Wendy, RSA., CETLA., CETYL., PC Ed ., and MA in TEYL, Hong Kong, China, (2004, May 25) *Subject: Phonemic Awareness*. [Message 1942] Message posted to ExtensiveReading@Yahoogroups.com.

Atlantis Rising Online(2004). *Carvings Spark Debate Over Alphabet:When Did Civilization Move Toward Its First Alphabet?* Retrieved October 30, 2004 from http://www.atlantisrising.com/xnews.html.

Bach, Emmon, Calabrese, Andrea, Caplan, Dr. David, et.al. (1996). *Letter From Massachusetts Linguists on WLL by David Klein*. Retrieved December 2, 2004 from http://mathforum.org/epigone/amte/swiraxkhay.

Blumenfeld, Dr. Sam A. (2001). *America's Ongoing Reading Problem.* Retrieved October 31, 2001 from www.ritalindeath.com/blumenfeld10.htm.

Bridgewater College and Daleville College Staff of Alumn. (1930). Staunton, Virginia: McClure Company, Inc.

Chenoweth, Karin, *Phonics Debate Linked to Nature of Educational Research.* (2002, March 28). The Washington Post, p. GZ05. Retrieved November 24, 2004 from http://www.nrrf.org/article_chenoweth_3-28-02.htm.

Columbia encyclopedia. 6th ed. (2004*). Parker, Francis Wayland.*. New York: Columbia University Press. Retrieved October 29, 2004 from http://www.bartleby.com/65/pa/Parker-F.html.

Corcoran, John. (1994). *The Teacher Who Couldn't Read:* Focus on the Family, Colorado Springs, Colorado.

Cronin, Eileen M. (1994). *Helping Your Dyslexic Child.* Prima Publishing: Rocklin, California.

CTVC-Independent Television Productions. (1999) London Weekend TV.

Cuadros, Paul, Land, Gregory, Scully, Sean and Song, Sara. (2003, July 28). The New Science of Dyslexia. *Time Magazine,* 56-59.

Cunnningham, Patricia M., Moore, Sharon A., Cunningham, James W. & Moore, David W. (1989). *Reading and Writing in Elementary Classrooms: Strategies and Observations.* New York: Longman.

Damerell, Reginald. (1985) *Education's Smoking Gun: How Teachers' Colleges Have Destroyed Education in America.* New York: Freundlich Books.

Deliyannis, Deborah Mauskopf. (2003) *Historiography in the Middle Ages.* Boston: Brill Academic Publications. New York: American Book Company.

Education Oasis. *Language Arts: Dolch Word Lists.* Retrieved October 31, 2004 from http://www.educationoasis.com/curriculum/Lang_Arts/dolch.html.

Encyclopedia Phoeniciana. *Phoenician Alphabet: The Alphabet Family Tree.* Retrieved October 29, 2004 from http://phoenicia.org/alphabet.html.

Freeman, Frank. (1936, December). *Journal of Educational Sociology*, December 1936. (as cited in *Remedial Reading* Monroe & Backus, 1937).

Gatto, John Taylor. (2000). *The Underground History of American Education,* Oxford Village Press, New York (Pre-publication edition).

Gatto, John Taylor. (2001). *The Underground History of American Education,* Oxford Village Press, New York.

Grossen, Bonita. (1997, November). *A Synthesis of Research of Reading From the National Institute of Child Health.* University of Oregon. Retrieved November 24, 2004 from http://www.nrrf.org/synthesis_research.html.

Hiskes, Dorothy. (1998, February). Right to Read Report. *Explicit or Implicit Phonics: Therein Lies the Rub.* Retrieved October 31, 2004 from http://www.nrrf.org/essay_Explicit_or_Implicit_Phonics.html.

Hirsch, E.D. (1987) *Cultural Literacy: What Every American Needs to Know.* New York, New York: Vintage Books.
.

Hirsch, Jr., E.D. (1996). *The Schools We Need and Why We Don't Have Them.* New York: Doubleday.

Hurford, Daphne M. (1998). *To Read or Not To Read*, New York, New York: Scribner.

Levine, Felice J. Ph.D. (2003, December 3). *Letter to Secretary Rod Paige.* Retrieved on October 27, 2004 from http://www.eval.org/doeaera.html.

Levinson, Harold N. (1984). *Smart But Feeling Dumb,* New York, New York: Warner Books.

Levinson, Harold N., and Addie Sanders. (1992.) *Turning the Up Side Down Kids Around,* New York, New York: M. Evans and Company, Inc.

Locke, John. (1693). *Some Thoughts Concerning Education*, 1693, The History of Education and Childhood. Retrieved October 27, 2004 from http://www.socsci.kun.nl/ped/whp/histeduc/locke/.

Loucky, John Paul (2004, May 26.) [Re: Msg.441] Message posted to ExtensiveReading@yahoogroups.com.

Martin, Janet. (2004, September 9). Unpublished Comments. Tempe, Arizona.

McGuinness, Diane, Ph.D. (1999). *Why Our Children Can't Read and What We Can Do About It.* New York: Touchtone Simon And Schuster.

McManus, Hannah T. and Haaren, John H. (1914). New York: Charles Scribner's Sons.

Modern History Sourcebook: *John Locke: Some Thoughts Concerning Education.* (1692). Retrieved October 29, 2004 from http://www.fordham.edu/halsall/mod/1692locke-education.html.

Monroe, Marion & Backus, Bertie. (1937*) Remedial Reading: A Monograph in Character Education.* Cambridge, Massachusetts.

Moore, David W., Moore, S. A., Cunningham, P.M., Cunningham, J.W. (1998). *Development Readers & Writers in the Content Areas K-12.* New York: Longman/Addison Wesley.

Morange, Wendy. (1997). *Dyslexia,* Brookfield, Connecticut: The Millbrook Press, Inc.

Montessori, Maria. (1912). *The Montessori Method: Scientific Pedagogy as Applied to Child Education in "The Children's Houses" with additions and revisions by the author.* New York: Frederick A. Stokes Company.

Mulcaster, Richard. (1581). *Positions Concerning the Training Up of Children, Chapter 5.* Retrieved October 29, 2004, from http://www.ucs.mun.ca/~wbarker/positions-txt.html.

National Reading Panel. (2000, April). Retrieved November from http://www.nationalreadingpanel.org/.

O'Brien, Reverend John A. (1952). *The New Our New Friends: Cathedral Edition.* (A Revision of the *New Our New Friends* by William S. Gray, A. Sterl Artley, and May Hill Arbuthnot). Chicago: Scott, Foresman and Company.

Partnership for Reading. *Bringing Scientific Evidence to Learning.* (2002). National Institute of Child Health and Human Development (NICHD). U.S. Department of Health and Human Services and the U.S. Department of Education. Retrieved November 24, 2004 from http://www.nifl.gov/partnershipforreading/.

Paige, Rod, Secretary, U.S. Department of Education. (2002, March 13*). Fund for Colorado Event: Remarks of Secretary Rod Paige.* Retrieved November 24, 2004 from http://www.ed.gov/news/speeches/2002/03/20020313.html.

Pensky, David. (1997, April 16). *Want to Read? Learn to Break the Code.* The Daily Report Card, Vol. 7, No. 33 #3. Retrieved October 31, 2004 from http://www.ofcn.org/cyber.serv/academy/rptcard/1997/drc733.html.

Right to Read Foundation, Inc. (1996). Sweet, Robert, Jr. *The Century of Miseducation of Teachers.* Retrieved October 29, 2004 from http://nrrf.org/essay_Illiteracy.html.

Right to Read Foundation, Inc. (1996). Sweet, Robert, Jr. *Illiteracy: An Incurable Disease or Education Malpractice?* Retrieved October 29, 2004 from http://nrrf.org/essay_Illiteracy.html.

Roe, Betty D., Stoodt-Hill, Barbara D. & Burns, Paul C. (2004). *Secondary School Literacy Instruction: The Content Areas*, (8th ed.). New York: Houghton Mifflin Company.

Sanders, Marion. (2001). *Understanding Dyslexia and the Reading Process*, Needham Hights, Maine: Allyn and Bacon.

Silverstein, Dr. Alvin. (1992). *Dyslexia,* New York, New York: Franklin Watts.

Song, Sara. (2003, July 28). *"Is Your Child Dyslexic?" Time Magazine, 56-59.*

Strauss, Stephen . (February 18, 1997). *Phonics Reading Method Best, Study Finds Whole Language Approach Significantly Less Effective, Houston Research Shows.* Globe and Mail in Toronto, Canada. Retrieved November 18, 2004 from http://www.aci.on.ca/lighthouse/globe.html.

Sweet, Robert, Jr. (1996). *The Century of Miseducation of Teachers.* National Right to Read Foundation, Washington, D.C. Retrieved November 24, 2004 from http://www.nrrf.org/essay_Century_of_Miseducation.html.

Sweet, Robert, Jr. (May-June, 1997). D*on't Read, Don't Tell.* Policy Review, Number 83. Retrieved November 24, 2004, from http://www.policyreview.org/may97/thsweet.html.

Sykes, Charles J. (1995). *Dumbing Down Our Kids: Why American Children Feel Good About Themselves But Can't Read, Write or Add.* New York. St. Martin's Griffin.

Thompson, C. Bradley. (2004, March 18). *Is Phonics-rich Instruction, as Pushed by the White House, Needed in U.S. Classrooms?* Insight on the News. Retrieved October 27, 2004 from http://www.insightmag.com/main.cfm?include=detail&storyid=634442.

Todd, CeCe (2002, April 8). *State Plans Retools Reading*, The East Valley Tribune, Mesa, Arizona.

Townsend Press Reading Series. (1999). New Jersey: Townsend Press Inc.

Townsend Press Vocabulary Series. (1997). New Jersey: Townsend Press Inc.

Toynbee, Arnold. (1946). *A Study of History: Abridgement of Volumes I-IV by D.C. Somerville.* Oxford University Press. New York.

Weaver, Constance. (1994). *Reading Process and Practice: From Socio-psycholinguistics to Whole Language.* Portsmouth, NH: Heinemann.

Wilson, Robert McCole. *Teaching Reading - a History.* Retrieved October 29, 2004 from http://www.socsci.kun.nl/ped/whp/histeduc/wilson/wilson10.html.

Winn, Marie. (1977). *The Plug in Drug.* New York: Bantam Books/Viking Press.

Worldbook Online. (2004). *Charlemagne.* Retrieved October 27, 2004 from http://www.aolsvc.worldbook.aol.com/wb/Article?id=ar106840&st=Charlemagne.